India Express

Also by Daniel Lak

Mantras of Change: Reporting India in a Time of Flux

India Express

The Future of
the New Superpower

Daniel Lak

INDIA EXPRESS
Copyright © Daniel Lak, 2008.
All rights reserved.

First published 2008 by Viking Canada.
First published in hardcover in the United States in 2008 by
PALGRAVE MACMILLAN®–a division of St. Martin's Press LLC, 175 Fifth
Avenue, New York, NY 10010.

Palgrave Macmillan is the global academic imprint of the above companies
and has companies and representatives throughout the world.

Palgrave® and Macmillan® are registered trademarks in the United States,
the United Kingdom, Europe and other countries.

ISBN: 978-0-230-61759-9

Library of Congress Cataloging-in-Publication Data is available from the
Library of Congress.

A catalogue record of the book is available from the British Library.

Design by Letra Libre, Inc.

First PALGRAVE MACMILLAN paperback edition: December 2009

10 9 8 7 6 5 4 3 2 1

Printed in the United States of America.

For Katherine Helene and Robert Liam,
who've shared so much of this with me.

Contents

The simple and astonishing truth about India and Indian people is that when you go there, and deal with them, your heart always guides you more wisely than your head. There's nowhere else in the world where that's quite so true.

—Gregory David Roberts, *Shantaram*

INTRODUCTION

BY THE SIDE of a leafy suburban street, in the South Indian city of Chennai, an old man plies his trade. He bends over a wooden plank suspended between two piles of ragged bricks, wielding an old-fashioned iron. His name is Ram, which means "God" to most Indians. It's a common name here. Dark skinned, wizened and wearing a white cotton loin cloth, Ram is what Indians call a *press wallah:* press, as in iron, *wallah,* an all-purpose Indian word that means someone who does something.

As Ram works, a pot of charcoal smolders beside him, even in the steamy summer heat. The coals go into a compartment in his ancient iron. Ram himself provides the steam to smooth the wrinkles from the clothes. He fills his mouth with water and sprays it between pursed lips at the most stubborn creases and ornery fabrics. Then he whips the hot iron onto the wet cloth, producing billows of steam and the hissing of a hundred snakes. Beside him, a makeshift clothes rack displays his finished work: crisp cotton shirts that sparkle in the sunlight, trousers with creases like knives, dark skirts with no pleat out of place, sari blouses so finely ironed and starched they seem to stand up on their own. These are the workaday uniforms of his white-collar customers, pressed and ready for another day at the computer console or the sales counter.

The press wallah at work is a common sight in India. Even now, as the country hurtles down the path to modernity, surprisingly few families own ironing boards. There is simply not enough time in the day for a working woman to slide an electric iron over her husband's shirts. She takes them to the press wallah. Most urban neighborhoods have one. They stand and work outside in all weather, with just a rickety wooden lean-to for protection against monsoon rains and the relentless summer sun. But Ram is no ordinary street worker. He is a part of the new India, a society that's bucking eons of tradition to raise itself out of poverty, already showing the developed world how to be an economic and political superpower. Even as he spits water onto wrinkled fabric and wields a ten-pound iron full of glowing chunks of charcoal.

Ram gets it. He understands what's needed to make changes in a society that regards him as a lowly, if useful, menial worker. Ram's customers probably assume, more or less legitimately, that his sons will be press wallahs, too. Or the equivalent in another line of work: tea shop waiters, domestic servants, ditch diggers, truck washers, *dhobis* or laundry men, assistant mechanics in a greasy roadside auto-repair shop, office boys or "peons," as Indians know them. These are the jobs to which Ram's lowly status in the Hindu caste system traditionally confined his progeny. It was ever thus.

But Ram had a different plan, and the guts to go for it. Not for him the tedious, unending cycle of poverty perpetuated by the caste structure. No, this press wallah pressed for change. One of Ram's most loyal customers tells the story of how the old man broke out of the caste system. A journalist by profession, the customer—call him Sujeev—stands close by Ram's ironing spot, at the end of his own driveway. Ram is intent on the pair of white linen trousers stretched tight beneath his iron. He pays no attention to our conversation, for he speaks only the local language, Tamil, and is illiterate.

"One day about ten years ago," Sujeev begins, while Ram's iron hisses in the background, "my wife dropped the clothes off with Ram, and he smiled and made a remark about the weather, as he always does. Then as she was turning to go, he asked for a moment of her time and told her about his plan for his two boys. He wanted to send them on a computer course, he said, at night school. They'd keep on attending day classes at the government high school and helping him with deliveries. But they would be learning another trade at night. They would be studying to be 'software men.' That's what he called them. Software men."

Back then, in the early 1990s, computers weren't at all common in India, outside of major institutions and big businesses. Today's well-known information technology companies were just starting out. There was no outsourcing of white-collar jobs from the West, no billionaire computer geniuses, no Hotmail, Google or Netscape. But Ram had heard of computers, and his plan was to borrow some money from his regular customers to pay for the boys' education.

"Not much, about a thousand rupees from each of us," Sujeev says. "About fifty dollars back then. But that was a lot for Ram to repay, and he was offering interest as well. We gave him the money and wondered a bit if we would see it back."

Sujeev said he and his wife considered the money they'd given Ram a gift, not a loan. They did the math. At the rates he charged for ironing, even with the quantity of work he processed, there seemed no viable way for the old press wallah to repay them. In all, he borrowed money from nineteen of his best customers. Tuition fees were expensive then at the relatively few computer schools that offered classes. There was no competition, as there is now, when India boasts a "software institute" on every city block. But Ram proved his doubters wrong. He worked harder than he had ever worked, Sujeev said. He came to his ironing board earlier and stayed late into the evening. He didn't take Saturday afternoon off. He took on extra work from other streets and local businesses. He pressed towels and sheets for hotels, uniforms for hospitals and restaurant tablecloths. His sons came on weekends and delivered his work on their bicycles. It was a scene of furious activity, and Sujeev and his wife were amazed. After a time, Ram's clients noticed there was something about the two boys that was different. They held themselves more upright, seemed a little less deferential, a little more professional.

"They were very confident," said Sujeev, "for low-caste boys."

This went on for nearly two years, and then one day Ram came to Sujeev's front gate accompanied by two tall, beaming young men wearing short-sleeved white shirts, with knotted ties and dark slacks, each with their father's trademark knife-edge crease. The press wallah had a small dog-eared notebook in one hand and a plastic shopping bag in the other. Each of his sons—the two businesslike young men by his side—carried what looked like a painting or a photograph in the crook of an arm. Ram was politely insistent that he needed to see both Sujeev and his wife.

Proudly, he presented his two boys and talked about their graduation. "Already they have jobs," he said, "in real offices where they wear clothes like these," gesturing to the heavily starched white shirts and narrow black ties. Framed diplomas were held up for inspection and passed around. Then Ram's sons consulted their father's notebook while the old man reached into the paper bag and counted out the money that he had been loaned, plus interest. Sujeev's wife tried to tell the press wallah that they didn't want to be repaid, but he was as firm as they'd ever seen him. Not impolite, but determined that they accept their repayment. Especially the interest. They saw that they must, so Sujeev and his wife took the money, chatted for a while, and then watched as Ram walked down the street and repeated the same scene at every household from which he'd been given a loan. Flanked by his two officially trained software engineer sons, the old menial laborer exuded pride and hope as he spoke to the upper-caste, professional folk on the street where he'd wielded his hot, heavy iron for more than twenty years. From a caste perspective, it was a once-unthinkable scene. The elderly lower-caste ironing man talking about his sons with Brahmins—people like Sujeev and his wife, at the pinnacle of the Hindu hierarchy—and proudly repaying the money they had loaned him. "It would not have happened twenty or thirty years ago," Sujeev says, still full of admiration for the two boys and their determined father.

In a sense, Ram represents India's arrival on the world stage. His is the story of an underdog, faced by more challenges than natural advantages, who manages to realize a dream. India really was once the underdog. It certainly was when I began visiting in the 1980s. At that time, the glory of winning independence from Britain forty years earlier was waning. For many Indians, that residual pride in besting the British was little compensation for the tenuousness of daily life. Poverty, overcrowding, disease and frequent outbreaks of religious or communal violence were not making it easy to be a citizen of the world's most populous democracy. Even the Green Revolution of the 1960s—when Indian farmers used new strains of wheat and more efficient agricultural technologies to banish famine and make their country self-sufficient in food—was old news. But the freedom struggle and the victory over famine were still being touted by the government as achievements to be proud of. Among the poor, both urban and rural, and the working classes, such barely remembered achievements were all too intangible. Decades of democracy were all well and good, but mere day-to-day survival was challenging. Political leaders told the masses that they were fortunate to live in a land of ancient culture and modern progress, but the poor were too busy staying alive to notice. Those who passed as middle class in those days didn't have a problem with survival. But they, too, struggled—with finding a job, decent housing and medical care and, most of all, with believing that the future held promise for their children.

The vast machinery of an all-powerful, central government employed many more people than a barely nascent private sector—from the graduates of top universities to the lowliest laborers. There were government-run oil companies, steel mills, banks and retail stores. Tens of millions of Indians worked for the state. India's private enterprises had all the employees they needed and then some. Starting your own business was unthinkable with a huge state regulatory apparatus waiting to pry loose concessions and bribes and often setting terms that all but guaranteed bankruptcy. What businesses there were survived largely by collaborating with the system because it shielded them from competition and gave them monopolies for largely inferior products and services. For a highly educated professional, or for an entrepreneur, going abroad was often the best option. Many of the estimated two to three million people of Indian origin living in the United States today either emigrated during the long years of state-dominated economics or are descended from people who did.

That was then. This is now. It's not easy to pinpoint exactly when India began to wake up from decades of post-independence slumber. Perhaps the period of figurative rest was necessary. Long centuries of invasion, oppression, colonial rule, and then the trauma of independence and its bloody aftermath, all had left deep scars. Perhaps India needed time to recover and find itself before it began to realize its potential.

Discerning the tipping point when that started to happen isn't easy. There are several contending narratives. In the late 1980s, the government decided to allow the import of telephone-switching devices that had been kept out of the country previously by prohibitive tariffs and duties. The technology was primitive by today's standards, but the decision to introduce it made an enormous difference in people's day-to-day lives. It led eventually to the establishment of a pay telephone office in almost every Indian village. These offices put a country in touch with itself for the first time ever. Parents could speak to children at boarding school, wives to husbands who had migrated to find work. Farmers could call agents to find out the market price for their produce instead of depending on venal local buyers.

Then again, the moment of truth for Indian modernization might have been the explosion in software companies in the 1990s, which made Indian firms such as Infosys Technologies, Wipro Technologies and Tata Consultancy Services famous in Western corporate circles. A country once renowned for exporting people was reprogramming the computer networks of the world. That led to the boom in call centers and Indian-accented voices guiding Westerners through their bank accounts, computer operating systems and cell phone invoices.

But most economists, commentators and even ordinary Indians identify a different moment as the time when their country began to move decisively forward. In April 1991, a new government was elected. The country's balance sheet was an utter disaster. Public spending was out of control. Tax revenues were a joke. But worst of all, India faced a balance-of-payments crisis. Heavy borrowing from foreign markets had left debts high and liquidity low. There were fewer than a billion dollars left in the kitty, barely enough to cover the bill for a month's imports. The country was poised to do something it had never done before: default on loan repayments. What emerged as the solution to the problem also bordered on the unthinkable. Put simply, it was decided to remake India's economy. Ministers and advisers drew up an audacious plan to allow the free market to flourish. This was entirely counterintuitive. From its inception, India had regarded itself as a socialist country. Its first prime minister, Jawaharlal Nehru, felt capitalism was too harsh and fervently believed that a benevolent socialist state would lift hundreds of millions out of poverty while developing an industrial base in a land of farmers and peasants. In the middle years of the twentieth century, as the Cold War intensified and nations were expected to choose sides, India allied itself more closely with Moscow than with Washington. Although still firmly democratic politically, Indian economics tended to favor a tough regulatory state that planned everything and licensed the private sector to do what it couldn't do itself.

This approach made some sense at the time. British colonialism left India with relatively little in the way of industry. The country was a source of raw materials that had to be processed abroad, in England mostly. Today, India has steel mills, oil and gas terminals, heavy machinery manufacturers, automotive plants and ports that might not otherwise have been developed. A small cabal of homegrown capitalists also benefited mightily from their government's distaste for the private sector. Huge family-run conglomerates stood astride the Indian economy, unchallenged by international competition and rarely troubled by competitors at home. Products were shoddy and customer service all but nonexistent. It was hard to tell the difference between the government-run companies and the private ones, as an Indian acquaintance once wryly observed.

What become known as the economic reforms of 1991 were introduced cautiously. Import restrictions were barely relaxed. Tariff barriers were lowered slightly. The vast Gordian knot of regulation on business and commerce was eased a bit. But enough was done to convince creditors to reschedule India's debt repayments so that the new policies could take effect.

It worked. Even the country's battle-hardened, unreformed Communists, who enjoy a solid if minority position in the Indian parliament, admit that the policy changes of 1991 represent the crossing of a Rubicon. There can be no going back. The balance-of-payments crisis went away, never to return. The economy picked up steam and soon growth was averaging more than 5 percent per year, often much higher. Indian consumers began to access the goods that the rest of the world took for granted. In almost every economic sphere, the country began to outperform expectations. Even poverty alleviation accelerated as jobs were created and the education sector was able to provide more school places in both public and private classrooms. Witness Ram's two sons.

If 1991 was India's wake-up call, then today the country is out of bed and on its way to the office. Metaphors aside, the pages that follow will be a journey through a vast land and society unlike any other in the world. Western urban civilization has come to pride itself on being a melting pot, a mosaic of cultural aspirations and shared values. India pioneered this concept thousands of years ago and continues to improve on it today. This is a country in which hundreds of millions of people speak one or more of the twenty-two major national languages, observe the rituals of dozens of religions and live in conditions ranging from unspeakably primitive to magnificently luxurious. This extraordinary diversity gives the country immense tensile strength while posing an often insidious challenge to civil order and national unity. The market system melds with this brew of ethnic, linguistic and religious heterodoxy to make individual Indians inveterate problem solvers and multitaskers. Indians confront immense challenges, from chronic power shortages to pollution, from impossible overcrowding to extremes of climate. Daily life is a constant process of negotiation, reassessment and acceptance of hardship that makes people tough, resilient and focused. Indians succeed because if they don't, there is no safety net to catch them. There is no second chance.

And it's not just the business sector that's thriving on diversity and challenge. India is proud of calling itself the world's largest democracy. Canada and the United States both have larger landmasses, but even together they can't muster an electorate of more than 670 million people. Nor does either have to hold elections on several days over a period of a month or more because of the massive logistical needs of getting hundreds of millions of voters to the polls. Democracy is one of India's great accomplishments, perhaps still its greatest triumph as a nation. It may be flawed, chaotic and corrupt, but democracy flourishes in India and has done so, almost without interruption, since shortly after the last British rulers left in 1947. With a powerful central government, twenty-eight state administrations and thousands of municipal, district, town and village councils, elections are a crucial part of Indian life. Voter turnout is almost always high, and the intensity of tea shop debate over the political crisis of the day has to be experienced to be believed.

The ever-expanding network of satellite television news channels in India has only added to the strength of its democracy. The frequent exposure of fraud and corruption in the system, as reporters thrust their way into political backrooms with hidden cameras and bundles of marked cash, has been a welcome bonus. Democracy thrives in India in part because it is the only way to run such a vast, diverse society. People who are denied the freedom to despise and criticize their government can be expected to revolt. There has never been a large-scale uprising in India, even among the lowest of the low, however grim their prospects. Arguably, this is because democracy provided the outlet for frustration, if not always the means for redress. Governments change with regularity, coalitions of parties form and reform, and the people gaze in wonder at the spectacle.

Not every Indian is an enthusiast for the free market or believes that his or her country is sufficiently democratic. With India possessing the largest number of poor people in the world, there's ample scope for antipoverty activists, along with their colleagues in the environmental, legal reform, human rights and other movements. Fueled by technology and the globalized media environment, Indian activism is growing in national and international clout. The people who speak and work for the poor have thrived as the country modernizes. Many are powerful, passionate voices against market economics and the changing nature of society, and their arguments have had an impact on perception and policy. Indians bring to social activism all the focused skills of the marketplace that they've nurtured in their cities and rural bazaars for thousands of years. Dr. Vandana Shiva, Arundhati Roy, filmmaker Anil Padmarjan, Palagummi Sainath, Swami Agnivesh—all are names that the world's activist community knows and respects, but their native land nurtured them and gave them their sense of outrage.

In this book I argue that India has arrived at the world's top table, and is awaiting its due recognition. Buddhism, a religion that began in India, postulates that human beings must discover their potential and find enlightenment, success if you will, within themselves. It is said that Prince Siddhartha Gautama, who became known as the Buddha, was "awakened" when he sat under a tree and discovered the way to end suffering and attain an enlightened state of being. For practicing Buddhists, all questions can be answered by drawing on inner resources, by contemplation and focused reflection. The Buddha's revelation was that the seeds of enlightenment already exist inside us. So it is with India's quest for development and status as a player in the contemporary world of politics and economics. This quest is based on qualities of character, toughness, problem-solving ability and tolerance of diversity. Imported notions such as Western-style democracy, legal systems, free markets and social activism only enhance Indian society's innate strengths. For too long, the outsider's view of India has focused on its weaknesses: the poverty, frequent natural catastrophes and social inequities. Or on the mistaken notion that the country is a spiritual supermarket, somehow less concerned with the material demands of day-to-day life. The reality of India transcends both those views. That India is a vast, fluid and complex land is indisputable. That its growth to global influence will be of vast benefit to all is a point that is now being proven. I hope that I can begin to convince the reader that India—like Ram the press wallah— will confound the skeptics and overcome the odds, come what may. Problems, pitfalls, doubts and perhaps severe crises will spring up as India's express barrels along. Unforeseen environmental, human and man-made catastrophes will take their toll. In 2006, as I was re-searching and writing this book, it was bird flu, terrorism and global warming that posed cross-border challenges and threatened interna-tional trade and development. Who knows what will come along next? Whatever it is will have an impact on India as hard as or harder than anywhere else. But perhaps the most crucial part of the process of becoming and being a superpower is coping with crisis, managing the unforeseen. To the visitor, India is teeming and chaotic. Its streets are impossibly crowded. Beggars with twisted limbs sit outside ex-pensive boutiques. Just keeping a luncheon appointment can be a challenge, let alone navigating a business deal through the many bar-riers of language, bureaucracy and mystifying poverty that charac-terize this country.

Yet, Indians manage all this and more, every day and at every level of society. In this book I argue that India's influence will continue to expand, along with its economy. The title of the final chapter, Asia's America, says it all. India is well on its way to being one of the world's dominant nations, and it will wield its clout in a distinctive yet ulti-mately familiar way. Like the United States, India will act as a liberal superpower, motivated by national self-interest but with pluralist, democratic values at the forefront. There will be those in India and abroad who object to India's emergence on the world stage.

China also has superpower ambitions, and relations between Bei-jing and New Delhi will have to be managed carefully. But in the end, the world itself will benefit as India assumes its place as a world power.

1

DEBUGGING THE MILLENNIUM

Y2K and India

IN THE LATE 1990s, the world was warned of an impending computer meltdown. The threat posed by the so-called millennium bug, or Y2K, was predicated on the proposition that most computing systems had not been properly prepared for the onset of the twenty-first century. All computers have a calendar, not just as a convenience to the user but as a component of every operation. The internal calendar that ran inside many computers—especially older models—employed six digits to display the date. The first two numbers in that sequence signified the year; consequently, "991231" was scheduled to become "000101" at midnight, local time, on January 1, 2000.

Therein lay the supposed bug. As the twentieth century drew to a close, what we kept hearing from the media and computer experts, in ever more hysterical tones, was that the appearance of those first two zeroes at the beginning of the date sequence would be so illogical, so impossible for processing systems to comprehend, that a complete meltdown was inevitable. All computers programmed using older languages with the six-digit date sequence were doomed. Planes would plummet from the sky when their onboard computers shut down the engines or disengaged the autopilot. Trillions of dollars would be wiped from banking systems because financial records would cease to exist. Food, gasoline, clothing and other important commodities would stop arriving at retail outlets that had become completely dependent on data-based inventory control. Municipal services would shut down; governments would stop functioning. It was even suggested that confused computers in Washington and Moscow would order the launch of nuclear weapons, as a kind of default response to a situation that even the most paranoid programmers had never dreamt of.

In business and government circles, these dire predictions were widely believed. Suddenly people understood just how much they relied on computer networks for nearly every aspect of their daily lives, and they panicked. Even if Y2K did not lead to World War III, it was certain to be costly and disruptive. Amid the cacophony of Cassandra voices, a few skeptical notes were sounded—and picked up by the media—but the overall tone ranged from deep concern to hysteria. Who can forget the scenes on the television news in late December 1999 of consumers across North America buying up cases of mineral water and laying in emergency stocks of fuel? In one particularly alarming news story, a gun-shop owner reported that he couldn't keep handguns and hunting rifles in stock, so great was the demand from those who feared the worst. As it turned out, India had a significant role to play in this unfolding drama.

The 1990s had been kind to the world's second most populous country. Not to all of its people, a third of whom still toiled in the deepest and most intractable poverty, but for those, virtually equal in number, who formed what was being described as the fastest-growing middle class on the planet, life was increasingly sweet.

A nascent information technology sector was developing in the now-famous southern city of Bangalore. Other cities across the country were establishing their own high-tech development zones. Around the world, Indian computer programmers were becoming ubiquitous, from Silicon Valley to South Africa. But perhaps most importantly, the word began to spread that India's relatively late entry into the global computing business had important implications for the Y2K crisis. Put simply, Indian programmers understood the language of Y2K, an early computer code called COBOL. COBOL ("common business oriented language") was invented in 1959 by a committee established by the U.S. Department of Defense. It is the oldest computer programming language, still in use in some obscure corners of the cyber-world. Banks, financial markets, governments and the military-industrial complex all programmed their computer mainframes with COBOL when they first entered the information age. And few of them, as we learned in the gathering gloom of the late 1990s, had bothered to spend the vast sums necessary to retool or update the programs when more advanced computers came along. Of course, COBOL itself was kept up to date by companies such as Microsoft, which had adopted it for server and mainframe use, but fewer and fewer cutting-edge programmers and IT experts in the West were versed in COBOL's mysteries. There were far sexier languages to learn and invent.

Not so in India, where a heavy-handed government obsessed with self-reliance in every economic sector had only reluctantly begun to explore computing in the 1980s. A decade later, COBOL was still widely taught and used. Although COBOL wasn't the only language with an alleged propensity to Y2K meltdown, its prevalence in India gave the country's IT companies a huge competitive edge when Western multinationals were caught up in millennial meltdown hysteria. The Indian government spent millions of dollars to advertise the nation's debugging expertise, belatedly discovering the IT bandwagon that the country's entrepreneurs had been promoting for years.

A veritable who's who of global capitalism beat a path to India. Insurance giants, banks, airlines, retailers and petroleum companies all came looking for Indian consultants, or paid to have Indian firms send teams to corporate headquarters abroad. The Indian government statistics office estimates that more than US$2 billion was earned in export revenue between 1996 and 1999. An even larger amount poured in as the final year of the century brought latecomers into the fold. At the same time, a flood of Indian programmers left to join foreign companies setting up their own millennium debugging operations. The Clinton administration abetted the trend when it convinced Congress to increase the quota of high-tech job visas several times over, in part to help American companies cope with Y2K. The legislation became known as the "Gates amendment" because one of the leading voices in its favor was Microsoft's Bill Gates.

So what happened? In a word, nothing. The millennium bug turned out to be a mythical beast, a chimera of immense proportions

and no substance. Around the planet, ecstatic, occasionally inebri-
ated crowds roared out the countdown to the start of the twenty-first
century while corporate executives and IT specialists awaited the turn
of the clock in a state of more or less heightened anxiety. A few companies put on a brave face. British Airways even offered a champagne
flight that night so the historic moment could be toasted five miles
above Earth. A BA spokesman said the airline's onboard computers
were perfectly prepared for the new millennium and there was no risk
whatsoever of a catastrophic meltdown. Other carriers reported a real
reluctance among passengers to fly when the onboard computer clock
ticked into double-zero territory. But it's now a matter of historical—
if not hysterical—record that Y2K did not happen. British Airways
passengers sipped their champagne, cheered along with everyone else
and returned to Heathrow Airport safely. Bank accounts were unaf-
fected. So, unfortunately for many, were outstanding credit card bal-
ances. Money markets experienced the usual flurry of buying and
selling that accompanies a historic occasion, but the computers
recorded their transactions faithfully and without faltering. No nuclear weapons were launched.

The world awoke—slightly hungover—to business as usual on
the morning of January 1, 2000. The companies and computer networks that had refused to retool, or debug, in preparation for the new
century were lucky. They took a risk and it paid off. The others had
opted for an expensive solution to a nonexistent problem. And India
had benefited hugely, not just from the initial wave of spending on
Y2K "solutions," as they came to be known, but from the massively
positive exposure that the phenomenon gave Indian computing.

While some auditors and accounting departments may have
questioned the cost of repairing something that wasn't broken, no
one blamed India for devoting so much effort to solving the Y2K
bug. Indian companies such as Infosys Technologies, Wipro Technologies and Tata Consultancy Services showed the world they could
deploy resources and talent to address customer concerns quickly
and effectively. How did American and European customers feel
about being billed for work that was unnecessary? "They seem to
love us," answered one Bangalore executive in early 2000. "We were
there when they needed us," S. Subramanian of Tata told a television
interviewer. "Our teams worked long hours, and everyone seemed

hugely reassured, and the new orders for new work are simply pouring in." Behind him on the television screen were dozens of office cubicles where smartly dressed young men and women sat glued to monitors and keyboards—a vision of the new, awakening India if ever there was one.

More than one media commentator found significance in the fact that Indian IT found its launch pad in Y2K. India is as self-critical a society as any, though it can seem prickly and proud to an outsider. In this case, a little humor and a little history combined to set the role of millennium debugging in context. It was pointed out that many important concepts in modern mathematics were either invented or perfected by Indians. One of these is the notion of zero. Early counting systems, based on fingers and toes, were hardly likely to come up with the concept of a digit representing nothing. Zero is a sophisticated idea. Without it, much arithmetic, let alone calculus or algebra, is impossible. But, as almost every Indian schoolchild learns, nothingness is intrinsic to Indian philosophy. Wise men and gurus alike have concluded that all life is *maya*, illusion, mere perception. In other words, zero. It's true that this idea was fully explored and entered numerical notation only when Muslim conquerors ruled much of the subcontinent. But that is another matter. Zero belongs to India.

So many people thought it appropriate that India gave the world guidance in the matter of zeros. "We have taught the world nothing, and we continue to do so," was the gist of one wag's comments on the New Delhi diplomatic cocktail circuit. It's safe to assume that however disparaging the remark may seem, it was said with quiet pride.

I VISITED INDIA for the first time in May 1989. The highway to the Indian frontier from the Pakistani city of Lahore was the Grand Trunk Road, which once connected Calcutta to the foothills of the towering mountain rampart known as the Hindu Kush. It was the same route taken by invading armies and travelers for centuries. In his novel *Kim*, Rudyard Kipling describes life along the Grand Trunk Road as frenetic and mysterious by turns. As the journey at the heart of the novel begins, the urchin Kim and his traveling companion, an elderly Buddhist lama, watch the comings and goings with awe:

Look! Brahmins and chumars, bankers and tinkers, barbers and
bunnias, pilgrims—and potters—all the world going and coming.
It is to me as a river from which I am withdrawn like a log after a
flood.
    And truly the Grand Trunk Road is a wonderful spectacle.[1]

IN THOSE DAYS, the subcontinent's most celebrated road, at least the
part near the India–Pakistan frontier east of Lahore, was much quieter. Relations between the two countries were tense, and cross-
border trade and travel almost impossible. My own journey was one
of the first of its kind and came during a lull in hostilities. The countryside is flat, green and well irrigated. On both sides of today's border, this is the land known as Punjab, from the local term for "five
rivers." It is the richest farmland in all of South Asia, but few places
saw more blood shed in 1947 when Muslims and Hindus fled ancestral lands for new countries, stopping only to fight and slaughter
people moving in the other direction. Now, decades after the carnage that ensued from India's partition and independence, the border still seems unnatural, a heavily guarded line that slashes through
communities that had been shared for centuries. And yet subtle differences between the two countries have emerged since they attained
freedom.
    In 1989, Pakistan had known decades of open trade and a mar-
ket-driven fiscal policy. The most obvious sign of the market philosophy it adhered to was an economy that had been penetrated by
Western brand names familiar all over the world. You rode a Toyota
or Nissan van to the border post. The man who collected your fare
had a Sony radio pressed to his ear, and there were countless billboards for Coca-Cola, Nike and other foreign products. India at that
time was more than forty years into a very different economic experiment. This became obvious after I crossed into Indian territory and
was sitting outside the customs post in the midday heat, badly in need
of a cold drink. I asked the border guard if refreshments were available and he smiled and waved his hand at a distant kiosk. A young
boy carrying a bucket came running, fetching up breathlessly by my
side and digging into the ice water sloshing around in his pail.

"Thumbs-up," was what I thought he said, then "Limca, Frooti, Campi Cola." I picked up the unfamiliar bottles and saw that it was actually Thums Up, and that Campi Cola had modeled its logo on Coke's cursive symbol. Eventually I learned that Coca-Cola and many other familiar American companies had pulled out of India in the 1970s after disputes over government regulation. Coke executives had chosen to forsake India's massive market rather than divulge the company's zealously maintained secret soft-drink formula to the government, as Indian bureaucrats had been demanding. Indigenous brands had prospered in the absence of foreign competition. India's hot, thirsty summers improved ever so slightly with a cold, beaded bottle in one's hand, even if the brand wasn't a name known to me. I reached into the boy's bucket and pulled out an icy Limca, the local equivalent of Sprite or 7UP, and downed it in one swallow.

Beyond the border crossing, we traveled in Indian-made vehicles. My first taxi was a Hindustan Ambassador, and later I took a trip in a smaller Premier Padmini. There were Mahindra jeeps and Tata trucks, Maruti subcompacts and Bajaj motorcycles. The very rich could import a Rolls-Royce or a Mercedes-Benz by paying taxes and duties that more than trebled the sticker price, but other drivers stuck to what was more readily available on the local market. Later that night in Amritsar, I relaxed over a bottle of Rosy Pelican beer. There was no Budweiser or Heineken to be had anywhere outside the expensive bar of a five-star hotel. I sat back, sipped a slightly musty lager and contemplated the Indian economy, forty-two years after independence.

India had been a self-described socialist state since its birth as a free nation in 1947. It was guided by economic mantras extolling self-reliance and hostility to foreign consumer goods. These were the legacy of the country's first prime minister, Jawaharlal Nehru—one of the most remarkable figures of the twentieth century. Nehru was a giant in the struggle to free India from British colonial rule and became head of government when the independent nation was born. He won three elections and died in office in 1964. His legacy is immense, both as a campaigner for Indian sovereignty and as a moral voice on the world stage, arguing against the nuclear arms race and in favor of better treatment for the world's poor nations. But he also fancied himself an economist and, before independence, reflected on the various economic models on offer. He came to admire the Soviet Union's planning process, in which economic goals and the means to achieve them were set in five-year plans that could be monitored for implementation and effectiveness. But as a committed democrat, Nehru rejected the coercive authoritarianism of Communist Party economics, declaring in 1929 that "the human cost of the Soviet system was too high."

When his government took office in 1947, it found an economy that had begun—under the last decade or so of British rule—to reacquire the technological and industrial base that had been lost to mercantile colonialism in the nineteenth century. An automotive industry, for example, based on Henry Ford's model of assembly lines and outsourced parts production, had been operating in the southern city of Chennai (then Madras) since the early decades of the twentieth century. But by and large, India was overwhelmingly an agricultural country. Some 90 percent of its gross domestic product came directly or indirectly from farming, much of it subsistence farming. The departure of the British had left the big plantation sector—indigo, cotton, jute for burlap bags and other export crops—in an uncertain state. The hostility of the Indian people to exploitative, large-scale agriculture made land reform an early imperative. Among Nehru's most successful economic moves were the breaking up of large estates and the redistribution of the land among serfs, farm laborers, sharecroppers and other sons and daughters of the soil.

However, Nehru believed that India's future was in industry, and he and his planners decided that the government would build foundries, factories, tool-and-die works, food-processing facilities and other big-ticket industrial plants. It would do this largely by itself, accepting direct foreign aid but no private investment based on equity. This would allow the government to occupy what Nehru called "the commanding heights" of the new Indian economy. There was to be a "socialist pattern of development" that emphasized the good of the people over profits. Indian companies were to be well run, economically viable and providers of employment and prosperity. The broad consensus of Indian society that had coalesced behind the freedom struggle included indigenous Indian capitalists who were well placed to take part in the industrialization process. They had access to funds and expertise in constructing and managing factories. Nehru tapped these people to be both builders and administrators, and, increasingly, he required them to establish and run enterprises owned by the government. Steel mills, oil refineries, shipbuilding, heavy equipment and transport manufacturing, as well as factories that produced countless other capital and consumer goods, were among the industries in which Nehru's government played a role.

At the same time, certain sectors of the economy were reserved for private companies, including vehicle production, textiles, soft drinks, some food processing and so on. Hence Thums Up cola and the Hindustan Ambassador car. To this day the vehicle of choice for Indian government fleets, the Ambassador is a clunky copy of the 1951 Morris Oxford, an otherwise long-forgotten and unlamented bit of British automotive design. Its competitors were largely based on foreign designs as well. The Premier Padmini, which still makes up the bulk of the taxi fleet in Mumbai, is modeled on a Fiat coupe from the 1950s. Like the Ambassador, its design barely changed over the forty-five years that it was manufactured between 1955 and 2000.

The corporate players were the traditional Indian business families that had risen to economic prominence under the British: the Tatas, Birlas, Mahindras and Bajajs. They ran a wide array of businesses, but a vast regulatory apparatus was set up to control each and every aspect of their enterprises, from hiring and firing to new production lines, capital investment, export licenses, imports, even advertising campaigns and finding new retail markets. A uniquely Indian name for this form of regulated enterprise was coined: License Raj. And India's business community, no stranger to the behavior of the earlier Raj, that of British colonial rule, observed that one replaced the other with a comparable capriciousness and appetite for willful obstruction. Yet Indian business owners did little to try to change the system because it protected them from international competition and allowed them to sell somewhat shoddy goods in a guaranteed market. In its defense, the business community might argue that it had no opportunity to improve its products because strict foreign exchange controls limited access to outside technologies and materials.

Neither Nehru nor the governments that followed in the 1960s and 1970s led by his daughter, Indira Gandhi, shied away from imposing even more restrictions on the private sector in the name of broadening those commanding economic heights. In 1953, the Indian government took control of Air India, at that point one of the developing world's most successful and respected private airlines. Indira Gandhi nationalized several Indian banks in her years in power, inevitably turning them into barely viable entities that seemed to exist largely to distribute loans to government supporters who had no intention of repaying them. The state sector in India, founded with undeniable idealism and with some early notable successes, was by the 1980s becoming a massive drag on development. Job opportunities for a growing population were limited at every level. The civil service, state-owned enterprises and private-sector businesses had all the employees they needed. Indian government regulation frightened off local investment, let alone wary foreigners and multinationals that might have created jobs and opportunities for India's young people. Something had to be done.

In the 1980s the administration, led by Indira Gandhi's son Rajiv, had modest dreams of shaking up the Indian economy and stimulating the country's hidden dynamism and entrepreneurial skills. After all, it was often pointed out, Indians were traders, merchants and capitalists centuries ago, ranging over the known world with sophisticated textiles, jewelry and other items that today's economists would consider exports and commodities. Centuries of domination by Muslim conquerors and European colonizers had sapped the country of its innate talents for market economics. Decades of state-led capitalism disguised as socialism, but really an enabler of political hegemony by the Indian National Congress, or Congress Party, had furthered the decline. The global economic boom of the 1980s was leaving India behind. The country, it seemed, couldn't win. The international financial contractions of previous decades had hit India hard, despite its protectionist policies. Now it was being denied a share of global expansion.

The 1984 election brought Sam Pitroda, along with a team of fellow young moderns, to advise the new government in New Delhi. As a child in eastern India, Pitroda says, he had never seen a telephone, let alone used one. In what he himself terms a miracle, he won a scholarship to study in the United States and was a multimillionaire by the time he returned to work with Rajiv Gandhi. His was one of the loudest voices calling for a relaxation of import restrictions and duties on telecommunications and technologies that would help India develop. Computers, for example, in the 1980s could be brought into the country only upon payment of a 350 percent tariff on their declared value. Locally made Indian computers were available, but they did only a fraction of what their imported counterparts could do and were manufactured in such small numbers that it took customers years to reach the top of a waiting list to purchase one.

Pitroda is known in India today for one remarkably far-reaching achievement. Having made his fortune in the United States in telecommunications, he was a great believer in the multiplier effect of good, widely available phone services on both the economy and the general welfare. So Sam Pitroda urged his boss, Prime Minister Rajiv Gandhi, to allow the import of some relatively simple switchboard technologies that, he argued, would eventually lead to cheap, locally developed phone services in practically every hamlet in the land. Predictably, there was bureaucratic resistance. A generations-long tradition of protectionism doesn't disappear overnight. But today, Pitroda's dream is made manifest in the ubiquitous PCOs, or public call offices—tens of thousands of them across India—in which local, national and long-distance calls can be made, monitored and paid for on the spot. Faxes too, and now the Internet, are accessible to everyone. India's PCOs are becoming cybercafés where young men and women send e-mail, apply for jobs and acquire information, all thanks to Sam Pitroda's telephone switches of the 1980s. Now retired and living back in the United States, Pitroda told an Indian interviewer a few years ago about how it felt to see his work in action:

> Once, when I was traveling in western India, there was a PCO where 30 girls in brand new dresses, were all lined up. I could not understand it for sometime. We went a little bit ahead, and then we realized that these girls were waiting to call their brothers in New Jersey because it was an important Hindu family holiday. Today, there are 20 million phones in the country out of which 10 million phones are from the technology that we developed after changing the import laws. It was that simple.[2]

UNFORTUNATELY FOR PITRODA and like-minded people in that 1980s government, the whims and tendencies of Indian politics reasserted themselves after only a few years. Financial scandals, changes of government and other crises put a brake on progress. Rajiv Gandhi was assassinated in 1991. The new administration that he might have headed—for his Congress Party won the subsequent election—immediately found itself faced with a frightening balance-of-payments crisis. Put simply, India did not have enough foreign currency in its national bank account to make payments on international loans. If something wasn't done, the country would have to default, for the first time ever. This perfect record was a point of pride for the Indian elite. More seriously, missing an international loan payment could be costly to the nation's credit rating and prospects for future lending.

It fell to Manmohan Singh, a former World Bank official, to deal with the looming crisis in public finances. Singh was appointed finance minister by the new prime minister, the wily and pragmatic P. V. Narasimha Rao. Rao was a veteran member of the Congress Party who had mouthed more than his share of anti-business, state-socialist slogans in the past but who was now prepared to take the radical steps that his minister proposed to avoid defaulting. Singh had spoken to his former colleagues at the International Monetary Fund and its sister organization, the World Bank, about what might be required to reschedule India's payments. He knew what they would tell him: that only a wholesale rethinking of economic policy would allow lenders to cut India some slack. Leftists in India are still infuriated by these demands, which they believed were a form of blackmail. India was told to make its economy more market-friendly. It was asked to ease import restrictions, cut red tape, allow more foreign investment into the country and sell off state-run businesses. These were—then, and more or less remain to this day—the usual conditions imposed on countries in financial trouble. As a solution to economic problems, they have a mixed record. Some countries have found that their economies worsen when placed under the yoke of market reform. But not India.

The immediate effect of the economic rule changes was to allow the debt payments to be rescheduled. That a proud country avoided defaulting on its international obligations perhaps was success enough for the early years of reform. But the global economy was entering a new phase in the 1990s. In the United States, personal computing and the Internet were converging to create a soaring global demand for telecommunications, software, web design, business consulting and other related services. A whole generation of Indian immigrants had gone to America in previous decades, seeking greener pastures and the opportunities denied them in their homeland. Many had settled along a corridor in northern California that ran south from San Francisco Bay past Stanford University down to San Jose and beyond. This, of course, is Silicon Valley, then, as now, home to the world's industrial leaders in information technology.

Bell Laboratories, the forerunner of Intel, set up its first research facility in Silicon Valley decades ago, as did Xerox and others. All sorts of specialist computer-chip design and manufacturing firms followed. So did the next wave of Internet ventures. Scientists and engineers were attracted by both the work opportunities and the sun-drenched California climate. After working for one of the big players, some started companies of their own. They were fiercely competitive, yet saw themselves as part of a team of top professionals in a singular setting. Silicon Valley spawned a unique culture of business mixed with applied research. The thinking was often wildly innovative and outside the box. Google, Yahoo!, Hotmail, Netscape and eBay are not ideas that any sane banker would have backed thirty years ago, however savvy his or her financial instincts. Even the Silicon Valley venture capitalists were pioneers. Like the scientific community, they were prepared to take immense risks. They enjoyed being at the cutting edge of commerce, funding the coolest new research and cashing in.

Indians took to the Silicon Valley "thing" early and almost instinctively. As immigrants, they wanted to succeed, almost at any cost. After all, they had all risked everything by leaving their homeland and the network of relatives and friends so crucial to traditional Indian society. They brought with them an incredible work ethic and often a first-rate science or engineering education. Their pleasures tended to be simple: food from home, family, often a quiet spiritualism and, of course, work, work and more work. At first, they frequently were code punchers and keyboard jockeys, doing what they were told to do by American-born entrepreneurs and computer professionals. But soon enough they became key players, inventors and investors themselves, starting up new businesses and marketing the next big thing on the

World Wide Web or in computer gaming. At the height of the white-hot technology bubble there were hundreds of thousands of Indians living in the San Francisco Bay area. Most of them either worked in high tech or were drawn to its margins, opening restaurants and shops to service the IT professionals from home.

India's own computer and software industry was insignificant. But both at home and in the United States there were many of Indian descent well positioned to take advantage of the world's growing dependence on desktop computing. One of them was Pradeep Kar. Now a trim, bearded man in his forties, Kar traveled to the United States in the 1980s on behalf of a big chemical company owned by the Indian government. Kar says he was chosen to go almost by chance, though his English-language skills and MBA undoubtedly helped. Ethnically, he was something of a pioneer. He arrived in the Bay Area just as Indians were emerging as a force to be reckoned with. They were there, they were working, but they weren't yet the dominant ethnic group in Silicon Valley, Kar says. But it wasn't hard to sense the trend.

"Even then, we knew or we believed that being Indian was something special. That we had a set of skills there that we could leverage for foreign customers, that our work ethic, our excellence in math and science, could all be put to use." Like many Indians who went through the Silicon Valley experience, Kar was struck by the contrast between attitudes in India and those in the United States, the openness of America versus the stodgy orthodoxy of home.

"It was a good time to be in the States, and to see what was possible in the right environment," he says. "I always wanted to go home, to do business in India, but I was inspired in California by the fact that business wasn't seen as evil, grasping and out to steal from the public. The Americans didn't feel that way at all. They saw business as socially useful, and the best way to create employment and prosperity."

Throughout the 1990s, India found itself at the nexus of a complex and beneficial web of developments: the global boom in IT demand and services; the connection with Silicon Valley; a generous visa policy in the United States that actively courted Indian expertise; changing aspirations at home that saw young graduates yearn for private-sector jobs, not the civil service; and, of course, the Singh economic reforms, which unleashed entrepreneurial skills and revitalized a steady but sluggish and underperforming economy. Add to this the catalyst of the Y2K millennium bug, when the world beat a path to India's door.

None of this is to say that Nehru's state-led economic model did not serve a useful purpose in the initial decades of Indian development. The vast inequalities that come from unfettered free markets were somewhat mitigated by Nehru's policies, and India was able to build a respectable industrial sector from almost nothing. An indigenous steel industry, shipbuilding and even rocket science and a space program all evolved behind India's huge tariff walls and state-driven ideals of self-reliance. The country's domestic consumer products left much to be desired, but they were priced for the local market and people grew used to them. Those soft drinks I was sipping in 1989, and even the clunky old cars that ferried me about back then, are still around, even as Coca-Cola, Toyota and Sony make inroads into the rapidly expanding Indian consumer market. Had Nehru opted for a more American approach to development, India might not have managed to build so many steel mills, factories and foundries. Imported goods would have displaced indigenous products long before the companies that made them in India were ready for international competition. Yes, computers might have arrived sooner, but overall the Indian economy would have been a very different platform from which to launch the country's IT and knowledge-economy aspirations.

India's economic progress in its first forty years of freedom was respectable by many standards. What came to be known derisively as "the Hindu rate of growth," a steady yet unspectacular expansion of the economy that continued through feast or famine, dominated India's early decades. This annual growth, reflected in an annual 3.5 percent increase in gross domestic product, was not enough to produce the jobs and prosperity that so many craved, but it was a source of stability in often troubled economic times. Indeed, India was able to meet its international obligations for so many years in large part because it kept its imports to a minimum. It used its foreign exchange mainly to purchase petroleum and other commodities that could not be produced in sufficient quantity at home. Likewise, free market orthodoxy emerged unchallenged in Western countries only from the

1980s onward. Before that, most Western governments, including that of the United States, tried to influence, coerce and regulate business in what were seen as the greater interests of society. Nehru's economic model was in step with his times. But as time marched on, the world chose a different approach, one that empowered the private sector and individual entrepreneurs to become major players in economic matters. Although India was at first coerced in difficult circumstances, it made the market-friendly adjustments demanded by its creditors. The rest is history. Economic reform is entrenched and seems to have broad political support. In the main, India has won what Pradeep Kar describes as "the second freedom struggle, the battle to wrest the economy from the License Raj and give [it] to the people. We won that in 1991 and no one wants to turn back the clock. No one."

THE STARTLING EFFECTS of these reforms are now evident in much of the country, at least in urban areas and bigger towns. Perhaps nowhere is this more true than in Bangalore, a sprawling metropolis of nearly seven million people that sits in the center of South India, equidistant from the Bay of Bengal to the east and the Indian Ocean to the west. This is the heart of the country's information technology boom, home to most of the big-name firms and to the Indian headquarters of foreign companies such as Sun Microsystems, Dell and Cisco Systems. In the coming years, the world may have to start calling Bangalore by another name. Its ethnic nationalist government has decided to rejig the official moniker of the city to Bengalaru, which apparently is a more accurate transliteration of the city's name in the local language, Kannada. But, as of early 2007, few if any of the city's IT firms and entrepreneurs have changed their office addresses: Bangalore it remains.

Once Bangalore was a quiet, sleepy city of green parks and quiet boulevards. Built, like Rome, on seven hills, it was a retirement community with an equable climate that has none of the extremes of heat, monsoon, or even winter fog experienced elsewhere in South Asia. The more lush and densely treed streets are still home to many former civil servants and army generals. But even before it began to thrum with cutting-edge IT creativity, Bangalore had acquired a reputation as being the brain of India.

Bangalore's universities specialized in the sciences, and the Indian government bequeathed to the city a series of important research and development organizations. The country's space program, which aims to put an astronaut on the moon within a decade, is based here, as are advanced military research institutes. India's last president, A. P. J. Abdul Kalam, a scientist who is generally credited with developing the country's nuclear weapons and ballistic missile program, did much of his work in Bangalore before taking up the largely ceremonial post of president in 2002. The city was a magnet for scientists and researchers even before the 1990s IT boom and Y2K firmly established its global reputation. Now the city is sometimes seen as a victim of its own success. The traffic is chaotic, property prices are soaring and electricity and water shortages have become routine.

Most of the IT investment in Bangalore is located in a suburb known as Electronic City. The signs yield few concessions to linguistic nationalism. No Bengalaru here. Consider Ascendium, Brionic, Teknic, Multipul, Syscon, Mphasis, Trolex and Thermonetric, among many others. These are names of IT companies that have sprung up, and there's more than an echo of similar strips and streets in Silicon Valley. They are meant to sound cool, sexy, hip and cutting-edge. And yet they give nothing away about the nature of the business conducted beyond the metal gates or inside the generic glass-and-steel office towers of Electronic City. Other, more familiar names are there too: BP Solar (the alternative energy branch of British Petroleum), 3M, Intel, Microsoft, IBM and, of course, Domino's Pizza. Even here in South India, home to some of the country's best cuisine, fast food and the computer business are joined at the hip.

One of the more impressive corporate headquarters belongs to Infosys, one of India's three largest companies in the information technology business. The other two of the three are Wipro and Tata Consultancy Services. Among them, these three trade off on various benchmarks. Tata has the highest turnover, Wipro is the largest employer, Infosys is a bigger global player. But taken together, they form an IT colossus that dwarfs every other knowledge-sector business venture in India. Between them, the three companies employed more than 120,000 people in 2007, and their global turnover looked set to be in excess of US$8 billion annually. Their corporate growth rates, by any measure, have been white-hot. Most recently, Infosys saw its business expand at around 30 percent in one year; the other two companies are more or less in sync. All three are competitive and yet oddly complementary. Wipro began as a vegetable oil company and is still largely privately owned. Infosys, which was started from scratch by seven founding partners, is a darling of the investment community, with its listings on Indian, U.S. and European stock exchanges. Tata Consultancy Services is part of the massive, family-owned Tata group, which includes steel, automotive, electrical power generation, tea gardens and other enterprises.

The Infosys campus resembles nothing less than a state-of-the-art technical university built with no expense spared. Its towering office blocks and other buildings are sheathed in reflective glass and grouped around a sprawling employee services complex that includes a sizable health club, a concert venue and fast-food outlets that are among the busiest restaurants in the country. Employees bustle about with cell phones glued to their ears or whir by on electric golf carts. All are intent on an array of complex and vital missions to the far-flung reaches of the Infosys empire. Software solutions to Silicon Valley's finest? That's in block B, where teams are in constant satellite contact with their counterparts in the field via a cluster of dishes on the roof. Corporate strategy for a Fortune 500 investment firm bundled into a bespoke software package that promises guaranteed results? More highly educated Indians huddle in cubicles in another building to formulate policy for boardrooms and shareholders half a world away. Other Infosys priority areas include call-center support, business services done as outsourcing and a long list of computer-related tasks that so many non-IT firms used to do in-house before Y2K opened the door to Indian-based specialists.

In 2001, the CEO of Infosys and a leading pioneer of India's information technology sector was C. Narayana Murthy. He is now retired, having chosen to leave his post in 2006 when he reached the company's mandatory retirement age of sixty, despite his lofty status in Infosys. But he remains a board member and has been given the title of "chief mentor" at the company he helped found in 1987. His wife famously stumped up the $250 that was his share of the initial investment. Murthy is an almost mythic figure in the Indian business world, an ascetic and spiritual Hindu, well read and fond of a good laugh.

Murthy also has a liking for the pithy sayings of the American baseball legend Yogi Berra. When I first met him several years ago, an exchange of Berra's best seemed a good place to begin. We opened with "nostalgia ain't what it used to be," then moved on to the more famous "it ain't over 'til it's over." Murthy chortled when I told him about "when you come to a fork in the road, take it." He in turn came back with "the harder I work, the luckier I get." Murthy then burst into laughter and said that that particular phrase had become his business mantra.

Like Yogi Berra, Murthy is short and a little stocky. "My gravity is low," Berra once said. But unlike the baseball player, the Infosys founder attributes his success—in the first instance—to God. Murthy admits under questioning that sheer business acumen and a measure of good luck also contributed. With further gentle pressure, he will also confess to being good with people and numbers, and to having what some like to call "the vision thing." But in the end, it always comes back to his faith. "I'd say we were blessed by the Almighty," he told me, "but we have worked hard and, thanks to God, have made some astute business decisions along the way." Murthy's piety is a quiet but crucial part of him. He observes all the rituals that high-caste Hindus are supposed to adhere to: daily prayers, a vegetarian diet, offerings of flowers and visits to temples and pilgrimage sites. He sees absolutely no dichotomy between success at the cutting edge of Indian information technology and belief in one of the world's oldest faiths. "Look, it's all about spiritualism," he said. "That's why I do what I do. Our lives are all about using what's given by God to do as much good as possible. This company is strongly ethical because we the founders just didn't want to start another business that was run like an authoritarian state. When we started, we said we'd never change our ethical approach, and we never have."

A favorite boast of every Infosys executive is that hundreds of company employees, thanks to the value of their shares, are millionaires. In fact, as we were having our tea in his book-lined office, Murthy told me that the man who served us was one of those millionaires. "He just bought himself a house worth four million rupees [about $90,000 at the time]." Murthy explained that the employee had raised the cash for a down payment by selling some shares and putting others up as collateral for a loan. The tea server later told me that he kept most of his stock because he likes owning a piece of Infosys.

"Nowhere else in India, or probably in the world, would someone as far down the ladder as our friend here have so much money or be so informed about the finances of a company. We're proud of this," Murthy said. In many other companies in India, neither would such an employee understand our conversation in English. The tea-serving Indian rupee millionaire did, and he smiled at his boss as he took our cups away.

Murthy's bookshelves in his corner office in the Infosys corporate block reflected his active, probing mind. There was Bill Gates, of course. A well-thumbed paperback edition of *The Road Ahead* had pride of place among other business books. Murthy also reads philosophy, thus Bertrand Russell, Milton Friedman and Karl Marx. Murthy is fond of explaining that he used to be an ardent Marxist. That was before 1974, the year he found himself in jail in then-Communist Bulgaria. He was making his way overland from France to India after spending a few years in Paris.

"I was on the night train through Yugoslavia and a girl and a boy were sitting in the same compartment. The girl spoke French, so I struck up a conversation with her. We got along famously, but I'd stumbled into the middle of something. The boyfriend must have got jealous because he spoke to the police when we got to the Bulgarian border and they came and dragged me off the train. I guess they thought I was some kind of spy, probably the only South Indian they'd ever seen." The young Murthy spent a horrifying seventy-two hours in jail. He was offered no food and very little water. Then, with no more explanation than had been given when he was arrested, his captors took him back to the railway station and put him on a train to Yugoslavia.

"They expelled me," he said. "And then they told me how lucky I was that India and Bulgaria had friendly, fraternal relations. I thought, If that's how these Communist regimes treat friends, then I don't want any part of it. You don't end poverty by redistributing limited wealth: you help the poor by creating more and more wealth. That's what we do here at Infosys—keep the pie growing so everyone can get some."

Murthy's sense of social obligation, expressed through his business activities, is common among the captains of India's IT industry. You hear versions of it from the likes of Azim Premji, founder of Infosys's main competitor, Wipro, and—around the turn of the millennium—India's richest man for several years running. That calculation is based on the value of the stock he holds in his own corporation and is certainly not reflected in his lifestyle. Premji famously drives a ten-year-old car and scorns the trappings of wealth. A journalist for India's *Economic Times* newspaper, Chitti Pantulu, once told me a tale that illustrates how Premji and Narayana Murthy see themselves.

When President Bill Clinton traveled to India in March 2000, he wanted to visit budding information technology centers other than Bangalore and so was invited to Hyderabad, a city more or less in the geographic middle of the Indian landmass. No expense was spared to make Clinton feel welcome in his few hours in the city.

Pantulu covered the U.S. president's visit. "There was a big function and Clinton was, of course, on the dais," Pantulu said. "Our local business leaders were pushing and shoving, competing with politicians to sit up there too. Murthy and Premji just sat quietly in the audience and you could tell that they didn't mind. Along with a few dozen other invited guests, they had met Clinton privately, and again it was a quiet affair, although the president knew who they were and was very enthusiastic and full of praise. Then, when it was over, all the VIPs went clamoring out the door with full security and sirens howling in convoys." Indians call this a *tamasha,* the seething show of self-importance and sycophancy that's very much a part of political culture.

"It was inconveniencing everyone in its path—the usual behavior of so-called dignitaries here," said Pantulu. "When the press contingent was finally allowed to leave by the security men, Murthy was sitting all by himself outside the venue, waiting for the valet to bring his office car around. There was no one pushing anyone else around. Nobody was making special arrangements for him. He was deep in thought and none of the pompous local idiots or the officious security staff was paying any attention. I think he liked it that way. And he was driving himself back to his living quarters because he'd given the driver the day off. I'd like to see one of our politicians or sons who inherited their family business do that. Many of them don't even know how to drive."

IT services sourced from India are now everywhere and growing in influence. Murthy, Premji and others have helped build a sector that is growing by leaps and bounds. By some estimates, more than two million Indians work in some aspect of the country's knowledge economy. This number includes people in small family firms that provide services such as gardening, catering and maintenance, as well as cutting-edge researchers and entrepreneurs. Infosys is a leading player, but there are dozens if not hundreds of smaller, hungrier companies starting up every week. From humble beginnings at independence, when India had to build an industrial sector almost from scratch, through years of protectionism and bureaucratic, state-led five-year plans, to the reforms of 1991 and the IT-fueled explosion of more recent years, India's economy is powering along. It's a potent force in a country that has long simmered on the global back burner.

2

FROM TECH SUPPORT
TO TUTORING

India's Online Revolution

WHERE BANGALORE AND information technology lead, other cities and sectors soon follow. After Bangalore came Hyderabad, then Mumbai, Chennai and others. Even Calcutta, a city long run by Communists, is becoming a hub for communications and IT investment. The Indian capital, New Delhi, has also been transformed from a city where politics was the only game in town to an information and back-office powerhouse. A few years ago, few people knew what back-office services were, according to a special supplement of *The Economist* magazine published in 2004. But now a notion that didn't really exist at the beginning of the 1990s—the outsourcing of jobs from West to East—had found its new home: the seething, rapidly expanding suburbs around India's political heartland.

That particular quiet revolution broke out in the late 1990s. For me, the opening salvos were fired early on a searing pre-monsoon May morning. There is no respite from the heat at that time of year. Some days, the pavement softens to black mud in the sun's relentless glare, and hundreds of thousands of air conditioners send the city's energy demand soaring. That means power cuts and brownouts, periods when lights dim and fans barely stir the thick, still air. By day, tempers flare in buses and cars so superheated that an open window provides no comfort whatsoever. Neither do nights bring much relief. The mercury drops a few degrees and power cuts continue. People sweat into their sheets or go to bed wet from the shower hoping that evaporation will cool them as they try to fall asleep.

Yet, there were then—and continue to be—places in and around the city where electricity and the hum of air conditioners are constant. One such neighborhood lies just beyond the fringe of Indira Gandhi International Airport, about twenty miles from the city center. This is Gurgaon, an industrial park that grew into a community. When I first visited Gurgaon in the late 1990s, there were the usual small neighborhood services and firms—furniture-makers, transportation companies, metalworking shops and brick kilns. But the area had also recently acquired a high-tech flavor since augmented with an astounding residential real estate and retail boom. India's trendiest shopping malls sprang up alongside condominium complexes that might have been airlifted intact from California or Toronto. Then, on my first visit, new-economy India was most evident in row after row of sleek modern factories that loomed along the planned grid of streets. As I drove past, I heard the discreet thrum of diesel-powered generators, muffled by soundproofing, for this was an area that simply could not afford the same kind of power cuts plaguing the residents of more traditional parts of New Delhi. Here the AC never stopped humming and the computer screens glowed without a break. This was nothing less than the Indian version of the legions of manufacturing plants that line China's coasts and throng its hinterland, producing cheap toys, clothing, shoes and electronic devices for Western consumers. Factories with global markets for their products, just like China—but here in the suburbs of India's capital city, what was being produced was wholly intangible.

One of the early pioneers of change in Gurgaon was a company based in the United States but with a global workforce and market for its services. It called itself eFunds. The firm got its start as a provider of services to the banking industry, from verifying customer identity and creditworthiness to printing personal data on checks. As banking embraced the World Wide Web, the company evolved too, and was quick to pick up on new technologies, particularly the use of the Internet as a tool for money transfers and accessing financial products. In India, eFunds and its U.S.–based competitors helped set up ATM networks for banks that for decades had kept only paper records and been run almost entirely by government departments. Over the years, eFunds began to transfer more and more jobs from its global businesses to India. True, Indian labor is cheaper, but this was not the only reason for the shift. There was also a growing consensus that India was an easier place for multinational firms to do business. It was the start of a whole new connection between India and the world. At first glance, in the late 1990s, it wasn't entirely clear what was going on in the vast workspace inside eFunds's main building. Hundreds of well-groomed young people were sitting at computer screens, wearing headsets. Almost every person in the room was talking. Some waved their hands and nodded their heads as they spoke. Others sat stock still, only their lips moving. The place was awash with whispered words distinguishable only as fragments of speech.

" . . . here to help, ma'am."
" . . . and what is the account number?"
"Sir, there's no need to shout or be rude . . ."
"I'm Bobby and I'm calling about an overdue . . ."
" . . . pay the Visa now, and the MasterCard . . ."
" . . . last three letters of your mother's maiden name."
"Really, it's the most we can delay the payment . . ."

Today, we're accustomed to the idea of call centers. We have spoken to Bobby (real name Bharat), his colleague Sue (Saraswati) or their equivalent and struggled to understand their unique Indian-American accent. During training sessions, they watch American films and learn how to interpret the various English-language idioms of North America, if not to master them themselves. They choose to go by nondescript diminutives and nicknames that won't startle less worldly customers in the suburbs of Orlando, Winnipeg or Phoenix. These names often are written on Post-it notes stuck to their computer screens as a reminder. Everyone wears a headset, and sound-dampening technology keeps the cacophony of one-sided telephone conversations to a dull roar.

To walk around a room like this is a quasi-voyeuristic experience, a forbidden glimpse into the financial affairs of thousands of North Americans, most of whom—then, in the late 1990s—probably had no idea that an Indian liberal arts graduate was accessing their account data on a computer screen. How could they know that the young woman telling them to be a little more regular in making credit card payments or to do something about those bouncing checks came from a family of devout Hindu jewelers where four generations lived in a single house? It was a glorious disconnect, back when such businesses were still rather new. Now India's success in the global market for business process outsourcing, or BPO, is undeniable. What began as a business opportunity is now an economic sector that earns the country more than US$13 billion a year in foreign exchange. This counts as an export, just as if the companies in question were sending abroad timber or compact cars. Both revenue and employment in call centers and other BPO firms doubled each year between 2000 and 2005. No one expects more recent statistics to be any different. At last count, more than seven hundred thousand Indians worked in the sector, and all of the country's major cities seem to be staging perpetual job fairs where established and new BPO companies try to attract the best of the many Indians who graduate from university each year.

Name a household brand in software, financial services, insurance or travel, and chances are that the company has a phalanx of Indians handling customer calls, doing the payroll or plotting corporate strategy. As with the IT business, at the outset it is all about time zones and cheaper labor, to be sure. Indians working in a call center earn a tenth of what their colleagues in the West take home. As well, the country is ideally placed geographically to handle the after-work, before-breakfast needs of Western consumers. But there's far more to the phenomenon than saving money and meeting customers' needs outside office hours. There is also the high quality of the work done by Indians in India. It is not only cheaper, it is also as good as or better than in the West.

On one side of the vast workspace in Gurgaon that day was a call-out section. The operators here dialed numbers from a computer-generated list and tried to sell credit card accounts or cellphone calling plans to whoever answered the telephone at home in North America. It was the least desirable station in the call center because one could dial numbers for hours without making a sale, and that was discouraging. Next to that tier of cubicles were the banking help desks. In this section, the operators handled complaints about service charges, explained how to make a deposit or arranged a money transfer. Then there was the credit department, where the operators scolded tardy debtors and even helped set up mortgages for aspiring property owners on the far side of the world. One of the young men sitting at the credit check desk was Rajesh, a rare example of an operator who went by his Indian name. On the day of my visit, Rajesh was helping a householder in Omaha, Nebraska, named Bill arrange a partial second mortgage on a home already half paid for. The money was required, Bill told Rajesh, because his family needed a larger garage. To accommodate his son's new car, he explained, as Rajesh nodded sympathetically, ten thousand miles and ten time zones away.

On his computer screen, Rajesh called up the mortgage template from the bank's website and began to ask a series of questions. He carefully filled in fields in the template using Bill's answers and income data summoned up from bank records. When he hit the return key after completing Bill's form, Rajesh could determine what the chances of approval were. A local manager, or perhaps someone in the loans department at head office in Omaha, would make the final call. But Rajesh was able to reassure Bill that "our bank" regarded him as a good credit risk and he was practically a shoo-in for the $25,000 extension to his mortgage, "all things being equal and no unforeseen snags," as he put it. Bill was ecstatic. He thanked Rajesh and then, out of the blue, told him that he planned to visit India one day.

"Now, sir, you know I didn't tell you where I am sitting. We're your community bank, for heaven's sake," Rajesh protested. Bill found this denial funny and wished Rajesh a good day before going off to— presumably—tell his wife the good news. It was just before supper time in Omaha. India is situated on the other side of the world in relation to North America—roughly twelve to fifteen hours ahead of most major U.S. and Canadian cities. Typically, Indian call centers are at their busiest overnight, as India takes advantage of the time difference. "We march across the country with the various time zones over there," a shift supervisor explained, "starting our day on the east coast, then heading toward California and even Hawaii and Alaska . . . just before we go home to our beds at sunrise . . . local time." India's advance on North American time was a huge business advantage that targeted working consumers in the United States and Canada who couldn't call their banks and help desks while they were at work.

One of the key figures in the short history of Indian outsourcing was Jack Welch, when he was still CEO of General Electric. He was "the Christopher Columbus, Albert Einstein and Archangel Gabriel of back-office outsourcing," according to one former executive who now works for a GE competitor. *Wall Street Journal* reporter Jay Solomon, who covered the outsourcing phenomenon extensively while based in New Delhi, writes that Welch began to realize India's vast business potential in 1989 when he made a sales trip to the subcontinent. He was there to sell various GE "old economy" products, such as airplane engines, to the Indian government. In those days, Indian Airlines and Air India still monopolized the skies over South Asia. Both government-owned airlines were in the market for new planes. The General Electric CEO had some fairly straightforward sales pitches to make. But in a meeting with Sam Pitroda, then chief technology adviser to Prime Minister Rajiv Gandhi, it was Mr. Welch who got pitched. "We want to sell you software," Pitroda told the visiting American über-capitalist. He went on to explain to Welch that India needed business for its emerging high-tech sector. According to Solomon's account of the meeting, the plain-speaking Welch gave a reply very much in character. "If I kiss your cheek, what do I get in return?" he asked. Solomon himself completes the story. "Fifteen years on," he writes, "the answer is clear: the global outsourcing revolution."[1]

The canny Welch proceeded discreetly. He was well aware of the potentially negative political implications of the deals he was about to set in motion. After that pivotal meeting with Pitroda, GE formed partnerships with numerous Indian companies whose names are now well known to anyone who works in technology or follows the business news. This included, of course, Tata Consultancy Services, Infosys and Wipro. Each got an early share of GE's business, which has been worth billions of dollars since then. According to Solomon, the Indian companies also got a quick lesson in the Welch business model, which mixed cost-cutting with customer service. That's a mantra that's repeated constantly by businessmen and women in India who talk about the prime importance of the client and the need to keep costs under control, even as trade expands and the services available from Indian firms grow ever more sophisticated. "GE was very brutal," Wipro executive Ramesh Emani told Solomon, explaining how the people whom Welch sent to India in the early 1990s played software firms against one another to force constant gains in productivity and output. GE began modestly, like the sector itself, concentrating on buying cheap Indian software and selling its own products there. Over time, some of these operations developed into joint ventures. But as the American economy moved from manufacturing to services, so did GE. A firm that began as an electrical supply company became a global player in finance, business services and information technology. In the 1990s, India was at the forefront of the Welch-driven strategy. Again according to Solomon, "the light went on for GE in 1997 as the [company's] financial unit was about to create an Indian office to process applications for a credit card joint venture with a local bank."[2]

One of the first things the new GE venture did was hire a man named Raman Roy away from the Indian branch of American Express. Roy has changed jobs several times since then and now works for himself, exploring the frontiers of business outsourcing. But he is a leading member of the club that brought BPO to India. He is also a direct, informal and friendly man who loves to tell the story of his groundbreaking role in bringing back-office work to his homeland.

He was wearing a crisp white shirt and dark tie when I met him. He apologized for the clouds of cigar smoke in his office. He smokes, he says, to curb his restlessness. This is a man who never stops moving, fidgeting, shuffling papers. He exudes energy and clearly enjoys what he does for a living. "I'm a workaholic," he says, gesturing with a cigar to a pile of papers and files on the corner of the desk, "but this is my job, my hobby and my life rolled into one." Roy says he and his colleagues have created tens of thousands of jobs in India, and they aren't about to stop any time soon. "Who could possibly quit working with a record like that to live up to?"

"Look, the first thing to say is that we created this whole outsourcing business by accident, a glorious lucky accident, and so many problems arose along the way—usually to do with disbelief, attitudes, lack of faith. The prize of certain success was what kept us going, sometimes when nothing else would." Roy, as he settles into his story, modifies slightly the significance assigned to General Electric in establishing the outsourcing trend.

"Well, it wasn't entirely GE, you know," he says. "They knew a good thing when they saw it, but lots of us were aware that India was on the move, even before economic reform and all that, that we had the English language, labor-cost and time-zone advantages that we could leverage to create jobs and earn profits. But the only companies around then were pretty hidebound local players or multinationals that just wanted to do retail business in India."

Roy was the manager of the India branch of American Express, which issued traveler's checks, processed charge card applications and operated a few banking services. India had strict currency controls limiting foreign exchange transactions, so most of the business, Roy explains, was with foreign visitors and tourists. "We had a tiny fraction of Amex global turnover," he says. "No one [at head office] would have noticed if we disappeared, no one. We didn't bring in that much money at all."

Being small didn't exempt the India operation from its business responsibilities. Monthly returns had to be prepared and faxed to headquarters, usually, according to Roy, to a deafening silence. "Nothing would happen, no reply, no specific enquiries, nothing. We kept doing it because that was policy, but we wondered sometimes, what was the point? Then one day I got word that our controller was coming to visit. I got a little nervous. I told one of my employees to get the office in order, cleaned up, files put away and so on. We had no idea why he was coming."

As it turned out, Amex was sending one of its top finance officials to India because head office thought the Indians weren't doing their job properly. The financial returns that appeared on the fax machine simply did not compute. "It was surreal," Roy says. "He [the controller] told us, 'You kids don't know how to make monthly statements; I'm going to teach you.' He spent three hours asking us questions and going over the books. He thought we were getting it wrong, writing our costs too low, and he kept saying that the quality of work was too high for such cheap accounting costs. In the end he realized that we were doing things properly, but he didn't believe what he saw. Costs in India were truly low, really low, and quality was pretty much as high as in America."

Thus the glorious accident that Roy sees as the beginning of outsourcing to India: the discovery by a senior Amex executive of India's low-cost competencies. Within months, American Express embarked on a major restructuring of its global operations. Most overseas processing centers were to be closed. Only a few of what had been forty full-fledged businesses would remain open. India survived the purge and took on work from other Asian countries. Roy set to work building up the infrastructure for his country's very first BPO operation. It wasn't easy.

"It took months to get phone lines, and they were bad," he recalls. "We needed bandwidth, a lease line, if we were to be in constant real-time communication with people, so we became the first private foreign company in India to ask for an uplink. Those paranoids in the [Indian government] telecommunications department, they thought we were CIA. No one had ever asked for that much bandwidth." Roy says American Express essentially told him to prove his own contention to them, that India could take on the work of fifteen or twenty of the processing centers that had closed in other countries, and do it accurately while maintaining those low costs that had so impressed the financial controller in the first place. Over the next two years, Roy's operation became American Express's most efficient cost center. The Indian government telecommunications department realized that it was not a front for the CIA. Business was booming, and then, according to Roy, "GE showed up."

General Electric, Roy says, "made me an offer I couldn't refuse." So he set up GE's first offshore credit card processing business. "We had [hired] six thousand employees in three years, and they were churning out excellent work, efficient, high-quality. Plus those were good jobs, very much in demand. We had the pick of the crop for workers. Eventually, I realized that my team and I were on to something that could be even better if we did it ourselves, so we decided to set up our own business."

In 1998, Roy left GE and founded Spectramind, one of the first really big Indian call-center firms. Within three years, he had fifteen thousand employees, earning up to US$10,000 per year for jobs for which American workers expected a minimum of $30,000. "Customers poured out of the woodwork—all the big names," he says. "And our competitors started setting up shop, but instead of taking business away from each other, we just made more of a market and kept raising the bar. Demand was unbelievable." The inevitable happened. Roy's company was bought by the Indian software giant Wipro, and its headquarters was moved to Bangalore. But Raman Roy isn't someone who rests on his laurels and counts his money. He has now moved on to develop new forms of outsourcing: legal services, corporate strategy, takeovers and just about any process that a big Western company can do in-house. "We do [it] for them, cheaper and better . . . but especially cheaper. It's amazing fun," he says. "Kind of like being an explorer in the Amazon jungle."

Roy's signature theme is that he is a pro-business capitalist who creates untold numbers of new jobs in India completely from scratch. More than the profits he earns, it's that theme that keeps him going, he says. He tells the story of a visit made to his office a few years earlier. An older woman came to see him unannounced, and she had to wait some time before being ushered in to see the boss. She spoke to Roy in a quiet, confident voice, a colorful cardboard carton balanced on her knees.

"The box had sweets in it, *ladoos*, the kind we Indians hand out in thanksgiving or celebration," Roy said. "She had come to feed me some from her own hand, as we do in our part of the world as a mark of respect. Her daughter worked in one of my call centers and the old lady was so proud. She and her husband had just bought a house, something they'd never imagined possible. And their daughter had given them the down payment and was helping with the mortgage. 'I never thought I'd live in my own house,' she kept saying.

"You do this work for money and prestige and all the rest, but it's really all about the thirty-five thousand jobs that we created . . . from nothing, providing income and enabling a whole generation of Indians to get what they want, to be free of the old ways and the old structures where there was never enough money to go around. My team and I created all those opportunities, and we'll continue to do so. And because it's bloody good fun."

Not everyone shares Roy's enthusiasm for BPO. There is a growing backlash in North America and Europe against the shipping of jobs to low-cost labor markets overseas. U.S. commentators such as Lou Dobbs of CNN have all but accused Indians of stealing jobs from Americans as more and more American firms move their service operations to India. In his book *Exporting America: Why Corporate Greed Is Shipping American Jobs Overseas,* the hugely popular television anchor says U.S. companies are obtaining services and moving operations abroad purely for financial gain. Firms, Dobbs writes, are guilty of "not only forfeiting jobs and perhaps your privacy, [but] also reducing tax revenues . . . and adding to the country's trade deficit and current budget deficit."[3] Internet chat sites and newsgroups buzz with criticisms of the outsourcing trend. IT professional N. Sivakumar says he was inspired to write his book *Debugging Indian Computer Programmers: Dude, Did I Steal Your Job?* by an anonymous newsgroup posting that read, "Greedy American companies are falling all over themselves to hire pathetically stupid and incompetent workers from India. Why? Because they are as cheap as the dirt that covers everything in India." Sivakumar and other Indian programmers feel strongly that there's more than a little racism fueling objections to outsourcing.

Then there are the dire warnings that the market will peak soon and India will cede dominance to Taiwan, the Philippines, Malaysia, Russia or some other place with a cheaper workforce and access to telecommunications. Theoretically, this is a potential problem for call centers and BPO operations based in India. According to a report issued in 2006 by the market research firm Gartner, Inc., the country's labor costs have increased by 20 percent or more since the boom began. These costs have yet to be passed on to customers as highly competitive companies scramble to keep and increase their share of the market. Some analysts predict that U.S. firms, hit with big increases in their bills for outsourced services, might simply choose other providers. But other analysts disagree, saying that India's companies established their competencies and skills early on and that this gives them the knowledge and awareness needed to stay competitive in the BPO market. More and more, these analysts point out, new business for Indian companies is coming from high-value clients such as law firms, American health management organizations and corporate strategy departments. "Once we leveraged our cheap labor," an Indian consultant told the *Business Standard* of New Delhi in June 2006. "Now we're using the expertise we've assembled from building our market share and going after the really lucrative businesses. There's huge potential there."

With typical flair, columnist Thomas Friedman of the *New York Times* taps into both the contentiousness of the debate and the outsourcing trend itself in *The World Is Flat,* his bestselling account of global trends in business and employment. His advice to those on

Dobbs's side of the argument basically amounts to: There's nothing you can do to stop it, so get out of the way and make sure your kids have the skills for what jobs remain, and will be created in the future. Globalization 3.0, as Friedman calls the borderless world of business services and information technology companies, has empowered Indian firms and individuals to such an extent that not even the mighty current of American public opinion can reverse the trend.

Friedman spotted India's awakening earlier than most. Peripatetic and a compulsive observer of the world economy, he maintains that the technology boom of the 1990s was indeed the catalyst for India's recent economic success and for the growth of its remarkable middle-class population—more than two hundred million people, by most acceptable measures. But Friedman also argues that the collapse of the high-tech bubble in the United States in 2000–2001 helped cement India's position in global outsourcing and back-office service provision, call centers and beyond. In the late 1990s, he says, when it seemed the bubble would never burst, European and American companies installed plenty of fiber-optic cables between India and the United States. The collapse of the boom left the data-carrying capacity of those cables underused and owned by banks that had foreclosed on bankrupt high-tech firms. No bank wants to be in the bandwidth business, so the unused cable capacity was sold at bargain-basement prices. In turn, Indian companies took advantage of dirt-cheap bandwidth to increase exponentially their business with the United States. As a Wall Street banker of Indian origin told Friedman, "For decades you have to leave India to be a professional. Now you can plug into the world from India. You don't have to go to Yale and work for Goldman Sachs."[4]

Hindsight may indeed be 20/20, but many Indian entrepreneurs already knew the truth of Friedman's assessment, even as the technology bubble was bursting. The NASDAQ, the electronic stock exchange where most high-tech shares are listed, reached its peak in March 2000 and then plummeted over the next twelve months. By some measures, US$7 trillion—that's $7,000,000,000,000—in share value disappeared, and thousands and thousands of companies went bankrupt. In India, the press coverage was gloomy. Commentators who had always mistrusted the technology sector saw their pessimistic predictions confirmed in the downward spiral. Demand for Indian software engineers declined and, after the Al Qaeda attacks of September 11, 2001, the U.S. Congress drastically reduced visa quotas that had once been largely filled by graduates of the elite institutions of India. Yet, as the world watched a bubble burst, there were more than a few people in India who had foreseen the opportunity that lurked amid disaster.

One was Kris Laxmikanth. In India, people in the job placement or head-hunting business are sometimes referred to as "body shoppers," but Laxmikanth, a balding, forty-something businessman from Bangalore calls his company simply The Headhunters Inc. With his wife and business partner, Saraswati, he connects jobs with people and he has long been one of the more successful entrepreneurs in a rather crowded sector. Before 2000, Laxmikanth had largely found American jobs for Indians, and Indian employees for American companies. He had extensive connections at the top engineering and science universities in his homeland and in high-tech firms in the United States' Silicon Valley and its equivalent in a dozen other countries. More than two hundred people worked for this high-powered couple, a number that grew even as the world technology markets were imploding. The bubble may have been bursting, but Laxmikanth wasn't worried.

"No way," he says, using one of the Americanisms he urged his job-hunting clients to acquire for their interviews. "This [market collapse] is natural and we welcome it." Money, Kris Laxmikanth maintains, isn't like matter or energy. It's not finite, and it can be created or destroyed. Markets make wealth and destroy it, in his view. People lose resources and jobs in a time of contraction, but they also gain immensely in times of expansion. This is fairly standard free market doctrine, perhaps, but Laxmikanth has the fervor of a true believer. He also has a dry sense of humor. Like Raman Roy, he sees business as an adventure, a way to inject a little risk into daily routines.

"Recently, we had a meeting at our office," Laxmikanth says. "People were saying, 'No one in California wants any programmers this week.' Someone else pointed out that we were getting calls and résumés from people already in the U.S. who'd lost their jobs. They wanted to come home to India and work. And I said, 'Exactly.' This is the growth area. India's own corporate sector will grow as America's shrinks, or at least rationalizes itself. More and more companies will set up or form joint ventures here. We'll be recruiting for them, and there are no quotas on start-ups or joint ventures, the way there are on U.S. visas. Now we can do even more business, even better business. It's bloody good for India, this bubble-burst business." He shakes his head and repeats that America's loss was India's gain, and that the loss was only temporary. "Do you think high-tech demand is going away because of a correction of stock market madness? No way."

History has proved that his optimism was just good business sense. Five years after the crash of the NASDAQ, The Headhunters Inc. was still flourishing. There were more employees, and there was a lot more demand for body-shopping services. As Laxmikanth expected, the return of Indian software people from abroad had catalyzed the corporate sector at home. The repatriated Indians brought both their expertise and their worldwide contacts with them. Ex–Silicon Valley people started businesses or—using Laxmikanth's expression—supercharged existing Indian firms. Meanwhile, recent graduates of the elite colleges—the seven Indian Institutes of Technology (IIT) and the six Indian Institutes of Management (IIM)—bucked long-standing trends and stayed home to work, preferring the heady feeling of India awakening to the now dimming allure of America or Europe. Pay levels, at least for top people, began to soar, and Indians found they could realize the Indian dream at home, with their family, familiar food and their own language and culture around them.

"It's been remarkable, too successful," said Laxmikanth, as ever searching for the next trend, the next opportunity. "We may just be on our way to a bit of a bubble here ourselves. Or more likely other problems, like expensive housing, too much demand for education and so on. But that's what happens with success. It comes at a cost."

Opportunities for Indian companies from the collapse of the technology boom came fast and furious throughout the early years of the twenty-first century. While the rest of the world was—understandably—fixated on Al Qaeda, wars in Afghanistan, Iraq and other issues driven by America, Indian companies were steadily growing and expanding. Like the firms run by Raman Roy and Kris Laxmikanth, they were also constantly looking for new niches. Business process outsourcing, which began as a cheap way to operate call centers, was on the march. According to Dayanidhi Maran, India's minister of communications and information technology, "[Our country] doesn't just want to do call centers. Call centers are the low end of the market. We want to climb the value chain." That is exactly what is happening.

TutorVista is a company at the cutting edge of the BPO sector, and it spawned a host of imitators within a few months of starting up in 2005. Just as Raman Roy found when his call-center idea caught on like wildfire, the competition served only to broaden demand for the service. As with so many of the other "products" that flow along fiber-optic cables between India and the rest of the world these days, what TutorVista sells is something that no one outside of science fiction would have foreseen just a decade ago. Basically, TutorVista employees help students with their homework. But its customers are in the United States and other English-speaking countries, and the tutoring takes place via the Internet and telecommunications links. It costs less than $100 per student per month, and business is growing fast. In late 2006, TutorVista had more than five hundred clients and employed some sixty teachers.

The company shares its office space with a technology college in Bangalore's Electronic City neighborhood. Cofounder Krishnan Ganesh is a youthful-looking man in his mid-forties who used to run OneSource, one of India's biggest call centers. He sold his founder's share in that venture to raise the money for TutorVista and also roped in another high-tech pioneer, Ravi Kannan, from the antivirus software company McAfee. The idea of tutoring students abroad came to Ganesh when he spoke to Indian friends who had immigrated to the United States and had found that the public education system wasn't all they'd hoped for.

"Indian families value education above everything else," he says, "and in the U.S., in some areas, anyway, there were problems. Schools had inconsistent levels of excellence, and preparation for SATs was uneven, often quite unsatisfactory. Also, face-to-face tutoring is very expensive." Families with lower incomes couldn't afford to give their children the extra help that might mean the difference between admission to a good college and a mediocre one, Ganesh says. The American government recognized this gap itself in 2002 when President George W. Bush signed into law the No Child

Left Behind Act. Among many other measures, the act provides funding for tutoring for families whose children attend underperforming schools.

"Even that [funding] isn't sufficient for a tutor at home, given American costs," Ganesh says. "So TutorVista just seemed like the way to go." One thing India does well is teacher training. Most employees of TutorVista have a master's degree in mathematics and sciences, the subjects that U.S. clients seem to need the most help with. Others are twenty-year veterans of teaching history, social studies and geography in elite Indian private colleges. Some are in their twenties; many are over forty. What they have in common is an unusual work schedule that sees them arriving at the office at one or two in the morning and leaving for home at 10:30 a.m. Tutoring across time zones requires the combustion of a great deal of midnight oil. Ganesh jokes that he's so used to being tired, "I don't remember what a good night's sleep [is like], but it must suit me. I get my best ideas when I've been up all night."

TutorVista's education director, Jarrod Brown, agrees. From Tennessee, he was brought into the company as an expert on American school curricula. A teacher by trade, Brown says he's there to give advice on tweaking the Indian approach to education so it better matches that of students in the U.S. Midwest or New York City.

"It's a real honor to be part of something like this," says Brown. "As a young teacher, I never dreamed that the Internet could be used this way, let alone that I'd have something to do with it. As for India, well, that's a whole other thing. I love this place."

Nearby, in a quiet office, forty-five-year-old P. Raj is online with a student from Memphis, working on some eighth-grade geometry exercises. He wears a headset and speaks slowly, almost painstakingly, occasionally repeating a phrase if his charge has trouble with his Indian-accented English. TutorVista teachers do language exercises before they start and throughout their employment, learning American and British idioms and watching Western television shows on DVD to try to pick up the cultural reference points that might help them bond with their students. They work with virtual whiteboard technology so that both tutors and students can write or draw and see what the other is putting on the screen. There's constant telephone contact between the two, which is being upgraded into quality digital sound along the lines of the popular Internet telephone application Skype.

At his workstation, Raj is urging his student to identify various angles and measurements from a diagram he has drawn. "Right," he says, "so where are the complementaries? Remember, they all add up to ninety degrees." A pause as lines appear on his computer monitor, drawn by a thirteen-year-old in Tennessee. It's after supper in the American South, 8:30 a.m. in Bangalore. "Excellent. Now there's just one more . . . see if you can find that, and soon you'll be able to watch Family Guy with the homework all done." It's impossible to hear the other end of the conversation, but the results of the session seem to speak for themselves.

"Raj is one of our best math people," says Brown as Ganesh nods in agreement. Mathematics is the subject that most parents seem to feel their children need extra help with. But TutorVista is offering a range of other subjects, too. There's growing demand for remedial training in Spanish, and Ganesh is looking around India for fellow countrymen and women who speak the language of Latin America and Spain. The firm is constantly hiring new teachers at salaries of between US$350 and $400 a month, which one of the employees describes as "competitive, but not quite enough."

TutorVista is at the crest of another knowledge-economy phenomenon in India: the growth of venture capital to fund new businesses and nurture ideas. Ganesh and his partner, Kannan, who knows Silicon Valley well, have managed to tap two important venture capital funds—one the Indian arm of a California company, the other based in Silicon Valley. They plan to use the money to hire more staff and expand the business into other tutoring areas. "Right now, we do K to 12 [kindergarten to grade 12]," Ganesh says, "but think of all those college students out there. Think of adults who want to learn languages or history or new skills, nurses and medical students on final exam paths. . . . Our form of Internet tutoring is set to take off, and we want to be ready."

In 2005, Indian companies attracted one-third of a billion U.S. dollars in venture capital. That's up from almost zero at the turn of the century, and it's bound to increase markedly in coming years. Among the waves of Indians returning from the United States and Europe to join the boom at home are many from leading venture capital firms. They're setting up local arms of the foreign investment firms that hired them in the West and convincing Indian investors to put money into their country's knowledge sector. It's an easy sales pitch, given that technology stocks have driven the Mumbai equities market to new heights for several years now and more and more Indian companies are listing their shares in New York and London.

India's start-up culture is very much like a company that is itself in an early stage of development, Ravi Kannan of TutorVista told the San Jose *Mercury News* in 2006. "It needs considerable care and feeding. I can come up with a good idea in one hour, but you need mentoring. You need funding. You need the ecosystem."[5] The country's traditional banking system, developed over decades of state-led, quasi-socialist economic policy, was ill equipped for the boom in private entrepreneurship that followed free market economic reform in 1991. Then, Indian banks were almost certainly government-owned, overstaffed and either bankrupt from bad loans to the politically well connected or allowed to provide money only to farmers, exporters or some other narrow business sector. Foreign banking services were severely limited by the almost xenophobic laws that governed their operation. The Indian private banks that have proliferated since economic reforms began were, at first, slow to respond to the increasingly sophisticated demands made by their prospective customers. Foreign banks have also set up shop in the liberalized Indian market. Some have quite a long pedigree. Canada's Scotiabank arrived in India in the 1980s and found itself a ready market niche lending small sums of money to families and women for purchases of consumer goods, appliances and motorcycles. The bank's long-term goal was to offer mortgages and now it's well positioned, along with a plethora of private Indian competitors and the likes of Citibank and HSBC, to take part in a property market boom that, in early 2007, was showing few signs of easing.

To THE OUTSIDER, India's emergence as a major player in the global knowledge economy and as a budding economic superpower might come as something of a surprise. A recent book on the subject by the British journalist Ed Luce, *In Spite of the Gods,* was subtitled rather provocatively *The Strange Rise of Modern India*. Luce is a veteran India watcher, and it's not hard to see why the country's quick ascent of the IT summit has confounded conventional analysis. We have grown accustomed in the West to thinking of South Asia as a region of poverty and disaster—at best as the home of highly motivated immigrants, at worst as the source of annoying phone calls. But while we were blinded by those stereotypes, India was defying them. Jack Welch got it early. So did Raman Roy and others, such as Thomas Friedman, all with their eyes on the future. Friedman's book in particular shows that the notion is spreading that India, along with China, is emerging as a pillar of the new world economy. But one question rarely explored dispassionately is the reason for India's surging success.

How did India manage to transform itself in less than a generation from a stodgy, disaster-prone repository of the world's images of poverty to a thrusting economic giant in the making? It's a question with many facets, and searching for the answer is something of a growth industry. Global consulting firms, governments, city councils, company directors and countless individual investors and entrepreneurs have made the pilgrimage to Bangalore, Hyderabad, Pune and the techie outskirts of New Delhi and Mumbai to study the Indian IT and BPO phenomena. They all are looking for the holy grail of knowledge-economy success. Journalists have been exploring this aspect of India's heady journey, too. Not just Friedman, but others, such as Michael Lewis, have enquired about the role of men and women from India in the world's IT explosion. In Lewis's highly regarded tale of the technology boom of the 1990s, *The New New Thing*, he tells how Jim Clark, founder of Netscape, queried a proposal for a new Internet venture by asking, "Where are the Indians?" His question produced the desired result. South Asian names began to appear on the business plans sent to venture capitalists.

It's almost conventional wisdom among those who know the knowledge business that Indians, or people of South Asian descent, invariably do well in IT, biotechnology and anything to do with the Internet. The list of those who have excelled is almost endless, not least because nationalistic Indians keep it constantly updated and easily available online. It includes many names in America as well as in India: Sabir Bhatia, the inventor of Hotmail; Vinod Khosla of the IT venture capital firm Kleiner Perkins Caufield & Byers; Pavan Nigam;

Vinod Dham; Kanwal Rekhi and so many others. At the height of the
high-tech boom in the 1990s, Indians were a hugely dominant ethnicity in Silicon Valley and in other high-tech centers around the
United States. They still are more numerous than most other ethnic
communities in such places. Drive through Palo Alto, the Raleigh-
Durham Research Triangle Park in North Carolina or Ann Arbor,
Michigan, today, and what do you see? Strip malls dominated by Indian restaurants, lavish gold jewelry and sari shops, and, of course,
Hindu temples, often in the elaborate style of South India, which
seems to produce the lion's share of exported Indian computer programmers and entrepreneurs. Posters advertise touring Indian musi-
cians and publications with names such as *India Tribune* are widely
available. There can be no doubting that people from the subcontinent have taken to high tech at home and abroad like fish to water.
But again, why?

The body-shopper from Bangalore, Kris Laxmikanth, thinks he
has the answer. He calls Indian computer prowess "the revenge of
the Brahmins." He postulates—compellingly—that India's highest
Hindu castes were denied access to their usual professions in government and law when strict quotas based on caste were introduced
in India in the late 1980s. These quotas, the most radical of India's
many attempts to address caste discrimination, placed impenetrable limits on the number of Brahmins—high-caste Hindus—allowed
into universities and the civil service. At first, Laxmikanth remembers, the caste quotas were seen as blatantly offensive by people like
him, for he is very much the epitome of the fastidious, cerebral and
highly educated Brahmin. For centuries, Brahmins had monopolized positions as priests and dispensers of knowledge, and they did
not take quietly to being displaced. There were widespread protests.
A few people even set themselves on fire and burned to death in public. But the quotas remained and have only broadened over the years.
In time, Laxmikanth says, it became obvious that he and other Brahmins had to move on, to find new ways to define themselves and to
earn a living.

"We had always considered business to be beneath us—perhaps
not explicitly, but it was hardwired in," he explained. "We were
thinkers, administrators, priests in the old days, keepers of the religious texts. But now that the civil service—our traditional career path

in this more secular age—and a lot of other things were denied us, we had to make our own luck. So people started going into business right around the time that computers, software, telecommunications and other fields were getting interested [in doing business in India]. Plus, so many of our people went to the U.S. to work in Silicon Valley. They were exposed to this new brain business, if you like. Smart people working for personal gain and inventing great products from nothing. It appealed to the Brahmin in all of us."

There's certainly some truth to this. Many of the highest achievers in India's information economy and in Silicon Valley–type situations around the world have been Brahmins from the south of India. Journalist and social activist Palagummi Sainath, himself a southerner from the highest Hindu caste, takes the theory one step further. He says many of the top people can trace their family roots to a specific neighborhood in Chennai, in the southern state of Tamil Nadu. Mylapore is a modest area located around the main Kapaleeshwarar Hindu temple at the center of the old city. Traditionally, it was home to priests and temple workers, and their families. Such Brahmin-dominated enclaves have long existed throughout India.

Sainath has written extensively about caste issues among Indian expatriates. "So many of the people who go to California or work here in IT have roots in Mylapore, even if they were born somewhere else," he says. "It's almost eerie, the connections between that place of high-caste purity" (here he makes quotation marks in the air with his fingers to indicate he uses the word purity in an ironic sense) "and American pockets like the Bay Area. And when they're abroad, those people don't change. They cook Mylaporean dishes, go to Mylaporean-style temples and want their sons and daughters to marry people descended from Mylapore families. In fact, the Mylaporean Brahmins here in India are much less into all of this than those abroad. That's what being outside your country does to you. Makes you obsessive about religion and successful in IT."

Sainath is far from being the only commentator in India to wonder if the arcane, impenetrable nature of Hindu lore and practice somehow predisposes its former priestly class to flourish in information technology. Like Hindu ritual, IT involves coded languages and a veritable priesthood of initiates to resolve problems and reconcile the mysterious and the mundane. Gurcharan Das, who has written several books about India's recent economic progress, thinks Hindus have an innate ability to excel at IT. "We proved by our history," he writes, "that we are inveterate tinkerers, people who can make things work in different ways at different times. That's perfect for software and other knowledge applications . . . In fact, the immense complexity of Hinduism . . . makes us tinkerers, hairsplitters, debaters, people who communicate, network and talk and get to know what works and what doesn't. That's perfect IT world behaviour and that's why we're the best at it."[6]

However, not every devout Hindu who excels at a high-tech job would agree. Naresh Balla, when I met him the head of a South India–based online college, says that spiritualism is important, but only because it grounds him, gives him focus and helps him separate work from family life while emphasizing the importance of both. "I have three pillars in my life," he says as his three-year-old son plays at his feet. "My family, my job and the spiritual side of things. Now for me, that is Hinduism. But not in any narrow sense. I'm intrigued by all religious faith, all aspects of the human spirit and the quest for meaning. When I'm not thinking about work or home life, I'm pondering—well, there's no other word for it—the infinite. I don't mean to sound pompous or anything. It's just where the mind wanders when it's done with immediate demands and necessary thoughts. The office or the kids or whatever. And I believe that I'm able to use that spiritual aspect to my life to solve problems that come up at work and at home."

I asked Balla if he saw the code that underlies every aspect of IT-driven development—trillions upon trillions of strange combinations of letters, numbers and symbols—as being in any way related to religious texts, the codified works that empower strange processes and are known only to a priesthood of initiates. This has been suggested on some of the wilder Internet sites that proliferate among expatriate Indian Hindus who become more passionate about their culture while living abroad. The suggestion made Balla laugh hard and long. "No, no, not at all. I'm not a mystic, and I don't read science fiction. It's just that I often find myself using my spiritual side to help me solve complicated problems. At the most basic level, I can relax, meditate my way through a crisis or overcome an obstacle, and I think that's pretty unique to Indian philosophy. Or at least to someone who takes the spiritual side of life seriously. You know, clear your mind, don't be distracted, and let answers come to you. Don't get stressed. Try to stay in touch with yourself. That's part of Hinduism, Buddhism, but I don't think it gives us any more skills than anyone else in the IT line."

Others find more prosaic explanations for the profusion of Indians in the knowledge economy. Pradeep Kar, founder of Bangalore-based company Microland, says the IT business just suits his nature as an informal, fun-loving yet hard-working guy. "A typical Silicon Valley keyboard jockey," he says, laughing. (It should be kept in mind that this typical keyboard jockey's company is worth tens of millions of dollars and does deals with the likes of Rupert Murdoch.) Although driven by his ambition to become a big player in the global high-tech economy, Kar nonetheless found time to start a club with his fellow Bangalore-based entrepreneurs, called BAIT, or Beer and Information Technology. Its members meet every Tuesday in a pub to talk business in an environment more festive than an office. Kar says his fellow club members and he have no time for the endless search for a magic formula for IT success among Indians. It's simple, he says, neither rocket science nor voodoo, just common sense.

"It's our emphasis on maths and science in education. And our work ethic. We're all driven to succeed by parents and family. Some government policies, like a ten-year income tax holiday on export profits, really helped. Fears of a Y2K meltdown—however much they may have seemed a sham after the fact—brought almost every important American company over here to get a problem fixed, and they went home convinced that India had arrived. You get things done here, cheaply, well and fast. And our core competency at writing code, programming, software—that matched the Internet boom perfectly. It also helped that it was an Indian, for example, who developed Hotmail." He continued, "Then there is the sheer size of our engineering workforce, [hundreds of thousands of] people graduating from science and engineering every year. In America, it's less than a third of that."

In his pithy, direct way, Kar probably hit the nail on the head. It is the inclination to put in the hours and the ambition to excel that Indians seem to have in spades—not some innate ability to manage arcana or surf the mystic codes of the infinite. In part, this may be because many people from India have either firsthand experience of poverty or deprivation or are, at best, a generation removed from penury. Even today, most urban Indians, at home and abroad, can talk about difficult moments in their upbringing when perhaps a wage-earning parent was laid off or ill. India is not now, nor has it ever been, a welfare state. Sickness or unemployment mean hard times. Whether the country can establish a safety net for its burgeoning middle-class workforce is a crucial question for the future. For the moment, if you're middle class and you don't work, you don't eat. Add to this the pressure exerted by a culture that values material success in adult life, in part so that children can be well educated and given the means to realize their own prosperity.

Religion helps, even if faith doesn't predetermine the Indian aptitude for computer work. Neither Hinduism, the majority religion in the country, nor Islam, the second-largest, disparages material achievement or the accumulation of property. On the contrary, material success is encouraged by most of the faiths that Indians follow, if only so that high achievers can become more contemplative and charitable in later life. Finally, the overwhelming success of people of Indian origin in IT has given attainable role models to a whole generation of young people who respond by clamoring to get into higher education and to work in the nearest call center or software technology park. Where once the civil service or academia was the career path of choice for educated Indians, the computer monitor and workstation beckon today.

India's rise to prosperity and global influence may still be surprising to many. Eclipsed throughout the 1990s and the early years of the twenty-first century by China's remarkable growth, India's ascent was comparatively unobtrusive. Innate strengths and skill sets enabled by economic reform policies and growing global prosperity began to coalesce in cities such as Bangalore and New Delhi. Government—often an obstacle to progress in India—stood aside and let creativity and entrepreneurial skills thrive, not as a dogmatic act of free market fundamentalism but because the resulting job creation and tax revenue from new, successful companies were of benefit to all. As Kris Laxmikanth says, "If India's economic success is the revenge of the Brahmins, then it must be history's kindest vengeance."

3

SILICON AND SLUMS

New Economy, Old Problems

IN LESS THAN TWO DECADES, Indian companies have become giants of the IT and BPO worlds, but global multinationals have also played a key role in the country's growing confidence and commanding position in the knowledge economy. Bangalore, Hyderabad and other centers of high-tech activity around the country teem with employees of foreign firms that have set up shop on Indian soil. These firms are drawn by the same conditions that have caused Indian IT firms to thrive, the low cost of labor paramount among them. An Indian programmer at Infosys or Wipro earns a sixth or less of what her counterpart gets in Silicon Valley or Europe. Yet, according to Larry Terrell, director of Hewlett-Packard India, there's little or no difference in the quality of work performed by his employees and those elsewhere in HP's global empire. "I am truly amazed, every day, by just how good these people are," he says, waving an arm to indicate a vast workspace full of young men and women at what HP calls its "Global Solutions Center, India."

That's a fancy name for a call center, which is the core activity in the gleaming cluster of buildings at the edge of Bangalore's Electronic City where, in late 2005, Terrell was leading a staff of four thousand. In what seems a sort of standard model for IT companies, several office towers hunker around a low, glass-walled complex where employees shop, eat and avail themselves of services such as banking, travel bookings and home-computer repairs. This is a significant advantage for an Indian employee: to be able to accomplish so many of life's necessary tasks at work.

Larry Terrell never expected to be based in India. He joined HP in 1978, just after graduating from the University of Memphis and serving in the U.S. Air Force. Terrell's small office sits in a corner of one of the call-center floors. As we spoke, hundreds of young men and women chatted on headsets at their workstations—an almost perfect replication of what I had seen in Delhi at eFunds some years earlier.

"I came [to India] on a recruiting trip in 2004," Terrell told me, "with no idea that I'd be staying or running things. I'm a company man and I'd risen through the ranks of what used to be a hardware manufacturer with many of the usual personnel and financial challenges. Now I'm in India as head of something that changes all of the time. It's pretty neat for someone who's fifty-five to be able to learn something new every single day."

Terrell says he thinks a lot about India and the lives that Indians live. "Every day I look out the windows of my car and I see amazing examples of the human spirit, of people working hard in adverse conditions, to get something for their kids. Here at HP, we've got good conditions, excellent pay and benefits, on-campus services galore, free transportation to work, things the ordinary Indian can only dream of. Yet no one has, in my time, slacked off or started to take any of this for granted." Terrell says it's impossible to overlook the growing gap between India's hard-core poor and the educated middle classes, especially in a boom town such as Bangalore. He says he hopes that the benefits of economic growth soon make their way to the deprived people of the city's slums. "You can't miss them [the poor]," he said. "They're right there outside the car window and along the side of the road. Everyone in this building is one of the lucky ones, that's for sure."

One of Terrell's team of managers at HP India, one of his "lucky ones," is Geetha Panda. She is one of the most senior female executives in a country where most businesses remain stubbornly patriarchal and glass ceilings are a fixture. "My go-to person," Terrell calls her, carefully avoiding the word *girl*. India's new-economy offices try hard for equal treatment of employees, irrespective of sex.

When I spent time with her in 2005, Panda had many responsibilities. She ran training programs, enforced corporate standards and managed teams of customer service supervisors. One of the toughest and most important was a military-style transportation service to ensure that HP's three shifts of employees (the company operates twenty-four hours a day) get to work on time, and, just as importantly, get home as quickly—and safely—as possible. It's a harsh comment on Bangalore's chaotic public transit system that almost every large employer in the city has to make comparable arrangements. Fleets of company-hired taxies and minivans ply the city's streets at all hours of the day and night, picking people up at home and from work, with time and safety the key considerations. Panda spends the beginning and end of each working day in "the control room," an open-plan office at HP headquarters where dozens of young men and women use computers and whiteboards to monitor the progress of thousands of vehicles bearing employees to and from the office. It doesn't always go as planned.

In late 2005, a twenty-four-year-old HP employee, Pratibha Srikantamurthy, didn't show up for her shift at one of the company's call centers in Electronic City, though her family said she had been picked up by a taxi purportedly sent by her employer. "We had no record of a pickup," Panda said. "Her driver had called in sick and we had been scrambling to find a replacement, so when we heard there'd been a pickup, we immediately called the police."

After a search lasting several hours, the young woman's body was found in a ravine close to her home. She had been raped and then strangled. The police soon arrested a man who they said had pretended to be an HP-assigned taxi driver. The killing was the realization of Panda's worst nightmare, she said, and had focused her attention on the importance of employee safety, even at the cost of inefficiency.

"You try and you try," she said, "to get people here on time, safe, comfortable and ready for work. And to get them home. You do so, improving timings and everything. But it all falls apart when something like this happens. Pratibha maybe should have checked the driver's number with our control room, which women working at night are supposed to do. But saying so doesn't bring her back. It's absolutely horrible."

The incident was a grisly *cause célèbre* in India. The media used it to illustrate the many shortcomings and flaws in the Indian dream of a highly paid job in the knowledge economy. More than half of Bangalore's two hundred thousand call-center employees are women, and the proportion is similar in other centers. It can also be argued that the attack was an indicator of the growing gap in wealth, income and aspiration between the country's burgeoning middle class and its equally large pool of poor people. Pratibha Srikanta-murthy was the living embodiment of the modern Indian dream, and her murderer was the very definition of a member of the alien-ated underclass—illiterate and a drifter. Not that a heinous crime can be excused because victim and perpetrator come from different backgrounds, but it's clear that clashes along the fault lines of wealth and achievement are emerging in a society that once boasted a low and relatively stable crime rate. Nowhere is this gap more visible than in Bangalore, where the material signs of IT and BPO success are ever present but so is evidence of deprivation and exclusion. It's es-timated that some 20 percent of the urban population is poor and living on less than two dollars per day. That's in a city where average housing costs have gone up by more than 20 percent in recent years. Life is not getting better for legions of people in India's hottest, hippest city.

Outside the main gate of Hewlett-Packard, a taxi ride to the near-est slum costs the equivalent of just a few dollars in local currency. The journey from Electronic City and its glitzy, high-tech office tow-ers to what is perhaps the more familiar international image of urban India, with its pitted pavements and crowded streets, takes no more than fifteen minutes. Stray dogs—absent in Electronic City because efficient garbage collection makes the pickings thin—start to prolif-erate. Some chase the taxi while others worry at scraps salvaged from roadside trash piles. The roads grow narrower, buildings look pre-carious and weatherworn and the day itself seems to grow darker.

To get to know the poor and downtrodden, I stop to find some guidance. Halfway along a street of stone-cutters and marble mer-chants ("From Italee" proclaimed one banner over a pile of dark, smooth slabs) is a sign pointing up a flight of stairs to an upper floor of a monsoon-stained tenement. "KKNSS" it read, an abbreviation for "Karnataka State Slum Dwellers Association" in the local language,

Kannada. I climb the stairs and enter a meeting room to find a portly man with a bristling mustache addressing about two dozen people, men and women, young and old, some obviously poor and others from the middle classes. Although seated, he is animated and vigorously passionate, waving his hands and making eye contact with members of the audience. People nod in agreement and occasionally speak, evidently uttering the Kannada equivalent of "right-on" or "you tell 'em." The man is J. P. Natraj, founder of the KKNSS and one of South India's leading antipoverty campaigners. He's in his late fifties and is happy to explain that he'll be fighting this fight until the day he dies.

India has more desperately poor people than any other country in the world, about 40 percent of all those on the planet who get by on less than a dollar a day. This figure includes both the urban and rural poor as the decline of agriculture sends more and more farm laborers to the city in search of work. Despite the demonstrable benefits that have accrued to many Indians from market-driven economic reform and globalization, vast numbers of the poorest of the poor have yet to see their lives improve at all. Even those who find work and get access to private services not provided adequately by government have to make unacceptable trade-offs. Many live as squatters in unsanitary conditions so they can be close to a source of income. Those who fall ill are forced to sell farm property to pay for medical treatment and then to move to city slums to get it. These are the people whom Natraj has championed all his adult life. He is part of a powerful social movement in modern India that is inspiring the urban poor around the world. In the mid-1990s in South Africa, an umbrella group for this movement was formed. The founders chose an emotive title for their organization. They called themselves Shack/Slum Dwellers International. As the founder of one of its member associations told a spellbound press conference at the World Urban Forum in Vancouver recently, "We call ourselves 'shack dwellers' to challenge those who live in houses where the roofs don't leak, and where human waste doesn't sit in stinking pools outside, next to the source of drinking water."

J. P. Natraj is opinionated, strong-willed and confident. His first words to me ensure that I am to be under no illusions about his feelings for people like me, who often write in glowing terms about

India's IT boom and the underlying principle that a rising tide lifts all boats.

"You're another one of those IT worshippers, aren't you?" he asks. "No, no, don't apologize, it's natural enough, given your background and your society's love affair with technology. But let me tell you a bit about some of your favorite capitalists and then tell me what you think."

An unapologetic leftist and trade unionist, Natraj talks about the time he and his comrades tried to unionize the canteen workers at Infosys, either India's richest or second-richest company, depending on fluctuations in the stock market. Of all the people who worked at Infosys locations in Bangalore and around the world, none were more lowly than the onion choppers and kitchen laborers who helped feed their co-workers, he said. "So we moved in there and organized a union." Helping exploited workers is part of his crusade on behalf of slum dwellers, he explained, "because everyone in our slums works somewhere, so if we can get them higher wages, they'll build themselves better houses. It's that simple.

"These canteen workers weren't getting time for holidays; there was no paid sick leave, no overtime, no job security. It was the worst job at Infosys and, of course, the company was so famous, it was easy to get people [to work for it]. So people could easily be fired and replaced from the crowd that hangs around outside the gates, waiting for a job. It happened all the time. On top of all that, the top [monthly] salary after long service was still less than three thousand rupees [approximately $65]. So we thought, great, this is the place for a union. It should have been easy. We approached people at home and off company property, signed them up and registered the union with the government. We were preparing to go see the company to start bargaining for better pay and conditions. But one Saturday evening, it fired the key organizers and hired new people at twice and three times the earlier salary. We couldn't do anything about it. The courts were closed [for the weekend] and our top organizers had either been bought off or were out on the street. That's your much vaunted Infosys."

Not that Natraj let this setback slow him down. His work and his passion lay in improving the lot of the poor, so that's what he continued to do. The KKNSS was founded in 1982 and still has strong ties to India's Communist political parties. It's not partisan, but it argues that the system is stacked against the poor, all the more so now that the country has adopted market-based economic reforms. The organization is unlikely to roll back those changes, but when it comes to using the courts and the media to fight for the rights of slum residents, J. P. Natraj fights to win.

"Our biggest victory was in the 1980s when someone in government decided that they wanted to 'beautify' Bangalore. That meant tearing down and demolishing slum housing that the rich found to be an eyesore, made them wrinkle their noses when they drove by in their cars. We fought that in the courts and by pointing out that the rich needed the slum dwellers to be workers, servants and hirelings. And those people needed a place to live. Eventually, politicians stopped the demolitions, but only because they wanted the votes of the poor. Then we fought for better houses, toilets, water and power connections for the slums. It's a fight that's still going on, and it's getting worse."

Slums—basically informal residential communities—have begun to proliferate in Bangalore again because of high land prices and the demand for menial labor fed by the IT and BPO economies. It was mostly construction projects that attracted the laborers, according to Natraj. He says big IT firms have no interest in hiring unskilled workers once their buildings are erected and their campuses secured behind fences and barriers built by the labor of the poor. Having given me plenty to think about, Natraj announced that it was time to visit one of the informal colonies that he and his people had fought to save from demolition.

The journey to Shaktivail Nagar from KKNSS headquarters in the stonecutters' market is through ever more crowded and dowdier streets. In India, the less well off the neighborhood is, the more churches and mosques one sees. Muslims are generally poorer than Hindus, and Christian missionaries cluster around the poor, looking for converts and dispensing charity. We passed a big red mosque that Natraj said was built with "Gulf money"—remittances from Muslim workers in Dubai. On the next block, outside the slum, was a partially complete brick building with a hand-painted sign that read "God's Garden, an air-conditioned church." Just past a narrow market, we came to an open stretch of ground just over an acre in size. My driver parked the car and we got out—Natraj, a young man from the KKNSS meeting named James Jayraj and me. The smell of human excrement mixed with rotting garbage was overwhelming. The car was parked next to the place where people relieved themselves.

Natraj noticed me breathing through my mouth to deaden the smell. He laughed. "It's a burial ground for the local Muslims," he said, "but these people"—he indicated a cluster of concrete shacks with tin roofs—"use it for it a toilet. The men in the daytime, the women at night. That's why we campaign for public toilets in our slums. So people don't shit in the graveyard or the park."

Our arrival had been noticed. Dozens of young children surrounded us, pushing and shoving to get close. Jayraj, who calls himself a community outreach worker, cleared a path through the kids and led the way into the slum before disappearing down an impossibly narrow passageway. Natraj watched him leave, then sat down outside the small branch office his organization maintained at the edge of the cluster of concrete-block shacks. He told me to find Jayraj and have a look around while he arranged to have tea and snacks brought to the office.

I wandered in shock through a maze of alleys so narrow that you had to turn sideways to get past open doors. I was just half an hour away from the high-tech splendor of Electronic City, and the contrast could not have been more stark. There you walked along immaculate paths between gleaming towers full of young, educated and privileged people. Here, you avoided the dangerous looking pye-dogs and tried not to breathe in the vapor from the stagnant pools that lay in clogged drains beneath the alleys. Jayraj beckoned me from around a corner and I joined him. As we walked, he greeted residents outside their tiny concrete homes, where they cooked over fires fueled by cow dung or on primitive kerosene stoves. One man said his name was John Peter. He was a laborer who painted buildings for about six dollars a day and who was raising his three boys in a single room no larger than sixty-five square feet. The family washed at a water pump and used the burial ground as their toilet. Kanawa, a tired-looking woman in her forties who appeared much older, crouched over a tray of wrinkled vegetables. If she sold them all, she earned about a dollar, and she, too, had three children. She was a widow. Bunya Swamy, a haggard and emaciated man, invited us in for a glass of tea. He went to the market every day and got work loading and unloading sacks of rice and flour. He earned two dollars if he was lucky and spent that on feeding his children. He had five.

I had been in many, many Indian slums and had met countless people like these. But rarely had I experienced such contrasts in a single day. Jayraj kept leading me down alleys and past homes, calling out names and professions and repeating phrases such as "a dollar a day" or telling me, "no work in construction anymore, so they have to unload trucks." He seemed to know intimately the patterns of life in Shaktivail Nagar. It was, he said, one of Bangalore's better slums. It was well established and the people had a form of land title that KKNSS had fought for. He pointed at the snarl of wires on nearby electricity poles. "Stolen power," he said. People couldn't get a legitimate electrical connection, so they slung a cable onto the exposed wires and bribed power-company engineers not to disconnect them. This meant that the otherwise dark, windowless concrete huts had a light so children who were going to school could read or do their homework at night. KKNSS made sure that all the slum's boys and girls went to a local government school and were supplied with at least the necessary textbooks and uniforms, until they were literate. "Some even go to matric," Jayraj said proudly, referring to matriculation, the last year of high school. None of the slum's children had ever made it to college.

Back at the entrance to the colony, J. P. Natraj had been joined by a man in a white porkpie hat who introduced himself as Mr. Alegesan. He was the "headman" of Shaktivail Nagar and owned the best house in the colony. It was a two-story affair of painted concrete, with a real tile roof and an official power connection. Alegesan worked for the government and had used some of his money to endow the Hindu temple that sat right next to a Christian shrine. Tension between Hindus and Christian converts was a bit of a problem in the slum, he said.

"But we're all together on the important matters. We ask God and the government for development, and if we don't get it, we go to court. We know this is a rich city, that land values are high. We have land here, why can't we get proper houses, bank loans, power, water, sanitation? You know why? Because people think we're scum, we're antisocial elements, we're criminals. We need to change that perception and then we'll help our people."

As he talked, glasses of milky sweet tea arrived, carried by a young boy who was clearly a child laborer in a restaurant. He was thin, with ragged trousers and no shirt, and had patches of eczema on his face. Mr. Alegesan talked on, Natraj nodding approvingly beside him. By this time I had grown accustomed to the pungent odors. A man was squatting in the middle of the burial ground, relieving himself as we spoke, but we barely paid him any mind. This is the Indian approach to the poor, the unpleasant, the overwhelming. You let your gaze skate over it, think of something else, hold your breath until you get used to the smell. Then you're okay.

Bangalore didn't have the worst slums in India, nor the largest ones, nor the most intractable poverty. Thanks to James Jayraj and his bubbling enthusiasm for his work, there were glimmers of hope. The efforts of the polished and passionate J. P. Natraj had led to progress. There were jobs, however paltry the pay, and the government school took students without demur, so long as KKNSS paid for materials and uniforms. This was a world away from some of the migrant-worker or displaced-person slums that festered in other Indian cities, such as New Delhi, Mumbai and Calcutta. Although the prospect of real change was fleeting and perhaps illusory, people were settled, and they could see the possibility of improvement in the lives of their children. Even the prospect of functional literacy or a menial job in the area, rather than far away, offered hope. Most other poor Indians had little chance of getting an education and had to go where the work was.

Not that anyone in Shaktivail Nagar had any hope of a job in one of the city's high-technology businesses or call centers. Those were for the existing middle classes and people with an elite education. No one in the slum worked as a driver, office peon or laborer in Electronic City. In Bangalore, even the lowliest office jobs require a reasonably high degree of education—often a matriculate or college degree. Despite the boom times, there are still more people than jobs in most sectors of India's modern economy. Natraj was scornful of Infosys, Wipro and the other Indian companies that were global players in the high-tech world.

"They are just the latest version of international capital," the old Communist said. "Their owners talk as if doing business were some sort of mission or sacred duty, as if they're spreading goodwill and charity and enlightenment. All they're doing is making money. That's their job, their duty, their purpose. We shouldn't lose sight of that. These new companies may say they want to change the world for the better, but all they want at the end of the day is to make their investors richer. I refuse to see them as any different from a foundry, a chemical factory or a coal mine. They're capital, we're labor." Natraj was nodding and pointing his finger at me, growing rather intense. "Capitalists and workers, nothing has changed. Nothing." He lapsed into silence. We got up and left, turning our car around in the shit-strewn burial ground on the way out and driving back through the narrow alleys to the main highway that runs between Bangalore and Electronic City.

Not every Indian living in a slum is from the lowest, most disadvantaged social classes. Increasingly, in cities such as Mumbai and Calcutta, land is so expensive that even working people with relatively secure jobs have been squeezed out of any hope of living in the better neighborhoods. This includes many government employees who in India have job security but are poorly paid. In the massive Mumbai colony Dharavi, often described as the largest slum in Asia, many of the inhabitants work for the local municipal government. Others toil in offices for private employers who can't afford to pay wages that will allow their employees to live in the massive city's formal housing market.

Among the inhabitants of Dharavi was Sadanand Palande. He earned his living by working nights on the streets of Mumbai, hunting down and killing rats. It was contract work, paid for by the city council. Those who could endure it for a few years, handing in the requisite minimum of twenty-five rats each night, were given a full-time job at the municipality. As a municipal employee, he would become a member of one of India's most powerful trade unions. This meant that he would be entitled to a pension and could never be fired for any reason short of public insubordination to a politician. He would be set for life. He could get married and raise children, maybe even get his sons into the employ of the Municipal Corporation of Greater Mumbai as well. But first, to qualify, Sadanand had to venture into odiferous alleys and piles of rotting garbage in pursuit of *Rattus ratus* and *Rattus norvegicus*—India's two most common urban rodents.

On the morning when I first met him, Sadanand was outside a
city government office where he and other rat catchers dropped off
the night's pickings. As we spoke, my eyes kept flicking to a bouquet
of hairless, pink tails sprouting from shopping bags—ten or more
bags, nearly three hundred dead rats. It was hard not to fixate on
them. Sadanand noticed and laughed at my morbid fascination with
his prey. Our conversation began with rats and moved on to more
general topics—food, weather and where each of us lived. Before long,
he had invited me to his home, a tin-roofed shack in one of Dharavi's many smaller "suburbs." To reach his hut, we walked down a
twisted lane that branched off from the road to Mumbai's Santa Cruz
Domestic Airport. As jets roar in on final approach to the main runway, passengers often fall silent, gazing out a window at evidence of
India's vast inequalities. Dharavi's clusters of huts, shops and tents
stretches from the inland side of Mumbai's jutting peninsula to the
airport boundary fence at the end of the runway. Just before your
plane lands, you can see people below plug their ears and stop talking, silenced by the screaming jet engines just overhead. Many don't
bother even to look up. They are used to hundreds of noisy landings
every day.

Sadanand's house was spotless and smelled of floor-cleaning liquid. A neighborhood woman kept it clean, he said, for which he paid
her a few dollars a month. He was fastidious about hygiene, food and
water. This was typical of devout Hindus, but Sadanand also understood that his occupation exposed him to unsanitary conditions that
could endanger his health. If he fell ill and missed a night's hunting,
Sadanand said, he would have no income until he was back on the
job. Nor do rat catchers take regular days off; they get just the high
Hindu holidays like everyone else, and those unpaid. They hunted
rats on weekends; they hunted rats when they were ill; they hunted
rats in bad weather. For twenty-five dead rats, they were paid the
equivalent of about three dollars, a few cents more for each extra furry
corpse. Sadanand had worked the rat-killing business for two years
when I met him, and he had another three to go before he'd get his
guaranteed job.

"I have no education," he said, through a translator, in his native
tongue, Marathi. "I can sign my name and read it, but I can't write or
read anything else. Sometimes there are literacy classes around here

but I have no time, none, between sleeping and working and going for fun." That last phrase referred to his favorite pastime, going to the cinema to watch the latest lurid offering from Bollywood. He watched films every week, sometimes the current blockbuster, but often pirated DVDs of recent hits or classics shown on television in a tea shop. What were his favorite movies? "Anything sad," he replied.

That night, after visiting Sadanand's house, I joined him on his rounds. Rat catching was a lonely, occasionally dangerous business. And not just because of the rats' sharp teeth and the diseases they carry. Other rodent hunters would sometimes try to steal your rats, Sadanand said. "It means they don't have to do any work; they watch you and count how many you've got, then they make their move. They snatch your rats and run or hit you until you give them up.

"It's terrible to be mugged." Sadanand said he'd once been attacked and lost all twenty-five rats from a full night's work. Now he carried protection, he said, producing from his waistband a crude homemade knife wrapped in cloth. So far he hadn't had to use his protection.

"It's enough that they know I've got it with me," he explained. Sadanand works with his cousin Jalande, who is also trying to land a municipal government job. If the two failed to meet their nightly quota, they pooled what they had and split the payment. When I accompanied Sadanand for a night's hunting, his cousin was there, too. Jalande seemed more like a twin brother, not least because the two men were dressed in similar outfits. Both wore light cotton leggings that clung to their calves, with bulky trousers over top and a long, loose tunic over a sleeveless undershirt. It was the rat hunter's armor, designed to guard against champing teeth. There was always the chance that the rat would be rabid. Not that Sadanand hadn't been bitten scores of times. He showed me scar after scar, including an alarming gap in his right palm. "All from sharp teeth," he said with a philosophical smile. Most of the wounds were from the days before he wore protective clothing. Sometimes, he explained, you think you've killed a rat with a decisive downward thump of your staff, but as you pick up the body by the tail, the beast comes alive and bends around in its own length to bite your hand, wrist or torso. It was after such a bite that he had to have anti-rabies injections, seven or eight painful needles straight into his abdomen.

Our hunt began at the same municipal office where we had met and mostly we ranged around the surrounding area, in and out of the storage warehouses and food shops where rats feasted by night. Shop and business doors were left open so Sadanand and other rat hunters could do their work. People invited us into their homes to chase rodents. We waded through thigh-deep garbage while rats ran through tunnels around our legs. Occasionally we felt their hairless tails brush against our feet and ankles. I am afraid that I used some rather choice words to cover up my fear, or more likely to telegraph it to my two companions—to their great amusement. My light cotton chinos were drenched in sweat and other less appetizing fluids. My well-fed thighs were there for the nipping but, thankfully, no Mumbai rats were tempted to partake.

The cousins worked as a team. When one spotted a potential victim, the other closed in for the kill. The tips of their long wooden staffs were smeared with smelly bits of rotting chicken. Even when we moved away from the decay and stench of the alleys, a pong of the charnel house lingered around us. When the two hunters managed to flush a rat, they worked closely together. If the beast dashed under something, or through a hole in the wall, they gave chase. When they knew their quarry was cornered or unable to flee into new corners or holes, they coaxed it out. One would make chillingly accurate rat-like squeaks. The other would put the tip of his staff near the hiding place, so the chicken stink could waft in. That usually elicited at least a look from the cornered rat, but the preferred technique—"best practice" they'd call it in management consultancy—was to allow the rat to come fully out of its hidey-hole before attempting the fatal blow. The three of us would stand stock still while one of the hunters uttered rat-squeaks, and the other kept the chicken juice–baited stick tantalizingly out of the rat's reach. When the moment came, whoever had the staff would thrust it down on the rodent's head or neck, quickly and savagely. A wounded rat would either run back into cover or, sometimes, attack its tormentor. Sadanand pointed to his feet. "Ankles and fingers," he said, looking at Jalande. "That's what they like to bite."

Once confirmed dead, a rat was picked up by the tail and slung into a shopping bag. The two hunters stopped every hour or so to tally up. Usually, well before dawn, they would have fifty or more corpses and would call it a night. Then they had to wait until someone arrived at the municipal office to count the dead creatures and make the appropriate entry into a ledger that entitled them to their weekly payments. Often the group of rat catchers that gathered each morning would share the task of waiting for often tardy municipal employees, taking charge of each other's rats and making sure full credit was given for every last crushed head and pink tail. On this particular night, Sadanand volunteered to stay behind so that I could film the official tally for a television documentary. His cousin and hunting partner wandered off into the night, singing a movie song and whistling. Sadanand laughed at his retreating back, made a few rat-squeaks and told me that he and Jalande both loved sad songs— a staple of the Indian cinema.

Rat hunting was a hell of way to earn a living, especially when home was a lean-to next to a river of sewage and toxic waste. But Sadanand knew that if he survived the years of night stalking, he had before him the prospect of a better house in Dharavi and a job for life. It was his version of the Indian dream. In his world, you worked hard or you lost your chance. One day, Sadanand would get married, and his children would go to school. "So they won't have to hunt rats," he said, shaking his head emphatically.

4

WATCHING THE NUMBERS

Early Warnings of India's Woes

IN MAY 2000, India passed a significant milestone: the one billionth Indian citizen was born. The moment was meticulously tracked and observed by government officials and by population and poverty activists. Partly, this was a celebration, but it was also the occasion for a renewed commitment to keep population growth as low as possible. Camera crews, politicians and foreign diplomats were called to the maternity ward of one of New Delhi's main hospitals to cluster around a slightly bewildered woman and her new daughter. Twenty-nine children are born every minute in India. The officials charged with deciding just who the billionth Indian was chose an infant who happened to be born within easy reach of the capital city's media and governing elite. This was, of course, a choice both arbitrary and convenient. But the message of the subsequent news conference was clear: Indian population control measures taken in previous decades had succeeded. Family sizes were shrinking and, within a few decades, the country's population would stabilize. But not before India passed China as the world's most populous nation. It was estimated that that would happen around 2040. Beijing's far more coercive family-planning measures have had a dramatic impact on China's population growth.

In part because of the Chinese experience, it is now politically incorrect to speak of "population explosions" or to espouse Malthusian theories about an increasingly crowded, resource-depleted planet collapsing under the weight of burgeoning numbers of poor people. Instead, experts now talk of sustainable population growth and of distributing resources more fairly. They point out that India's billion-plus people consume far less energy than the population either of the United States or Europe. The average North American child uses thirty-three times more resources to grow to maturity than his or her Indian counterpart. Closing that great gap, rather than bringing populations "under control," is the goal of global development these days.

One of India's leading thinkers on these matters is Professor Ashish Bose, known to the many who beat a path to his door as his country's demographer-in-chief. Now in his seventies, Professor Bose has studied Indian population trends all of his adult life. His inspiration comes from something he regards as akin to a sacred text. This is the Indian census, a vast exercise conducted at ten-year intervals that supplies him with the material for his remarkable analyses. Need to know how female literacy improved during the 1980s and 1990s? Ask Ashish Bose. Trying to discover whether Indian Hindus and Muslims have different birth rates, as some anti-Muslim bigots have alleged in their effort to raise fears about Islam swamping Hinduism? Go to the good professor for an eloquent rebuttal grounded in the latest data. How many computers, watches, motorcycles and CD players decorate or enhance middle-class Indian households? Bose knows.

Over the course of a lifetime, Professor Bose has developed and vigorously espoused many theories to explain his country. Some of his ideas are controversial; others are received wisdom; but all are expressed with compassion, eloquence and humor. Bose is one of life's teachers, a guru in the Indian philosophical tradition, one who imparts wisdom to those who seek it. His study, in a southern suburb of New Delhi, is a cluttered warren of papers and computer disks; countless scribbled Post-it notes are pinned and stuck to every available surface. Shelves groan under the weight of hundreds of books and bound reports from India's various statistical departments and government ministries. Theses sent by fellow academics and students sit open on his desk, their pages annotated and creased. This is where Bose's ideas emerge from apparent clutter and chaos, theories like the notion of BIMARU, probably his most famous contribution to Indian demography and statistical analysis.

India is divided into twenty-eight states and a few small territories ruled directly by the central government. Indians states don't have as much authority devolved to them as Canadian provinces or German *Länder,* but they do look after important areas of social policy such as health and education. The states vary hugely in size and population. The largest, Uttar Pradesh, in the north, has around 170 million people; the smallest, Sikkim, fewer than six hundred thousand. State governments are profoundly influential in the lives of their people. Professor Bose's theory of BIMARU is an attempt to hold local administrations to account for their failures and shortcomings. The word *bimaru* means sickly, or ill, in the Hindi language, spoken by about one-third of Indians. But as conceived by Bose, it's an acronym made up from the first letters of the names of India's four least-developed states, as measured by a variety of statistics.

These states are Bihar, Madhya Pradesh, Rajasthan and Uttar Pradesh (Bihar, Madhya Pradesh, Rajasthan, Uttar Pradesh). In the 1980s, when Bose was poring over data from previous censuses, he noticed that those four states finished consistently at the bottom of the league tables for crucial indicators such as literacy, maternal mortality, birth rate, infant health, doctors per square mile and so on. What was worse, he observed, while in other Indian states these indicators reflected an improving trend, in the BIMARU states most were either stagnating or growing worse. These were, he concluded, sick states in need of harsh, effective medicine, or at least a healthy dose of public awareness of their failings. Thus BIMARU was born. Bose told the media and his fellow academics that four of India's states were dragging the country down. If the numbers from BIMARU could be magically excluded from Indian development data, the country would leap up the global league table from near the bottom to somewhere in the middle. The BIMARU states, the professor said, were as badly off as a sub-Saharan Africa basket case. The plight of women and children was especially difficult.

The reaction to his announcement was mixed at best. "People in general were enthusiastic," says Bose. "If they lived in one of the forward-looking states, they could be proud of improving literacy and women's health and all that. But in BIMARU itself, the politicians were furious. They denounced me." That was decades ago and the backlash did not adversely affect Ashish Bose's standing as the maestro of Indian demographic analysis. In fact, it gave him a boost. "Overnight, I became famous," he says. "Journalists were entranced by BIMARU, and I was able to tell them much, much more about how this country was shaping up at the time, where the real positive and negative trends were, and they worked hard to work the idea into their coverage."

Slim and fit and still with a full head of steely-gray hair, the professor's eyes gleam when he is in full flow. "Everything was wrong in the BIMARU states," he says. To a certain extent, things are still badly out of kilter in at least two of them. In Rajasthan (a desert state southwest of New Delhi) and Madhya Pradesh (at India's geographic center), there have been improvements in women's health and literacy, the birth rate is declining to a more sustainable level and recent governments have won praise for their efforts to erase corruption. The two states were among the first in India to bring in improved data management systems under so-called e-governance programs championed by the World Bank and the central authorities in New Delhi. But BIMARU as a concept is alive and well because the two remaining states—Bihar and Uttar Pradesh—have not improved significantly in any key areas.

Apart from BIMARU, Ashish Bose is known for another major discovery arising from his work with statistics and population data. Unlike for the BIMARU thesis, Bose doesn't draw attention to it just to embarrass politicians and stimulate conversation. When the professor talks about this particular trend, he is deeply troubled and filled with righteous anger.

"In many parts of this country," he says, "we are killing off our female population, and though it's illegal, we seem unable to stop it."

Demographers usually expect that females will outnumber males as populations grow older. Women live longer for a variety of reasons: their overall health is generally better, they are less likely to cultivate self-destructive habits such as drinking and smoking, and so on. But in some of North India's most prosperous states, there are far more men than women, especially in the younger echelons of society. To put it bluntly, families are striving for sons and eliminating daughters before they are even born.

Many couples are using ultrasound or amniocentesis technologies to determine the sex of a fetus in the womb and then aborting females. "It's an unholy marriage of technology and tradition," Bose says. "The relatively well-off don't move beyond the backward attitudes of their orthodox ancestors: the belief that sons represent free farm labor, income and care for aging parents. The flip side is that daughters are seen as a drain on resources." The dowries that are theoretically illegal in India but still widely expected in much of the country are simply becoming more expensive. "In [the North Indian states of] Haryana and . . . Punjab, even among certain communities here in Delhi," Bose says, "a bride must come with a new car, and not some small, inexpensive one either. It has to be big and have air-conditioning. Wide-screen TVs, DVD players, computers—all these are often expected by the family of the groom, given a certain level of technological sophistication." Such items are costly, Bose says, and the same high regard for technology is driving the growing gender imbalance. "Ultrasound clinics are everywhere in these parts of the country. You don't have to look far to find one in Delhi. And they are being used to make decisions to abort female fetuses. This is not only legally and morally wrong; it's very, very dangerous."

In January 2006, a Canadian-led study published in the British medical journal *The Lancet* claimed that up to ten million female fetuses were selectively aborted in India over the past thirty years. The report made for grim reading, though it contained no surprises for Ashish Bose. It showed how mothers and families with a high school education were twice as likely to seek to abort a female fetus as were an illiterate couple. Bose said his statistical work over the years about India's worsening ratio between women and men had prepared him for the conclusions of the Canadian study.

"After a while, I start to ask whether anyone in this country cares anymore [about female feticide]," he says, shaking his head.

Among the well-off, it is said to be preferable to travel to North America to get the testing and abortion done in a private clinic there, away from the prying, judgmental eye of the Indian legal system. In most U.S. states where abortion is legal, getting rid of a female fetus because a couple prefers a male is rare, perhaps even unknown, so no laws or regulations prohibit the practice. But among some members of the Indian community in the United States and Canada, demand for ultrasound and other fetal sex-selection services has been steadily growing for decades. Doctors and medical professionals in both countries have expressed concern about female feticide, and some obstetrics clinics are reluctant to share the sex of a fetus with the parents. In Surrey, British Columbia, in 2005, a local Punjabi-Canadian medical activist accused Indian community newspapers of encouraging feticide by carrying advertisements for ultrasound clinics that promised "you will always know the sex of the baby." Despite such growing unease, there is no explicit ban on abortion performed to favor one sex over the other. The right to choose is the right to choose.

In both Canada and the United States, clinics exist to serve wealthy South Asians who want boy babies and can pay for it. Ashish Bose shakes with fury that other countries enable his fellow Indians to do what he considers to be a crime against humanity.

"Gender-based abortion should be illegal by international law, and Interpol should go after anyone in any country who allows it. Period. There's no halfway measure. It's wrong and it's the greatest slaughter of women ever on the planet, taken over time. It's a holocaust."

The Indian authorities are deeply concerned that their laws against female feticide, passed in 1994, are flouted so openly. There have been police investigations and occasional raids on abortion clinics, but governments are also taking more innovative steps. Some open bank accounts in the name of newborn baby girls. This is supposed to enable the parents to begin saving for the girl's marriage, a way of offsetting the traditional belief that female children are a burden on family finances while males provide labor and assistance. There are public information campaigns. Indian celebrities have spoken out on the issue. But Bose's "holocaust" is not going away. Male children remain the raison d'être for most marriages in India, however affluent or educated the parents. Sons inherit parental property, but under certain circumstances, a daughter without brothers who marries into another family can, theoretically, take the property with her.

In such cases, ancestral land—with long-standing blood ties to a particular family—is lost. Religious tradition also plays a part. Many devout Hindus believe that a father's funeral pyre must be lit by a first-born son or other important male relative, never a female. All of this, according to Bose, explains why so many Indian families are reluctant to have girl children, at least until sons have been born.

"They seem to want an heir and a spare," he says, "before they smarten up and realize how important it is to have women in the household, in the community and in the country. Only after one or two sons are born do they relax and welcome a daughter. This is madness, and it must stop."

A demographer can hardly be anything other than a feminist, Bose asserts. As someone who studies population trends and matches them with crime statistics and other social indicators, he says, it is evident to him that women are more civilized than men, more socially useful and constructive in their approach to life. "Look at history, anywhere, any time, any place. Large numbers of unattached and underemployed men are simply bad. They are unproductive and eventually dangerous. They get involved in crime, terrorism and, in this country, political thuggery. Our gender, mine and yours, we cause wars, we commit crimes, we fuel and carry out violence for all sorts of reasons. Women are peaceful, more moderate, more intelligent than us, and without them around in sufficient numbers to stabilize the population, we will go into steep decline."

Even in those parts of the country where female feticide is almost unknown, Indian women have generally faced an uphill battle. Most public fields of endeavor are men's worlds, from politics to business, medicine to government service. One meets impressive women in public and professional life all of the time in India, but they are the exception that proves the rule among the wider populace. For most Indian men, it's safe to say, a woman's place is where it has always been, in the home. Thankfully, in most new economic sectors in India, this is changing. The call-center business was an early pioneer in giving preference to the hiring of women over men, or at least in trying to achieve a balance between the sexes. Raman Roy, who helped get the offshore call-center business started in the 1980s, says women are far and away the best workers in the offices that he has set up and run.

"They are so much more reliable [than men]," Roy says. "They keep to timings, they work better in teams, they make less trouble, and I've rarely had to let a female employee go for repeated lateness or sloppy work. We noticed this early on and it has not changed over the years. 'Bring on the women' is our motto."

That's why the ratio of females to males in Indian BPO (business process outsourcing) firms and call centers is already past fifty-fifty in favor of women, according to the India-based news website Rediff India Abroad. The challenge is matching the reality of this modern workforce with attitudes on the street. As the murder of Pratibha Srikantamurthy shows, the streets of India aren't yet ready for large numbers of young women making their way to and from work. That puts the onus on employers to guarantee their female workers' safety, but it doesn't stop them from trying to correct the gender imbalance in the workplace.

Information technology firms have workforces that are still more than 60 percent male, in part because the engineering degrees necessary to get a job at Infosys or Microsoft seem to be more coveted by young men than by female students. That's despite the fact that women outnumber men in postsecondary education. The media workplace in India is becoming more equitable, though there are comparatively few female editors and senior television executives. Most female doctors practice in traditional women's areas such as obstetrics and gynecology. Often, this is because many female patients prefer to be examined and treated by women, a form of reverse sexism not unknown in Western countries. Government employees in India are largely men. As with medicine, many female civil servants work in family-related areas or as clerical workers. There are high-profile female bureaucrats, but they are few and far between, and they tend to be from the educated elite, overcoming the natural disadvantages of their sex through family and class contacts. Electoral politics in India is utterly male dominated at the top national and state levels. It's generally thought that women do not make winning candidates, that rural voters prefer strong men to represent them and that male representatives are more able to bring home funds and government jobs from the man's world that is Indian politics. Attempts in New Delhi's (male-dominated) parliament to pass laws requiring at least one-third of all parliamentary seats to be reserved for women have failed many times. Fewer than 10 percent of Indian MPs are female. Not so at local (village and municipal) levels. There, 33 percent of all councilors are required by law to be women. This has produced remarkable—if mixed—results. Strong female leaders have emerged, even in the most orthodox and patriarchal parts of the country, as women have learned to manipulate the ropes of power. However, male politicians have managed to stay dominant in some districts by nominating female relatives, wives or the widows of local strongmen. In such cases, the women vote and act as proxies for traditional party interests on village councils or *panchayats,* the basic elected bodies of Indian representative democracy.

It still can be argued that there have been subtle improvements to the lot of women in India, even if their role in politics is passive or controlled by men. In Rajasthan, one of Ashish Bose's BIMARU states, some of the country's lowest development indicators for women exist alongside a high female profile in local politics. Rajasthan is where most of India's child marriages take place. It is also a state where *sati,* the practice of devout Hindu widows leaping onto their husbands' funeral pyres and dying in the flames, reputedly continues to take place. Indian human rights and feminist groups contend that women from communities where sati has occurred are often pressured into a horrific act by the weight of centuries of tradition and that, given a choice, they would choose to live. Sati is illegal and rare in contemporary India, and when a case does occur, it generates immense interest and bitter controversy. Similarly, tribal and traditional customs, such as marrying off prepubescent girls to adult men or isolating women during menses, are finally on the wane thanks to law and advocacy campaigns that raise female awareness of women's rights.

Many Rajasthani Hindu women cover their heads with a Muslim-style headscarf and rarely meet men outside their families once they get married. It's a custom that dates from the days when much of India was ruled by Muslim sultans from Central Asia or by equally orthodox Hindu maharajahs and warlords. Yet, in 2005, state government in Rajasthan was dominated by three powerful women: Chief Minister Vasundhara Raje, State Governor Pratibha Patil and Speaker of the Assembly Sumitra Singh. The chief minister had also served as India's foreign affairs minister in New Delhi and is a forthright, capable politician who hasn't let her sex get in the way of her career. She is descended from one of India's most revered former royal families, the Scindias of Gwalior, and her mother was one of the country's early female MPs, elected to parliament for the first time in 1962. For her part, Governor Patil went on to become, in mid-2007,

India's first woman president. Her election as the country's ceremonial head of state was controversial, with many opposition leaders questioning her credentials and saying she was chosen largely because she was politically loyal to the then-dominant Congress Party. There was more than a whiff of sexism in some of the criticism of Patil.

In Rajasthan's colorful capital city, Jaipur, broad streets and new shopping malls sit alongside the fairy-tale castles and architectural follies of former maharajahs. This is India's jewelry capital, and the city's traditional wealth comes from its communities of goldsmiths and gemstone merchants, now among the country's leading exporters of finished goods. A brand-new office block that houses wholesale dealers in precious metals and stones is called Gold Souk. Increasingly, though, the modern economy of Jaipur is based on services—software, retailing and tourism. Such transformations, says Ashish Bose, are happening all over India, and this is good news for women. Jewelry manufacturing was always a man's world. Sons inherited the business from their fathers, and rigid orthodoxies based on Hindu caste or religious community governed behavior—for example, most gem sellers are Muslim, most retail merchants Hindu. But a medical college or a call center hires the best people for the new jobs it creates, with no historical patterns to direct the course of business. That often means, as we've seen, women getting preference over men.

Professor Bose is a frequent visitor to Jaipur, where he lectures at local colleges and discusses the changing nature of India with friends in academic, business and government circles. He is an old friend of the former governor, now president, Pratibha Patil. He has also met with Chief Minister Vasundhara Raje and finds her supportive of his views on women, if not overly thrilled that he still considers her state to be part of BIMARU. Bose likes to press the top women of Rajasthan to not lose sight of the lot of their sisters in villages. Neither demography nor social reform stops at the edge of the city, he says. It's particularly in the villages that change is both necessary and happening too slowly.

Jaipur began as an oasis in the vast Thar Desert, and just beyond the urban sprawl of today, the sandy wasteland reasserts itself. This happens rather abruptly. The road winds past strip malls where restaurants with names such as "Hunger Station" and "Chick-Inn" serve fast food to middle-class families. Clusters of residential developments sit half built, and new cars zip between them and the city center. But a few short minutes away, the scrub bush and blowing dust of the Rajasthan countryside are all the eye can see. The city skyline fades quickly in the rearview mirror. Wooden carts carrying vegetables and firewood are drawn along the shoulder of the highway by dromedaries. This is camel country. An occasional stand of mango trees in the distance marks the site of a village or hamlet. Often these communities are surrounded by patches of tentative green, the winter crops of cabbage and beans, breaking through chunks of dry, tilled earth. The road surface is smooth and newly paved. Chief Minister Raje's government puts a lot of emphasis on having good roads between farms and markets.

About twenty-five miles outside Jaipur is Chaksu, a village that has become known to feminists and women's advocates all over the world for the political nous of its female population. The women of Chaksu have long been involved in local politics; they have lobbied national governments in New Delhi and many have been abroad to campaign for the rights of peasant farmers in a global market that prefers to deal with big agribusiness companies. Fearless and committed, these women are used to visits by outsiders like Ashish Bose, who come in search of the secret of their success in raising awareness about the needs of rural women in a changing world. When the demographer and I arrived in their midst in late 2005, fifteen women aged between twenty and fifty-nine were gathered in a house just outside the village. They had been asked to come from their scattered hamlets and homesteads by Sharad Joshi, the local activist who had first started organizing them to fight for their rights. They all stood up and greeted Bose with palms pressed together in front of them, saying *namaste* and bowing their heads politely. All wore colorful headscarves and looked every inch the orthodox Rajasthani Hindu. After returning the gesture, Bose pointed at an elderly lady in a purple sari who sat just inside the door of the room and asked her to tell us her story.

By way of answer she reached into a shoulder bag and produced an object that she laid on the table. It was a brand-new Indian passport, and her calloused fingers held it open to the picture page. She indicated the date of issue and grinned broadly. Yesterday. And her name, Nathi Devi, was printed alongside her photograph, the Indian

state seal engraved on the paper—as emphatic a proclamation of cit-
izenship as any nation can offer. Nathi Devi had the loudest voice of
anyone in the group, and her explanation of the passport was long
and complicated and punctuated with bursts of her cackling laughter. Here, it seemed, was a woman none too shy and ready to take on
the world. And she had the passport to prove it.

"She says she's going to Hong Kong," Bose said. "She's going to the
World Trade Organization meeting on agriculture to give them a
piece of her mind. Think of it. Hong Kong via Bangkok, and before
getting this passport she had hardly ever traveled even to Jaipur." The
professor laughed, explained his amusement to Nathi Devi and then
asked her what she would do or say in Hong Kong. The old woman
launched into a monologue that—on translation—turned out to be
about how agricultural subsidies in rich countries kept small poor
farmers like her trapped in rural poverty. She said she'd also be telling
the delegates about how American and European corporations were
trying to patent traditional Indian crops such as turmeric and basmati
rice. "She's against the genetic modification of plants and crop
species," Bose said, shaking his head in wonder. All of these are popular causes with the activist left in India, and Devi had imbibed the
nuances thoroughly.

"How dare they tell us we can't have seeds from our plants," she
said passionately in her native tongue, Hindi. She was referring to the
"killer gene" biotechnology that makes certain plants sterile so farmers can't grow their own seeds but must buy them every year from a
big corporation such as Monsanto or Cargill. "How dare they force us
to use only one brand of weed killer or fertilizer. There are millions
of us out here who have a louder voice than all of the big companies,
and we intend to shout together in Hong Kong. No one is taking my
farm or my land. No one." As she spoke, Nathi Devi waved her passport like a weapon. Here was a woman well aware of her rights and
willing to fight for them, in India and around the world. Yet she was
illiterate and came from a rural culture so riddled with orthodox social and religious attitudes that she covered her hair in the presence
of men and drew water only from wells that had been dug by people
from her own Hindu caste.

Devi was being taken to the WTO ministerial meeting by Sharad
Joshi's Chaksu-based nongovernmental organization, the Centre for

Community Economics and Development. It had been founded a few decades earlier after floods in Rajasthan left many small farmers without crops or resources and thus deprived of access to the usual channels of assistance: government grants, foreign aid and soft bank loans. Led by the charismatic Joshi, a bulky, towering man with a sense of quiet competence about him, the organization had placed itself squarely on the front lines against globalization and corporate agriculture.

Other women at the meeting spoke about the more down-to-earth challenges that Joshi's organization tackled. These included addressing land disputes in the villages and ending caste discrimination that prevented village farmers from using water supplies reserved for others. Mostly the women talked about nonviolent civil disobedience and using the courts and media to draw attention to injustice. One woman told a poignant tale of bringing a schoolteacher to justice after he raped several low-caste students. "The government was protecting him, politicians were protecting him, the police were protecting him," she said. "But we got him and now he's in jail for fourteen years."

Sharad Joshi said that ordinary people who appeared in public to make the case for justice or social change had a lasting effect, "whereas we in the NGO sector come and go and rarely surprise anyone with our public advocacy. No media outlet would cover me talking about injustice," he said. "But they seem to listen to the likes of Nathi Devi pretty easily, especially if she surprises people, challenges their preconceived notions by waving her passport around." Other women had been sent to global gatherings, including the trade talks, Joshi said, and the result was largely positive. More than just getting international attention, though, the goal of organizations such as Joshi's was nothing less than to liberate the political energy of Indian women, to make them a force for social and economic change in their villages and around the world. Most of the women in the room at what we later found out were Joshi's headquarters had served their time on village councils and knew how to use the system from the inside.

"We don't just agitate and cause trouble in Delhi or Hong Kong," Joshi explained. "We use the council chambers and courts, too. We press for schools, clean water, investigations [of village crimes] and social justice. In India, you have to vary your tactics." It wasn't enough, Joshi believed, to highlight the most egregious forms of sex discrimination in India, such as female feticide, child marriage, sati and the sex trade. All these were necessary steps in the overall process of achieving true equality, of enabling society to benefit from the liberation of women and to unleash their economic and creative energy to solve problems beyond home and hearth.

"We start with politics," Joshi said, "but the sky is the limit."

Finally, it was time to leave. A tall woman in a black-and-white headscarf asked for a ride back in the direction of Jaipur. As we rumbled along the highway, Bose spoke to her in the local dialect and said her name was Shakuntala Devi and that she had met Bill Clinton.

"She's even had a dance with him," he said.

"*Clinton, ha ji, Clinton mai maloom hai,*" she said, "Clinton is known to me." She went on to explain that then-president Clinton had spent several hours in Rajasthan during his 2000 visit to India. He had asked to see projects that helped local women, and Sharad Joshi's organization was chosen to accompany him on this part of his visit. He was driven to Chaksu and sat in the same room where Bose and I had met Nathi Devi and the others. When the talking finished, the president leapt to his feet and joined the women of Chaksu in a high-stepping folk dance that was part of the ceremony in his honor. At the time, the television pictures of Clinton holding hands with a line of brightly dressed village women, swinging his legs in time with theirs, were a media highlight. But Shakuntala's encounter with the president went one better. Not only had she joined Clinton on the dance floor, she was one of the few who got to spend face time with him.

"He wanted to meet some of us privately, and I was due to go to a UN session in New York on community government and devolution of power," she explained, the normally unfamiliar words rattling off her tongue as if she were a veteran development worker. "So they put me forward, and I was cleared by his security people before the visit. When he got there, we went into that same room where we met in Chaksu and we talked, with a translator, for half an hour. At first I was nervous and only answered his questions, but he made me feel confident and appreciated so I told him what I felt about just about everything."

Shakuntala said she told Clinton about poverty and local government and how the two were related. She agreed with him that land titles and unfettered access to the process of law would greatly improve things for poor farmers. Clinton was fond of the ideas of the Peruvian economist Hernando de Soto, who insists that poverty would significantly diminish if only assets already held by the poor—land, farm implements, houses—could be registered in their names and used to acquire credit and social status. Shakuntala told Clinton a few stories about trying to register land at government offices in Jaipur and having to cope with corrupt officials. "He's very thoughtful, he nods while you speak, looks you in the eye and asks very intelligent questions. He listens to you," Shakuntala said of Clinton.

By contrast, the peasant woman told us, when she met the Indian prime minister in 2003, the septuagenarian Atal Bihari Vajpayee, she got barely two minutes of his time, and he hardly seemed to pay attention to her. "There were people coming and going, putting papers in front of him, interrupting me. He seemed confused and not really interested in me." Vajpayee was, she agreed, somewhat elderly and seemed to be easily distracted. The prime minister was a much-loved father figure of Indian politics during his time in power, but the degree to which he actually mastered the nuances of office is definitely open to question. A June 2002 *Time* magazine article even wondered whether Vajpayee was fit to serve as prime minister. At the time, the Indian government reacted with fury. The reporter who wrote the story, Alex Perry, very nearly lost his right to work in India as a vengeful Prime Minister's Office looked for ways to quash the notion that Vajpayee was asleep at the wheel.

Just when it seemed as if Shakuntala Devi had exhausted her anecdotes of the village woman and the wider world, she launched into the tale of her trip to the United Nations, several years earlier, for a grand summit and gathering on local government. "New York was like nothing I'd ever seen. Tall, tall buildings everywhere.

"It was frightening. We stayed on the forty-fourth floor of a hotel and I got lost all of the time. The view from the window made me dizzy, so I kept my curtains pulled. The first time I had to push the button for my own floor in the elevator, I ended up somewhere down under the ground. Then there were the meals. The food was terrible. There was too much of it, and everyone around us was eating beef. All of us women from India had a meeting and decided that we'd go on a sacred fast until we left New York, just as we do when it's a holy day in the village. We only ate fruit and drank only water." She grimaces at the memory. "Not that that was easy. Those big American bananas and oranges, they have no taste." She began to laugh. What she didn't tell us, and we learned only later, was that she had given the opening address to the conference and had been a huge hit.

Her speech had been powerful and direct, much like the woman herself. Give more power to communities, to women, she had said, and societies will prosper. As leader of the local council, or *panchayat,* that ran her village, she was speaking from experience. Her closing arguments earned her a standing ovation and coverage on the local TV news. Truly empowering women will get you clean, sensible government that delivers real services, she had argued.

After Bose and I dropped Shakuntala off at her village, we reflected on how she seemed to combine both modesty and passion, tradition and desire for change. We could discern what Bill Clinton saw in this remarkable Indian woman from Rajasthan.

Ashish Bose's India is a place of constant change and demographic tumult. He is fond of telling stories about his family as a metaphor for the historic passages that his country has been through in the twentieth century. India was a British colony when his father was born at the turn of the nineteenth century; an insurgent nation-in-the-making fighting for its freedom during Bose's boyhood; a newly independent country on the world stage when he was in his teens and twenties; a largely poor, somewhat disaster-prone place as he learned his trade and carved a role for himself as a demographer; and now a budding global superpower and information technology hub as his sons prosper and raise families of their own. Asked to explain how three generations could experience so much change, Bose waxes philosophical. He tells the tale of how his father came to be tutor to a tiger-hunting, turban-wearing maharajah back in the days when at least half of India was made up of independent princely states. These were theoretically sovereign entities, which cooperated with the British Empire but often maintained a stubborn, political independence from London. Several of them were huge, the size of some European countries. Quite a few were little more than small towns and their surrounding fields. There were fabulously wealthy princes who sat on golden thrones and rode elephants in grand parades. Others lived simply, or even in relative poverty, with none of the luxuries of Oriental satrapy.

"Papa was in his twenties," Bose begins his tale, "living in his home village in Bengal [in eastern India] when he saw an ad in the [Calcutta newspaper] *The Statesman* for an English teacher in a place called Kolhapur. Not only had my dad never heard of the place, he didn't even know if the job was still open, as it took a week for the newspapers to reach his village. That could have meant that someone had already applied and got the post. But he took a chance anyway and wrote to the address given in the ad—just that, no explanation of what school or what post, just 'English master needed, apply Kolhapur.'"

His father's letter explained that he had degrees in English, both a bachelor of arts and a master's. He heard nothing for more than a month and was beginning to give up hope that he'd get the job. Then, says Bose, a telegram arrived from the other side of India, containing just the single word, "Accepted," and brief instructions to proceed to Kolhapur by a certain date. "Again," says Bose, "there was no explanation of what exactly the job entailed. But there was no time to lose."

The young man left his village by riverboat and then caught a big paddlewheel steamer up the delta of the River Ganges to Calcutta. There he made the two-night journey by mail train to Bombay. His destination was still another six or seven hours along the rail line south of Bombay's stately Victoria Terminus. In all, it took the young teacher four days to travel from Bengal at India's eastern edge to Kolhapur on the country's western flank. En route, he read a book about the princely states of India and learned that he was traveling to one of the country's smaller but wealthier principalities, a place known for its schools and for the martial skills of its small army, which was often proudly deployed in support of British forces overseas. The royal family was descended from a Hindu dynasty that resisted both Muslim and British conquest for many generations and was still venerated for that reason. At the same time, the current maharajah was said to be a social reformer, Anglophile in outlook and fond of a good *shikar*, or tiger hunt.

At Kolhapur station, Ashish Bose's father stood out from the crowd with his Western dress and dark complexion. Kolhapuris were fairer-skinned than Bengalis, he observed, and most dressed in traditional *lunghis,* long, flowing sarong-like garments. A horse-drawn carriage was waiting to take him to the main high school—the best educational institution in the state—where he was to head the English department. Later, he would ask the people who hired him why his application had been successful. They had wanted an Englishman, they told him, as most suitable to tutor their prince, but none was available, so a Bengali would have to do. People from Bengal were renowned then, as now, as intellectuals, good communicators and sticklers for accuracy and truthfulness. It was an act of racial stereotyping that changed the course of Bose family history.

At the time of his arrival, the elder Mr. Bose wasn't married, but his family soon took steps to rectify that. Most Indians regard marriage as the necessary, stable platform for adult life, and the Boses were no exception. Following centuries of tradition, they found a partner for their son, negotiated with the girl's parents and set a wedding date. "My mother's family was very wealthy," Bose says, "but my father had an advanced university degree, so that more than offset his humble background. In Bengal they value the mind more than money. Good thing, too, or I'd have never been born." The happy couple settled down in Kolhapur in the 1930s in what the firstborn son, Ashish, remembers as a wonderful time. "Life was sweet. It was wonderful to be a child in that place and in that time," he says now. "It was green with forest and lush fields. The city was shielded from the worst extremes of heat by a range of hills. We played sports all of the time, went on hunting trips to watch the royals chase tigers."

As this idyllic childhood was unfolding, India's freedom struggle was in full swing. World War II was a distraction from the quest for independence, but not much of one. Bose was largely oblivious to all this, aware only that his homeland was not yet a sovereign country, though it was on the verge of great change. "My history teacher was an American, a leftist," Bose recalls. "He didn't like the British and he kept up with current events, the war, the freedom struggle, of course. He said he believed in democracy and that, one day, India would be free, a democracy itself, like America. But what I remember about him most was that he refused to spell words in the British manner, [he spelled] *labor* without a *u,* that sort of thing. It was a point of pride with him."

The teacher's politics weren't shared by many in Kolhapur, Bose says. There, the British war effort was hugely popular with the royal family, local army commanders and the people. In other parts of India, leaders of the freedom struggle were refusing to back the war unless India was guaranteed more autonomy in return for its military support. Some pro-independence groups were urging Indian soldiers in the British Indian army to desert their regiments. Others joined with Japan to actively fight Britain in South and Southeast Asia. By contrast, the crown prince of Kolhapur, Bose's father's student, was in combat with his personal regiment in the Horn of Africa, fighting Italian forces in Somalia. There were spontaneous cheers, Bose says, when news came in that the regiment had won a particular battle and the crown prince was given a British military medal for his efforts at the head of his troops.

Within a year of the end of the war, the Boses found themselves on the move. Back from battle, the crown prince graduated, and his tutor's family moved three times in the ensuing years. Bose says his life at that time gave him a taste of a force that was to transform India's settled rural economy. "Basically, we were at the cutting edge of the mobility of labor," Bose says. "It's far more common today for people to chase jobs and move from city to city, state to state, even out of the country. We were ahead of our time—a typical, modern peripatetic Indian family that happens to be from one part of the country, Bengal, but lived mostly elsewhere. It made us feel somehow . . . Indian."

Bose's brothers all moved abroad and were successful wherever they ended up. "But India is the place for me," Bose says with more than a little pride. "I've made this country my life's work and my life. The more I get to know about it, even the bad things, the more I love it—the diversity, the energy, the extremes of everything, emotion, climate, terrain, politics—and it's constantly changing. . . . It's a dream come true for a demographer."

5

FIGHTING FOR FREEDOM

A Colonial Legacy

THE TWENTIETH CENTURY began with India firmly under British imperial fiat. India was the jewel in the crown of an empire that stretched from South America to the South Pacific. The same century ended with the economy of independent India on a Y2K-fueled roll. In most minds, the heavy hand of British colonialism was a distant memory. Some more favorable vestiges of rule from London remain in the country today. India's favorite sport is cricket; its national drink is tea. More substantially, perhaps, British-style parliamentary democracy thrives in India, as does the rule of law through an independent judiciary. Indian lawyers often cite precedents from English law when making their lofty arguments in the higher courts. There's also a vigorous free press that owes more to the robust and opinionated newspapers of London's Fleet Street than to the much-trumpeted—if not always carefully observed—objectivity of much of the American media. The education system, stressing secular, liberal social values, has its roots in Britain. India's massive rail network—the world's biggest by almost any measure—was largely built during British rule, as were many irrigation projects, roads and even the capital city, New Delhi.

By far the most lasting and valuable legacy of colonial rule in India is the English language. Some 350 million Indians speak some

English, according to a recent study by a linguist from the University of Wales. Admittedly, that tally includes a great many who mix English words with their native tongue, a trend reflected in an increasing number of Indian television commercials. Coca-Cola, for example, tells consumers, "Life *ho to aisi*" (Life should be like this), and Domino's Pizza asks, "Hungry *kya?*" (Are you hungry?). Soon, it's estimated, the number of Indians speaking a dialect of English, or a mix of English and their own mother tongue, will outnumber the combined total of native speakers in Britain, the United States, Canada, New Zealand and Australia.

Wander down almost any main street in any Indian town or city and there will be signs for English lessons, either for beginners or the advanced courses that are necessary to get into an elite educational institution both in India and abroad. English is not an official language in India, but it is used widely in government, media and the courts. Debates in the Indian parliament are carried on in many of the country's national tongues, but English is used most often to make a telling point, or to accuse an opponent of malfeasance.

Business and trade are carried out largely in English, especially in IT and the knowledge economy. Computer and Internet users, of whom India had close to a hundred million in 2007, can often choose between English and local-language versions of popular software such as Windows or Internet Explorer, but many opt to have both, to enable simultaneous, bifurcated communications both inside their circle of friends and with the wider world. Most Indians speak more than one language anyway, their mother tongue and others acquired, for example, when the family moves to another city or state. Or they may pick up a version of the most often spoken language, Hindi, by watching Bollywood movies and satellite TV news. English mixes easily on the palette of tongues with which Indians shape their daily discourse.

Of course, not everything about the British legacy was positive. Indians often are infuriated by any hint of nostalgia for British rule. Thoughtful scholars are critical of the mixed inputs and outcomes of British rule, beyond parliament, railroads and the English language. The Scottish writer John Keay, in his masterful *India: A History*, contends that while Britain may have more or less unified India and given the subcontinent its current political shape, this achievement came at considerable cost. Unapologetic historians of empire often write proudly of the Pax Britannica that Britain imposed on India and other hitherto divided colonial possessions, but, as Keay points out, that peace was fully financed by India, not London: "The order and stability which British rule undeniably brought did not come cheap. In the experience of most Indians, Pax Britannica meant mainly 'Tax Britannica.'"[1]

For the most part, this pithy phrase describes precisely how India's British overlords—first the commercial appointees of the East India Company and later viceroys and ministers from London—raised money: by taxing the people. Farmers; traders; users of roads, ports and waterways; bazaar merchants and others all paid tribute to the company and later to the British Indian government. This was classic colonialism—we conquer you, you pay us tribute and are grateful for our kind attention. It also led to a phenomenon that inspires Keay to the extended metaphor "Axe Britannia." Before the British came along, India was covered by large tracts of tropical and subtropical hardwood forest—the jungle in Rudyard Kipling's *Jungle Book*. (In fact, *jungle* means "forest" in Hindi.) Today, India has less tree cover than almost any other country in Asia; the process of deforestation began in British times as Indian farmers and landholders cleared more and more agricultural space to generate the revenue needed to pay their taxes, which in turn were spent to further the conquest of their own country.

Recent economic studies of colonial India have concluded that being part of the British Empire was far more costly than beneficial for Indians, both qualitatively and as measured by the quantity of money lifted from local pockets. Take railways. It's true that these were largely built during British times, but they were paid for by Indian revenues or by British investors who repatriated their profits to London. India was left with a rail network, but Indian farmers and taxpayers either funded it or saw distant capitalists earn the dividends that accrued from its operation. Most public works in colonial India were developed on the same principle: water and sewage in major cities, irrigation canals and electrification. India paid its way in the British Empire.

Britain and other European nations were originally attracted to India precisely because its economy already produced so much wealth. Spices, textiles, dyes, timber, handicrafts, jewelry and other products were traded around the known world in Asia and farther afield for money and products in kind, gemstones, precious metals, more spices and, latterly, tea from China. Thus, India—or its various component states—already had a considerable economy when British merchants and military forces arrived to open up the Orient to trade, as per the prevailing view at the time. But as British control spread, and as the need to produce more profit for British shareholders became paramount, the conflicting interests of colony and colonizer became plain. Britain needed raw materials for the manufacturers that sprang up during the nineteenth century's industrial revolution. Its own domestic economy was surging ahead, driven by steam technology, a mobile labor force and trade and military might. If India needed consumer goods, then Britain would provide them, and the profits would flow back to London through both imports and exports. Britain's dominion rang the death knell over India's once sophisticated and independent trading economy. Cottage industries collapsed, and ancient technologies were lost or fell dormant. The woolen mills of Lancashire in the north of England shipped heavy cloth to a tropical land and received payment in cash or kind. India sent raw cotton grown on vast tracts of cleared land to be processed on gins and steam-powered looms run by the English working classes. Vast plantations provided the raw materials for the dyes that were manufactured in the English Midlands, particularly the indigo that produced the most distinctive and long-lasting azures and tourmaline tints. It can be convincingly argued that British policy in the 1800s forced India, in effect, to bankrupt itself by paying for the military and economic conquest of its own territory.

It can also be demonstrated that Pax Britannica was either illusory or a particularly cruel semantic trick, because the British brought very little peace to India. The empire's expansion may have been driven by the profit motive or, later on, by the fictional yet alluring notion that its representatives were spreading "civilized" values around the world. But this perhaps dubious achievement was largely accomplished through a series of military conquests and wars in far-flung places. Britain either started or joined in conflicts of one sort or another almost constantly throughout the nineteenth century, and right up to the beginning of World War I. Many of these military adventures were in India itself as Britain extended its authority by putting down rebellions and conquering the patches of territory that remained in defiant native hands. The soldiers who fought wearing British uniforms were Indian-born but commanded by British officers. As imperial Britain skirmished its way through the nineteenth century, much Indian blood was shed at home and abroad.

So too at this time began the modern phenomenon of Indian labor emigrating to find work as economic crunches in the subcontinent hit hard on the poor and working-class communities, whose plight seemed to bother London little, if at all. Today's ethnic Indian populations in the West Indies, Mauritius, Malaysia, Fiji and Africa all have their origins in the flight of their ancestors from discrimination and want in British colonial India. Often British companies and capitalists brought Indians to these faraway lands to be indentured laborers on plantations that fed the mills and factories of industrial-revolution Britain. A more vicious or exploitative system would be difficult to find.

British rule, then, helped transform a once-vibrant trading and industrial economy into a source of raw materials and a passive market for imported, manufactured goods. Railways and other infrastructure helped draw the colony together and gave new opportunities for rural people to change their lives for the better, but this was hardly a charitable exercise. But in the end irony favored the underdog. No matter how much Britain exploited its proudest Asian possession, Indians were eventually able to use British values, and British methods, to liberate themselves from colonial rule. These same instruments of language, custom and infrastructure remain hugely relevant in India today, helping create a functioning, if slow-moving, legal system and a liberal democracy.

India's freedom struggle was inspired, sustained and steeped in British traditions. The towering figures of the campaign to end British rule were often London-trained lawyers and English-speakers who could talk to colonial authorities and Westminster politicians in their own idiom: gentlemen speaking to gentlemen. These figures included Jawaharlal Nehru, India's first prime minister, and Mohammed Ali Jinnah, the founder of Pakistan. Even the moral and spiritual leader of the movement, Mohandas Gandhi, had worked as a barrister in London's Inner Temple—its hushed confines a warren of legal expertise and tradition to this day. In later life Gandhi eschewed Western clothing and the English language because he believed Indians had been conditioned by colonialism to loathe their own ways and that this kept them subservient. Nonetheless, Gandhi and others drew on British notions and attitudes to further their ambitions for sovereignty. Foremost among these was the belief, long cherished by Britain's elite, that their country was somehow wedded to the principles of fair play, legal norms and the rule of law.

Gandhi's campaign of nonviolent civil disobedience was aimed not just at acquiring the moral high ground but also at making the British keenly aware that they were in the wrong. Because of this strategy, the Indian freedom struggle gained support in Britain in liberal and leftist circles; among many Christians, including the Quakers; and with lawyers and constitutionalists troubled by the expansion of state power as a general principle. There was also much support for the Indian freedom fighters in the United States, among labor unions and social reformers. The dignity that Gandhi and other leaders displayed when they were arrested and jailed for their part in peaceful protest had a deep impact on many in Britain and around the world. When baton-wielding British-led police charged Indian men and women on hunger strike or demonstrating legally and peacefully in a public square, each press photo showing the resulting carnage was a nail in the coffin of colonialism. This is not to suggest that the freedom struggle was a focused, well-planned movement that proceeded logically from step to step. Rather, it was a series of provocations and reactions, often driven by emotion and frequently mired in discord and confusion. But the clarity of the underlying moral position weighed heavily in determining the outcome.

The British authorities were often extraordinarily violent in their attempts to quell the campaign for independence. In the northern city of Amritsar, on April 13, 1919, a seminal event took place that had repercussions for relations between Britain and India for generations. The city was tense because riots over the arrest of nationalist leaders earlier in the week had claimed two European lives. Tough new measures placed strict limits on public gatherings. But it was a religious festival, not politics, that drew thousands to Jallianwallah Bagh, a park in the center of town. Amritsar is the site of the holiest shrine of India's Sikh population, and many of those in the

Bagh were bearded men wearing dark turbans and women in flow-ing *dupattas,* Punjabi shawls. Of course, Sikhs were prominent in the freedom struggle, so there undoubtedly were activists among the pic-nickers. But it is highly unlikely that any of them had planned a con-frontation with the authorities, given the press of women and children in the park.

The authorities thought differently. Acting under orders from the Punjab government, General Reginald Dyer came to Jallianwallah Bagh in command of a squadron of Gurkha soldiers from Nepal. The Gurkhas were hardy hill men known for their fierceness and absolute loyalty. "They always obey orders," I was once told by a modern British Gurkha officer. "All orders. Immediately and without ques-tioning or hesitation." So when Dyer marched his fifty Gurkhas through the only entrance to the enclosed park and deployed them to block access in and out, it was brutally clear what his intentions were. A quick announcement that the gathering in the Bagh was illegal was followed by orders to open fire. True to their reputation, the soldiers from Nepal didn't hesitate. Bullets slammed into frantic hordes of people trying to flee. Many were shot in the back. Men, women and children fell and lay moaning. Blood spattered the lawns and paths. There was no cover save a deep well in one corner of the park. Scores tried to escape by hurling themselves down the well shaft and found instead more horrible deaths, either dashing their brains out on the bricks below or falling into a struggling mass of wounded humanity and slowly smothering. Still there was no order to cease fire.

Today Jallianwallah Bagh is an Indian national monument shown to schoolchildren and visited by tearful locals. A plaque on the edge of the well says 120 bodies were retrieved from its depths. There is still disagreement about the total number of casualties that day. The British government count was 379. Indian sources insist that three times that number may have died, so dense was the crowd and so intense the gunfire. Both the authorities and local people ac-cused each other of spiriting away bodies. Whatever the correct number may be, there is no doubt that the killings at Jallianwallah Bagh were the worst massacre of civilians ever committed by the British authorities in India.

The world responded with disgust and outrage, but in Britain there was widespread popular support for what General Dyer had done. A vote in the House of Lords commended him for his actions; so did his boss, Sir Michael O'Dwyer, the Punjab governor. Buoyed by all this, the general was unrepentant. He said he was firing on a revolutionary army and would have used machine guns if he had had them. After several months, an official enquiry concluded that Dyer had grossly overreacted, and he was demoted to colonel before finally resigning from the army. But in 1920, his return to Britain was the occasion for a hero's welcome. British opinion in India was much the same. This reaction to the massacre, as much as the killings themselves, outraged Indians, who saw the atrocity and its aftermath as further evidence that they had been colonized by brutal racists with no intention of either sharing power or granting independence. Such enlightened developments were reserved for the largely white colonies of Australia, Canada and New Zealand, which in 1919 were already autonomous dominions within the British Empire, practically sovereign states. Evidently, brown people weren't worthy of the responsibility of self-government, even if they had fought bravely and died in large numbers on the battlefields of Europe in World War I. A hitherto fractious national freedom movement coalesced around the outrage and began to make itself known across India and in the rest of the world.

I saw for myself how the Amritsar carnage still resonated in contemporary India when Queen Elizabeth II visited the subcontinent in 1997. The occasion for the royal tour was the fiftieth anniversary of Indian independence, a time to look back on the freedom struggle and its aftermath, and to look at the new state of relations between the former colonial power, Britain, and India. That same year saw Tony Blair's Labour Party win a landslide election in the United Kingdom. A new political climate was supposedly in place; nostalgia for the British Raj in India was simply not on the agenda. After all, it had been the Labour government of the late 1940s that consented to Indian independence in the first place. Blair seemed a different sort of politician, with none of the snooty, class-ridden attitudes of past British leaders. But from the outset, the queen's visit to India did not go well.

It was clear that many of the diplomats and officials around her hadn't done their homework. They appeared to be unaware of the sensitivity of India's elite toward many things British. This prickliness was not necessarily shared by the younger generation of Indians, who knew only freedom and saw the Brits not as former colonial masters but as citizens of a European country that played reasonably good cricket and had a few desirable universities. But the sensitivity was real enough among those who remembered earlier times. The queen provoked a furor in India even before her arrival there because of a speech she made in neighboring Pakistan, which was also marking its independence. She had said something that seemed innocuous about self-determination and freedom for the people of South Asia, including those in the disputed region of Kashmir. In India, where tensions with Pakistan over Kashmir had sparked several wars and border skirmishes, the speech was condemned as an unwarranted intervention in internal affairs. So the royal party found itself embroiled in controversy from the get-go.

To smooth some of those ruffled feathers, it was decided rather abruptly that the queen would travel to Jallianwallah Bagh as a mark of British contrition for the long-ago actions of General Dyer. All at once, what had been a fairly low-key royal visit became serious news. The Indian media wanted to know if Her Majesty would apologize for Dyer's actions, and if so, what would she say? The British High Commissioner at the time was a robust character named David Gore-Booth, and he was adamant that there would be no apologies for an event that neither this monarch nor the British government of the day had anything to do with. Rather, the queen would lay a wreath at a shrine erected in the Bagh in memory of the victims of Dyer's brutality. That seemed to mollify at least some critics.

The international media, me among them, headed for Amritsar to see if memories of the massacre could be dredged up, and whether the city cared at all if the British queen made an act of contrition for a reprehensible historical episode. We gathered on either side of the entrance to the park, leaving space for the queen to walk through and lay her wreath. It was a solemn and moving moment, and she carried it off with aplomb and what was apparently deep respect. The shrine is a sacred site in India, so visitors have to remove their shoes. The queen wore what appeared to be cheap woolen socks over her bare feet, and a few commentators remarked that she seemed to have stolen the cabin booties provided by British Airways on her flight to South Asia. But this was nit-picking, and it seemed as if the ghosts of Jallianwallah Bagh might finally be laid to rest.

Then, as the queen and her entourage left the garden, the notoriously outspoken and abrasive Duke of Edinburgh stopped to talk to
some Indian journalists. They asked him whether Britain regretted
the massacre of 1919. Drawing breath, Prince Philip opened his
mouth, only to place his booted foot firmly inside. "I served with
Dyer's grandson in the Canadian navy," he said in his characteristic
bray, "and he told me the whole thing was a great exaggeration." Philip
referred to a plaque near the shrine that set the number of dead at
two thousand and said, "That's not right, the number is much less."
Then he wandered off toward his waiting vehicle. Among the Indians
watching him leave was a palpable sense that getting rid of the British
Raj had been well worth the effort.

The public strain on relations between Britain and India wasn't
matched by precipitate action. No one withdrew diplomats. The
duke's ill-advised comments had no effect on business, trade or international cooperation. The two countries have too many common
interests and shared attitudes to let a row over history poison their
ties. India and Britain are each other's second-largest trading partners. They exchange goods and services worth some US$10 billion a
year. Many of those flashy software, IT and BPO companies in Bangalore have their customer bases in the United Kingdom. British companies, including Reuters (sold to a Canadian firm in 2007 but still
based in London), British Airways, Pearl Assurance and others, have
outsourced large numbers of white-collar jobs to India. The largest
Indian brewery, Kingfisher, is a close global business partner with a
Scottish beer-maker. The British cellular giant Vodafone is a major
player in the Indian mobile market. Britain's Indian community is
one of the world's largest, and many, many Britons live and work in
India. In short, both countries have long since got over the vicissi-
tudes of the freedom struggle.

In fact, that struggle and its outcome go a long way in explaining India's strengths and newfound economic confidence. Just as free
market–friendly economic reforms touched off the firestorm of
business-led development in the 1990s, so did the successful battle
for independence produce a legacy that still resonates in the Indian
psyche and society. In part, this legacy is the conviction that all things
are possible, that even a formidable challenge can be overcome
through politics, the law and alliance-building. The freedom strug-

gle brought together the modern and the traditional, the rich and poor, the political left and India's capitalists. Uniting the disparate streams of Indian society isn't easy. Indians' first loyalties are usually to family, caste and religious sect, in that order. Even within Hinduism, the religion of a vast majority of the people, there are many divisions and disagreements. For centuries this diversity made it easier for outsiders to conquer Indian territory. Local chieftains and power brokers found disunity more natural than unity. The freedom struggle changed all of that. From its early days in the late 1800s as a gathering of liberal elitists in Bombay to discuss increased local input into colonial governance, to the crowning achievements of Nehru, Gandhi and others in liberating the world's largest ex-colony by 1947, Indians had come together en masse and spoken as a body, a community, a nation.

The movement to liberate India from British colonial rule culminated after World War II. The war had devastated Britain. The country was left virtually bankrupt, a far cry from the glorious global power it had been at the beginning of the twentieth century. It could ill afford its vast colonial possessions, with their attendant military, financial and administrative burdens. A Labour Party government led by Clement Attlee came to power with a mandate to affect sweeping social change. Attlee was a democratic socialist whose voters expected him to act quickly on the provision of universal health care, unemployment insurance, mothers' allowance and other welfare measures. Not that the postwar Labour government was anticolonialist. There were sharp divisions over the question of Indian freedom, for example, but the case in favor was made on many levels. India had been fighting for its freedom for generations, and Britain's prominent role in the fight against fascism was at odds with the maintenance of political control of a people who wanted to be free. A consensus among Labour Party leaders and supporters gradually formed around the idea that a way had to be found to end British rule in India. There was also widespread horror in India and Britain at the policies of the wartime government of the outgoing Conservative prime minister, Winston Churchill, which had restricted food supplies to famine-stricken areas of Bengal in 1943, in part out of pique at the Indian boycott of British war efforts. Millions died in the last brutal act of British colonialism.

The freedom struggle led by Gandhi and Nehru kept its moral stature by being officially nonviolent, by stressing civil disobedience and passive resistance to the ravages of the authorities, but there was no shortage of tension and bloodshed in India when Attlee's newly appointed viceroy, Lord Mountbatten, arrived to take up his post in March 1947. It had been obvious for some time, though not officially acknowledged, that Britain was preparing to leave India. The subcontinent was in turmoil. Splits in the freedom struggle had long been simmering along religious lines. India's substantial Muslim minority—or at any rate its largest faction, led by Jinnah—wanted no part of a largely Hindu and independent India and was demanding a separate state. Some Muslim leaders and many ordinary people supported a united India as advocated by the Indian National Congress of Jawaharlal Nehru and Mohandas Gandhi. Nehru and Gandhi had not waged their fraught and emotional nonviolent struggle for freedom so that Indian territory could be split asunder. Indeed, the British tendency to favor one religious group over another, and exploit their differences, had long been a complaint among leaders of the freedom struggle.

The movement for Pakistan, Jinnah's Muslim state, had begun just over a decade earlier and, though it had considerable emotional force, it was not particularly well organized. It was also an idea that spread downward from the elite, not a grassroots movement at all. British India's large Muslim minority was a diverse community united by little more than a shared religious faith. Most Indian Muslims were laborers, artisans or poor subsistence farmers with little time for politics. They may have had their grievances with their Hindu neighbors and with the more oppressive features of British imperial rule, but these were not galvanizing influences in their lives. Similarly, in the bazaars, middle-class Muslim merchants and traders were more concerned with commerce than with the anticolonial struggle. At best, they paid lip service to Pakistan and freedom. It was chiefly among the Muslim political elite that Jinnah and others had made Pakistan their cause. For this relatively small group, anything less than the redrawing of the map of South Asia was unacceptable. None in this circle paid heed to arguments about the dangers of separating communities of people that had intermingled and cohabited for centuries. Indeed, Jinnah's supporters failed to ask the hard questions.

No field work was commissioned, no thought given to the aftermath of a wholly political process driven almost exclusively by an appeal to emotion.

No surprise then that violence was starting to spread over this issue. Not, in early 1947, on a national scale, but steadily, regularly, bloodily. People were turning on each other in Punjab, Bengal and other places where Hindus and Muslims shared villages or slums. Reports of deaths, rioting, rape and hate crimes were coming in every day in the final months of India's time as a British colony.

This was the dangerous and seething environment into which Lord Mountbatten was introduced. Within hours of setting foot in India, he was privy to the bitter divisions within a once-united freedom struggle, meeting Gandhi, Nehru and Jinnah. At first the Indians and the viceroy sat together in the same room, but later they would meet separately. In that and subsequent gatherings with the viceroy, none of the three Indian leaders hesitated to employ his own (British) legal and rhetorical skills—appeals to emotion, bombast and even threats—to convince Mountbatten of a particular position.

The viceroy found the idea of dividing British India frightening and potentially disastrous. He was also drawn more to what he saw as the reasonable attitudes of Nehru. Patrician, moderate and eloquent, Nehru had more than a little of the British upper crust about him. This exterior, however, belied a man deeply sympathetic to the hardships of the freedom struggle. He had been moved by the poverty and deprivation he saw around him and had formed an iron determination to end British hegemony. Mountbatten was awed by Gandhi, by his ability to appeal to the religious nature of Indians and by his commitment to nonviolence. But the viceroy soon learned that the frail old campaigner in his loincloth was the toughest and least predictable of India's leaders. As for Jinnah, the British aristocrat and the Muslim lawyer did not get on well at all. Mountbatten found the future founder of Pakistan "cold, very cold" and "impossible to argue with . . . a psychopathic case."[2] Jinnah rarely deployed charm or gentle persuasion with his opponents. Generally, he wielded his considerable intellect as a blunt instrument, even against newly arrived high officials from London who had plenipotentiary powers.

Eventually, in early June, one of Mountbatten's advisers came up with a plan to divide the subcontinent—over Gandhi's objections—

into two states, India and Pakistan, that would remain within the British Commonwealth as independent dominions. They would be sovereign but maintain links with the Crown. Jinnah was ecstatic, Nehru reluctant but resigned to such a solution. Gandhi withdrew from the talks in sorrow, giving the process his grudging consent, and devoted himself to quelling sectarian violence in urban slums and villages. Mountbatten moved quickly. He set August 15, 1947, just two months ahead, as the day British rule would end on the Indian subcontinent. It was a wholly arbitrary decision. Mountbatten later wrote that he decided on this rigid and impossibly short timetable in the hope that it would focus minds and minimize bloodshed. With so many tasks to be accomplished in order to create two new nations, including the precise division of land, assets and infrastructure, he hoped to make the seemingly impossible a fait accompli.

Many still are horrified by Mountbatten's sudden timetable and wonder if it exacerbated the carnage of partition. Others believe that his decision to move quickly may actually have saved lives. Such ruminations count for little beside the historical reality: millions were killed and many more displaced as and after Pakistan and independent India came into being. The months of slaughter that followed partition have been chronicled in dreadful detail by survivors, historians, photographers and, indeed, fiction writers. In his grimly dark short story "Toba Tek Singh," Saadat Hasan Manto imagines an exchange of mental patients between India and Pakistan in the years after 1947: schizophrenics and psychopaths who once lived together wonder if they'll go to one country or another; men cackle and moan as they lurch between rooms of the nameless asylum in some insane netherworld between the partitioned bits of India.

It could be said that Manto himself was a victim of partition. He left Bombay for the new Muslim land of Pakistan in 1948 but drank himself to death in less than a decade. He was only forty-three years old. In India, he had been a noted writer of fiction and screenplays. Secular and skeptical yet also suspecting that there was no place for him in largely Hindu India, he left reluctantly for the new land that had been established for Indian Muslims. Pakistan chose to ignore or be offended by his talents. He died alone, and his passing was not marked or eulogized at the time. It was only decades later that his adopted country recognized his worth.

Both the bloodshed and political wrangling that accompanied partition should have been anticipated. The dislocations were immense as millions left ancestral lands and traveled through hostile territory to reach an unfamiliar and uncertain haven. What is surprising, perhaps, is that the tasks of partition and independence were managed at all. Think of it. British India was a collection of eleven provinces and over five hundred notionally sovereign princely states. Each of these states had its own treaty with the British Crown and, technically, London's commitment to Indian independence didn't include the princely states. Each had to be convinced or coerced into joining one of the two new nations. As if dividing all of pre-independence India wasn't difficult enough, some provinces that existed as integrated entities would themselves have to be partitioned into Hindu and Muslim areas. Armies and weapons would have to be shared out, treasuries counted and split according to population and need. The civil administration, the backbone of British India, had to be divided, and workers had to choose which country they would belong to, just like the lunatics in Manto's asylum. It was a legal and accounting nightmare on a scale never seen before nor attempted since. And it took place against the backdrop of some of the worst spontaneous violence the world has known. It was a two-way genocide: Muslims expelled and ravaged their Sikh and Hindu neighbors in what would be Pakistan, and Muslims were killed, maimed, raped and beaten in India. In both cases, neighbors murdered neighbors, people who had worked together turned on one another's families, women were raped by men they had known for years. Trains carrying fearful refugees were stopped by armed gangs and, later, carriages bearing only corpses would pull up at the main stations in Lahore or Amritsar, on either side of the sundered land.

The legacies of partition are many. Foremost among them is probably the sixty-year-old dispute over Kashmir—the main reason to this day that India and Pakistan continue to overspend on military budgets while so many of their citizens are hungry, unemployed and exploited. Partition deprived Muslims in India of large numbers of their community's educated middle class. Tens of millions of Indian Muslims went to Pakistan because they had no choice: they lived in volatile border areas or mixed communities where they were no

longer welcome. Or, like Manto, they simply could not imagine themselves remaining in India after so much blood had been shed. Many
of Pakistan's first citizens were the Muslim lawyers, administrators,
military officers and businesspeople of North India and those
princely states that ended up inside the new Hindu-majority country.
India's loyal Muslims, or those who simply couldn't afford to leave,
were bereft of the role models and leaders they needed to recover
from the blow of partition.

Meanwhile, in the territories that became Pakistan, an essentially
agrarian and largely feudal economy had to modernize in a short period. Political institutions never took hold, nor was there an adequate
expansion of the industrial base that would provide jobs to a growing population of young men. Pakistani governance has never settled
into stable patterns of accountable, electoral democracy or policies
that benefit the people, in large part because of the trauma and lack
of foresight in those early years of freedom. Instead, the army and
feudal landlords continue to run the country to this day even as it de-
generates into a lawless, fratricidal state where Muslim extremists
such as Osama bin Laden are more popular than democratic political leaders.

And yet it's hard not to be amazed, as well as appalled, by partition. For there's no denying that many Indian, soon-to-be-Pakistani
and British bureaucrats, lawyers, military men, planners, economists
and others rose to the challenge thrown at them by Mountbatten.
They had ten weeks in 1947 to establish the infrastructure for two
new countries. They did it. The costs were immense but the exercise
was successful. Certainly in India's case, the sheer speed and com-
pulsion of the goal of "Freedom at Midnight" gave birth to an approach to crisis management through administration and law. This
was a hugely modern notion. In the past, borders usually were re-
drawn and populations shifted through the effects of war. Sometimes
pestilence, earthquakes or waterborne disaster would have the same
result. But in the aftermath of Mountbatten's announcement, what
might be called the Indian approach to problem solving was born.
No matter how gargantuan or seemingly impossible the task, it was—
and is—tackled with gusto and determination on political, administrative and human levels.

This approach was to serve India well throughout its early years. Traumatized, bloodied and poor, the new country began its modern sovereign existence with few advantages. Food supplies were unreliable. War flared periodically with Pakistan over Kashmir. A restive Muslim population was awaiting its fate within the borders of the new India. Hindu triumphalism was morphing into hatred of Islam, even of Gandhi, who was assassinated by a Hindu fanatic in 1948 amid accusations that he acceded to partition and was soft on Muslims. America was fixated, understandably, on rebuilding Europe and Japan and was leery of involvement in the new country. Britain was broke and glad to be quit of its former colonies. There was as yet no real agreement on the system of government. There were regional discontents based on language and other distinctions. All seemed chaotic and more likely to fail than survive and prosper.

That hasn't happened. Despite decades of poverty, corruption, occasional political instability, war and frequent manmade and natural disasters, India is alive and well. The economic strides of recent years and the expansion of the middle classes have come after decades of challenge. But in the manner of the ten-week dash to independence initiated by Mountbatten in 1947, India got here by, well, getting here.

6

DEMOCRACY, DYNASTY AND DEVOLUTION

Transferring Power in India

IN 1997, WHEN INDIA was celebrating its first fifty years of independence, pollsters often asked Indians what they thought had been the greatest single accomplishment of the past five decades. Was it the steps that had been taken to ease poverty? Improvements in grain production thanks to the Green Revolution of the 1960s? Military victory in three wars with Pakistan? Or, perhaps more importantly, the numerous defeats of Pakistan's cricket teams, which seem to matter more than war? Each of these answers had their adherents, but most Indians replied that the country's greatest achievement was its political system. India is a democracy, they said, and we are proud of it. Many, in the same breath, would also express distrust of, even revulsion for, politicians and political parties, describing them as corrupt, inept and without merit. They loved democracy, in other words, but loathed its practitioners.

The success—indeed the very survival—of Indian democracy is surprising when demographics, history and the vast diversity of Indian society are taken into account. The country has more than a billion people, of whom, at last count, nearly seven hundred million are eligible to vote. Dozens of different languages must be accommodated, along with a vast array of special interests, each with specific needs and demands. These are the conditions that Indian democracy must deal with when its political players campaign and then enter parliament to enact policy. Before it became sovereign and democratic, India was administered as a colony of the United Kingdom, with little or no autonomy and almost no local influence over its own affairs. Even further back in history, Muslim conquerors from the Middle East and Central Asia ran the subcontinent as a succession of feudal authoritarian satrapies. For thousands of years there had been little that could pass for responsible, accountable government. By the standards of the modern era, India came late to democracy and, on paper, it seemed ill equipped for the challenge.

When British rule ended in 1947, the newly sovereign state embarked on a political and economic course that was described as socialism but that achieved mixed results. Historians on the political left often describe the culmination of the freedom struggle as "the transfer of power" from a foreign elite to its domestic counterpart. India's early leaders were largely British-educated and they retained many colonial laws and attitudes. In the countryside, people toiled much as they always had, many still in thrall to large landowners and feudal overlords. Not that Nehru was unaware of this. Among the first steps taken by India's early administration was a program of comprehensive land reform. That program may help explain why democracy survived and became so stubbornly entrenched. That land reform had its limits, and that local landed gentries were able to cling to huge holdings by placing them in others' names, is now widely known. But the early years of independent governance in India were marked by a determination to give land to the landless, and many a successful family of today got its start in those early years of freedom. Thus, too, was born the persistent political power of rural over urban India.

Across northern and central parts of the country, large holdings were broken up and land and authority were handed over to local farmers. A whole new class of people with their own land and the means to produce agricultural surpluses became, in effect, a rural bourgeoisie. Those landed farmers, vested with real political power by land reform, became one of the country's first interest groups. Using their votes and their voices, they made their interests known to political leaders, many of whom still had feudal instincts and believed themselves entitled to respect and power. The farmers changed all of that. What they wanted, they got: access to irrigation, price-support policies, subsidized fertilizers and, later, free electricity. These successes set the pattern both for other interest groups and for politicians. Political turmoil in India today is largely shaped by the increasing urbanization of the country and the struggle of city dwellers and the middle class to make their voices heard in the fray of farm interests and traditional power brokers. Yet it's also clear that what has evolved as democracy in India is only partly about making the voice of the majority heard in the circles of power. More importantly, it has become a process by which key blocs of voters exchange their political support for government patronage. This may take the form of funding for local projects or the representation of less tangible group interests in the daily business of government. Not that the Indian electorate has not made bold, sophisticated decisions over the years, throwing out inept or corrupt government or rewarding successful policies; it has. But in the main, the "democracy" that Indians were so proud of in 1997 was still largely about patronizing key clients in exchange for support at election time

Nothing gives a greater sense of the breadth and challenges of Indian democracy than a general election. India follows the British and Canadian system by which elections must take place—at most—every five years but can be called sooner if the prime minister so desires or if the government loses the support of parliament. The 2004 election in India was the sixteenth time since independence that the country's voters were called to the polls. The national electorate is now larger than the combined populations of the United States, Russia and Brazil. Extending to all of them the opportunity to vote efficiently, freely and fairly is the job of the Election Commission of India—an independent branch of the government that is among the most respected institutions in the country. Getting a significant percentage of that mass of people to the polls is not simply a matter of setting an election date and signing up voters in a door-to-door registration drive, as in most democracies. An Indian general election has five or more days of voting spread over a period of weeks. Counting takes a few days more and lately, with no single political party able to win a clear majority of parliamentary constituencies, the actual formation of a working government takes even more time after the numerical outcome has been declared.

Extraordinary security measures have to be taken during Indian elections. Millions of soldiers and police are deployed to protect voting areas and to stand guard over the ballot boxes and counting centers. In recent polls, Indians have begun using electronic voting machines (with surprisingly few of the glitches experienced in the United States), and these are moved around in army trucks, guarded by heavily armed commandos. Counting takes place in highly secure locations, and information about the count is not supposed to leak out to the ever-rapacious Indian media.

These measures are not the result of official paranoia. On occasion in the past, elections in India have been rigged, stolen or influenced by coercion and violence. Not on a countrywide scale, but at the local and state levels, especially in more remote places, there are often dozens, if not hundreds, of incidents reported in the Indian press as "booth capture." The phrase describes instances in which a gang of armed or apparently bloodthirsty individuals take over a polling station. A standard modus operandi, straight from Thug 101, goes as follows: The police guards are neutralized, beaten or tied up. Other thugs turn away local voters, dispersing any lineups and making sure the word gets out that voting is over for the day. The gang leader sits in the returning officer's chair and cracks jokes as his men take the pads of ballot papers and mark all of them for their candidate. The ballots are then carefully folded and stuffed into the ballot boxes, which have been emptied of all previous, legitimate ballots. The returning officer's seal, obtained by force, is used to close each box so it looks official. Threats are uttered against the life of anyone who dares to tell the authorities what has happened, and then the bad guys slip away. At one time, this form of tampering worked rather well in certain areas, but now, with huge numbers of journalists and officials traveling almost constantly between voting districts, it's much less likely to succeed. Still, vigilance is maintained.

The close outcome of India's recent elections has produced unstable coalition governments that frequently fall in parliament, meaning another trip to the polls for the voters. In one of a spate of general election campaigns in the late 1990s, I visited a rural polling station in the crime-ridden state of Bihar, several hundred miles east of New

Delhi. It was in a lush farming area with green rice plants sprouting in flooded fields and groves of flowering mango trees outside each village. Bihar is notorious for many things in India: corrupt government, caste violence, poverty and inequality. The demographer Ashish Bose refers to Bihar as a "criminal state," the source of all that's wrong with India's reputation. But I object mostly to the state of its so-called roads. They are holed, ridged, buckled and often all but impossible to negotiate.

Getting to this constituency south of the state capital, Patna, was agony as our locally made Ambassador sedan clattered and strained along highways that were little better than goat tracks—goat tracks made by an elderly, drunken three-legged goat, I dare say. Finally, after much lurching and grinding over the potholed surfaces, we saw in the middle distance a ragged line of people. They were standing next to a low concrete building around which paper banners fluttered from trees and bamboo poles. It was a village primary school, and the polling station was under a canvas shelter in the schoolyard.

I was there to prepare a television news report, and my colleagues and I plunged into the lively chaos around the voting place. Posters urged people to cast their ballots and promised safety and secrecy in return. "Democracy—India's pride, India's strength" proclaimed one poster in Hindi script. These were the work of the Election Commission, which retains a touching enthusiasm for the democratic process, despite what must be rather dire inside knowledge about the behavior of certain political parties and their leaders on the campaign trails. During campaigns and especially on voting days, the three election commissioners have extraordinary powers to deploy the security forces, open and close roads and airports, and generally do whatever is necessary to keep things running smoothly. More than a few chief election commissioners have let this vast authority go to their heads, angering political leaders by pursuing them on corruption charges. Usually public approval for the commissioner in question intensifies in inverse proportion to the objections of politicians.

The chief election commissioner of the day, the gentlemanly M. K. Singh, had suggested we visit this village because Maoist guerrillas were active in the area and threatening to disrupt the proceedings. Various Communist militias that pay homage to the ideas of Mao Tse-tung roam the poorest, most backward areas of India and fight their most tenacious battles against democracy and its exercise. So it was in the late 1990s in Bihar, and so it is even more so today. In the 1990s, when we spoke to people in the queue outside the polling station, it was clear that they were aware of the possibility of violence and were afraid. At the same time, they were hopeful and committed to democracy. "We have to be here," Bishnu, an elderly, low-caste farmer, told us. "Voting doesn't change much but it's what we do in India. I'm poor, but I can vote." He spoke both with pride and resignation, and the nods and mumbles of agreement from people around him were ample evidence that this was a widespread sentiment, even in Bihar, where vote-rigging, violence and fraud plagued the electoral process.

We moved on to interview the women voters standing in a separate line. Queuing in India is often segregated for the simple reason that few people observe the etiquette of lining up, and women in their own queue can't be shoved aside by stronger, larger men. Instead, they shove each other. As I approached the women's queue, I heard the distinctive crack of a rifle shot, fired some distance away. The sound had not been preceded by the *whush* of a bullet through the air, so the shot wasn't directed anywhere near the polling lines. Nevertheless, it precipitated a panic. The queues dissolved as people dove for cover. More rifle fire came from the direction of a nearby hamlet as I ran to a tree to steal a look around its protective bulk. There they were, the gunmen—five or six men with rifles held to their shoulders, pointing them straight at the voters as they emerged from a building in the hamlet. I gestured to my cameraman to join me behind the tree. I told him to set his camera on a branch so he wouldn't expose himself to the marauders. But he was made of sterner stuff and stood out in the open, his camera mounted on a tripod while he took a long, steady close-up of the men who were shooting. Then he turned and filmed the voters as they scrambled for cover behind upended tables and the even flimsier shelter provided by the tent that served as a voting booth. A senior policeman ran over to me and motioned toward the thick trunk of the mango tree, telling us to stay out of the line of fire.

"Communists," he barked in the local dialect of Hindi. "Diehards. They won't come over here. They just want to scare everyone, to discredit the election. If they were from the political parties, they'd come steal the ballot boxes or stuff them full of votes for their guy. These guys, Maoists, they don't want anyone to vote."

What the policeman was saying was true. All of India's mainstream political groups use tactics that are most appropriate to where their candidates are running. So in the modern neighborhoods of the city, an eloquent lawyer gives moving speeches and appeals to reason. In other places, the most progressive of parties will run candidates with just the right appeal to caste or tribal loyalties. If that person is also a local gangster or feudal landlord, then so be it. Here in Bihar, guns had become the way you influenced elections, whether you were on the Hindu nationalist right or the Communist left. The Maoist guerrillas who were shooting at us were from the armed wing of a tiny hard-line political party. If they scared away enough voters to discredit the process of democracy in a particular constituency or even a single polling station, that was victory enough for them.

We were slightly disappointed that we didn't have the opportunity to film an actual "booth capture," but were still anxious to make the most of the opportunity that the Maoists had provided. Disregarding the policeman's advice, we made our way in a roundabout fashion, through ditches and behind irrigation dikes, to the place where the gunmen were entrenched, still shooting toward the polling station. They had chosen the grounds of another village school as their fortification. When we got close, I realized that the police were shooting back at the Maoists and that we'd foolishly ventured into the cross fire. We hunkered down behind an earthen mound to await an end to hostilities. That eventually came after the gunmen apparently melted away into the surrounding countryside, perhaps to wreak havoc elsewhere.

Back at the polling booth, work had already begun on getting things up and running again. Election workers, scrutineers from the various political parties and the police were picking up tipped-over chairs and tables and rearranging things so that the vote could go on. Voters were emerging from hiding, greatly diminished in number but ready to try again. The same old man I'd spoken to earlier gave me a cheery wave and mimed ducking behind the person in front of him in the newly re-formed queue, a wry smile on his face. As we headed back to our car, we could hear bickering about whether or not people should resume their former places in line. Democracy in India is nothing if not stubbornly resilient.

It is also unpredictable. Indian adults have been able to vote for the candidate of their choice for all of the country's decades of independence, and they have made some pretty spectacular choices, especially in state politics. It is fashionable in elite circles to decry the people's sometimes erratic choices as a product of illiteracy and rural backwardness, but there's another, more positive view: that some of the wilder and wackier election candidates actually prove the efficacy and sincerity of democracy. Indians are taught that theirs is truly an open system, where men and women run on behalf of the cause or party of their choice. If that party will have them, that is. Indian ballots are traditionally crowded with the names of candidates who have been turned down for a major party ticket and are running instead for political organizations set up in haste or anger. Often the name of the new party is almost identical to the original, and the competition for pictorial symbols to represent the party to illiterate voters on posters and ballot papers is fierce and partisan.

In the south of the country, where high-technology, pharmaceutical and automobile industries thrive, voters look to their film idols for cues on how to cast their ballots. Just as the United States has Arnold Schwarzenegger and the late Ronald Reagan and Greece has Melina Mercouri, the south Indian state of Tamil Nadu has M. G. Ramachandran, known universally as "MGR." MGR starred in over a hundred full-length feature films before he took to the political stage with a landslide state election victory in 1977. Typically in his movies he played a dashing hero who saves the day at the darkest moment, and he carried that image over into politics. For ten years, MGR governed Tamil Nadu as the head of a regionally based political party that championed the weak and poor and that overturned Hindu caste barriers that favored the Brahmin elite. He wore a white fur cap and dark wraparound sunglasses and was the object of intense, almost religious, veneration. More than one hundred people tried to kill themselves when his death was announced in 1987. They did this by dousing themselves in gasoline and striking a match. No one died, but a great many young men were severely burned. Concrete MGR statues—idols really, complete with hat and shades—dot the landscape of Tamil Nadu, erected after his death by devotees and sycophants.

So immense was MGR's impact that his last mistress (and he had a great many) assumed his mantle and has won election twice to the post of chief minister. This woman, Jayalalitha, is also a well-known South Indian actress. Her main opponent and bête noire is a scriptwriter in his seventies who continues to write and direct highly successful films, even as he manages to win elections and sit in the chief minister's chair. The two have a visceral hatred for each other and use the courts, violence and fierce rhetoric of the most personal sort to pursue their respective vendettas. Imagery from films dominates state politics; actors and scriptwriters vie for power. And yet the state of Tamil Nadu is one of India's most advanced by almost any measure.

In neighboring Andhra Pradesh in the 1980s, an even wilder intersection of film and democratic politics took place. There, the film industry was dominated for decades by a leading actor named Nandamuri Taraka Rama Rao, NTR for short. Not only did he act in nearly three hundred films over his lengthy onscreen career, NTR also often played the part of the Hindu god Krishna. It was in that role that he campaigned for high office. During two terms in power, in the 1980s and, after an interregnum, nearly a decade later, he rode huge chariots to election meetings and addressed the crowds wearing godlike headgear and costumes from his movies. He was Lord Krishna to the masses, the playful divine who dispensed justice and enjoyed himself with his fellow gods and goddesses. His public events were near bacchanals, ecstatic gatherings of voters to whom the deity was manifest in the spectacularly robed politician on the platform.

In fact, NTR's two terms in office were disastrous for the state of Andhra Pradesh. He had no discernible ideology, save pride in the local language, Telugu. He was prone to making wildly unpredictable policy decisions. Most devastating were the twin pillars of his election victory in 1994: state-subsidized rice and alcohol prohibition. At first blush, both policies made sense to his poor supporters, especially women, who formed a narrow majority of the electorate. The prospect of cheap food was obviously attractive to a poor family, especially if the husband in that family habitually frittered away his income in the local speakeasies or returned home only to beat his wife and children in a drunken rage. Unfortunately, the two policies combined to bankrupt Andhra Pradesh within a few years of their

enactment. Most revenues at the state level in India come from ex-
cise taxes on alcohol and other restricted products, and from road
charges paid by transport companies and long-distance truck drivers. Without income from legal alcohol sales, and with the state treasury depleted by expenditure on rice subsidies, public finances were
soon deeply in the red. NTR was jostled from power by his own son-
in-law in the mid-1990s.

Heroes and gods from the silver screen may play a dominant role
in South Indian politics but, in the rest of the country, politicians
themselves are the famous faces, the household brand names that
their parties turn to at election time. Just as the personality of the
presidential candidate is emphasized in the United States, so the face
and projected character of the leading politician is what matters most
in Indian campaigns. This is especially true in rural and less developed areas, and in constituencies where large numbers of poorer people live and illiteracy is rampant. Vast wooden cutouts of the
candidate, painted garishly and usually showing him offering a patrician wave of the hand, loom over election rallies. Everywhere the
candidate's face grins or looks grim—as reputation dictates—from
posters and signs. The thrust of the strategy is not entirely different
from that of the South Indian film-star politicians. This man (and it
is usually a man) will resolve your problems because he is benevolent
and powerful. Sometimes the face on the sign sports dark sunglasses
or the head is covered with a local style of turban or headdress: he is
one of us. A cap similar to that worn by Gandhi in the 1920s links the
candidate to the Mahatma, the father of the nation, and promises
compassionate, clean government. The sunglasses denote a modern
approach. The clothing is almost always a traditional robe or volu-
minous trousers and a waistcoat. He is aware of his roots and yet a
contemporary player; this is what the getup signals.

Family dynasties are everywhere in Indian politics. It's a rare successful politician who doesn't try to anoint his son, or occasionally
his daughter, as successor when it's time to retire. Wives play various
roles in their husband's political career. Sometimes they have careers
of their own, but not often. Most wives who get involved in their husbands' political trajectory are their extensions, their surrogates. Infamously, in Bihar, Chief Minister Lalu Prasad Yadav was forced to
resign in 1997 when police uncovered evidence they said implicated

him in the theft of government funds. But his resignation was merely symbolic. Lalu persuaded, or more likely coerced, his party to select his illiterate wife, Rabri Devi, to be the next chief minister, even though she had never held a job or been politically active. He commanded a huge majority in the state legislature, so the vote to confirm his choice was a foregone conclusion. As a result, he was able to stay in the official residence and effectively remain at the helm of the government he was accused of plundering. There are countless other examples of wives playing similar roles for less colorful politicians—or taking over when their husband dies as the widow entrusted with her husband's legacy. Patriarchy runs deep in Indian life and politics.

The most famous dynasty in Indian democracy is the Nehru–Gandhi family. A member of that clan, either by blood or by marriage, has run India for most of its independent existence. The first was Jawaharlal Nehru, prime minister from 1947 until his death in 1964. He himself was no dynast, according to numerous biographers, but a Western-educated social democrat who wrote and spoke as if he believed in merit and achievement as the measures of political worth. Nonetheless, his daughter, Indira Gandhi, became his successor within two years of his death. She had acquired the politically useful name Gandhi from her estranged husband, himself a politician but no relation whatsoever to the mahatma, leader of the freedom struggle and apostle of spiritualism and nonviolence. The Congress Party after independence was not a disciplined, ideological political movement but, rather, a broad church of freedom fighters, Indian businessmen (there were barely any women in the business communities in those days), members of the old royal families of the princely states, special interest groups and the like. Nehru himself was a beacon to the poor and excluded Indian masses, despite his own patrician upbringing, and he developed an almost mystical tie to the downtrodden.

Indira Gandhi's accession to the leadership of India, and the beginning of political leadership as family business, seemed accidental. Nehru's immediate successor in 1964 was his close political ally and Congress veteran Lal Bahadur Shastri. It was a bad time for India. The country had lost a war with China a few years earlier, and conflict with Pakistan broke out within a year of Nehru's death. That resulted in an Indian victory, but Prime Minister Shastri died unexpectedly of a heart attack at a postwar peace conference. This cleared the way for Indira Gandhi to assume power.

Gandhi built on her father's appeal to the poor with her campaign slogan "*gharibi hatao*"—banish poverty. She nationalized remaining private enterprises such as banks and factories and slowly planted the seeds of a personality cult in her late father's beloved Congress Party. Gandhi governed India at perhaps its most tumultuous and chaotic time. On the domestic front, she thrust her image and governing style into every walk of political life. Beyond her country's borders, perhaps feeling that as a woman in a patriarchal setting she had much to prove, she was aggressive and seemingly fearless. Just six years after victory over Pakistan in the 1965 war, she again ordered the Indian army to war with her country's neighbor. This time the conflict led to the creation of the independent state of Bangladesh. In 1974, Gandhi's government staged India's first nuclear weapons tests, a wildly popular move at home and just as intensely deplored around the world. But Indira Gandhi's most powerful legacy in India was a departure from the tradition Nehru established: she is the only leader of her country to suspend the constitution and use emergency powers against her political opponents, an eighteen-month experiment in authoritarian rule that cost thousands of lives, nearly wrecked the Indian economy and lost Gandhi the next election. That was in 1977. She returned to power three years later, when her successors in New Delhi proved to be spectacularly incompetent, but she never really regained the respect that she had once enjoyed among voters. An election campaign ad in the late 1960s proclaimed that "Indira is India." That was never again the case.

If Indira Gandhi learned a lesson from her election defeat, it wasn't obvious. Returned to office in 1980, she sought to cement her party's position by manipulating, undermining, co-opting or dividing her political opponents. Nothing was sacred, not even religion. Her meddling in the internecine politics of the Sikhs had exacerbated already simmering tensions within the faith. Violent militants were courted and sponsored at her orders as a way to dominate more moderate Sikh politicians who didn't side with her. Early in her mandate, separatist sentiment and alienation boiled over into bloody violence in the largely Sikh state of Punjab. There were battles between armed Sikh militant groups, and bloody sectarian attacks by those militants on Hindus. Many of those responsible for the terror in 1984 holed up inside the Golden Temple in Amritsar, the most sacred shrine of the Sikh faith. Over the objections of military and civilian advisers, Gandhi ordered the security forces to attack the temple and oust the militants within. This they did, but only after destroying much of the temple and at the cost of infuriating even the mildest and most apolitical Sikhs. Such hubris cost her her life. The two bodyguards who sprayed Indira Gandhi with machine gun bullets on October 31, 1984, were enraged Sikh soldiers who had been loyal to the Indian state for years. Rajiv Gandhi, the elder of Indira's two sons, had been an airline pilot and had avoided politics. The untimely death of his younger brother, Sanjay, in 1980 changed all that. Heeding the siren call of his clan, he came back from the world's flight lanes to become his mother's political confidant. When Indira Gandhi was assassinated, Rajiv took over as Congress Party leader and shortly afterward won a landslide election victory.

At first, the latest member of the Nehru–Gandhi dynasty was immensely popular. He was young and handsome. He had a striking Italian wife. And he was widely perceived as being above the corrupt power politics practiced by the older generation of Congress leaders. That image soon dissipated and the young Prime Minister Gandhi found himself besieged by problems at home and abroad. A disastrous attempt to send Indian peacekeepers to Sri Lanka turned into a war with the island's Tamil Tiger rebels. India had to withdraw in ignominy. Worse still for Rajiv's squeaky-clean image, he was accused of involvement in a corruption scandal when his defense minister, V. P. Singh, alleged that the prime minister had taken kickbacks on government arms purchases. Rajiv dismissed Singh from office only to lose the 1989 election to a coalition led by the very man he had fired.

Rajiv's assassination in 1991, by a Tamil Tiger suicide bomber, interrupted the dynasty for a number of years because his wife, Sonia, refused to get openly involved in politics. She was grief-stricken at the loss of her husband, fearful for her children's safety and uncertain whether an Italian-born widow had any place in Indian public life. But Sonia Gandhi did emerge as a power broker in the Congress Party in the 1990s, especially when the party was out of government later in the decade. Evidently a late bloomer, she emerged on the political scene in 1998 when she made a stirring speech at the site of her husband's assassination. The following year, she won election to parliament and became leader of the opposition. Even partisan observers say she often performed with dignity and aplomb in parliament. After her party emerged from elections in 2004 with enough support to lead a coalition government, she surprised everyone by naming the respected economist and architect of India's economic reforms, Manmohan Singh, as prime minister. Few, though, doubted that she was the de facto leader of India. It is widely believed that her main ambition remains to groom her son, Rahul, now a sitting member of parliament, to take over the family business.

Thus the Nehru–Gandhi dynasty still holds sway over the Indian National Congress, the party that helped lead the country to independence six decades ago. But the days are long gone when Congress can count on Indian voters to hand it a majority government, or any role in government at all. The party suffered three successive election defeats in the 1990s, emerging with insufficient support either to govern or even to form and lead a coalition administration. Yet Congress and the Nehru–Gandhi dynasty are intrinsically linked to each other, if only because the party lacks a coherent ideology that transcends the appeal of personality and family names. In that sense, dynastic politics remain hugely relevant in India, but there are other forces that play an increasingly significant role in public life.

One of the most potent has been the overt exploitation or deliberate aggravation of religious tensions for political gain. India is about 80 percent Hindu, with Muslims making up most of the rest of the population. There are small percentages of Christians, Sikhs, Buddhists and followers of other creeds as well, but using religious conflict as a political weapon almost always means inflaming discord between Hindus and Muslims.

The Islamic faith first arrived in India not long after the prophet Muhammad established it in Arabia. By the eleventh century, Muslim generals and sultans were ruling large swathes of Indian territory, and their hegemony continued for nearly seven hundred years. In that time, many Indians converted to Islam, and other Muslims from Afghanistan and farther afield settled in the land they had helped conquer. Hindu warlords and resistance leaders fought Muslim domination but with only limited success. By the time European colonizers and traders began establishing a presence on the Indian coast in the seventeenth century, Islam was predominant among the subcontinent's ruling elite.

This fact rankles many Hindus. Whole ideologies of the right postulate that Hinduism needs to be remade as a militant faith whose followers are willing to die for their community's glory and its fundamental right to rule India. This is the side of the political spectrum most willing to use religious tension to inflame and inspire an electorate, but other parties, including the allegedly secular Congress, have not shied away from doing so themselves. Infamously, Congress activists massacred Sikhs in New Delhi when Indira Gandhi was assassinated in 1984. Some three thousand people died in an organized pogrom led by politicians and policemen equipped with voting lists who went from house to house and butchered anyone who had a Sikh surname. Women, children, young men—no one was spared. It was a horrific display of the dark side of the sycophancy that grips the Congress Party. Even Rajiv Gandhi, quickly sworn in to replace his slain mother, said when he was told of the killings, "When a mighty tree falls, the ground shakes." No Congress official has ever been punished for instigating those crimes except, of course, by the loss of trust among members of the Sikh community. Only in recent years have party leaders apologized for a reprehensible episode.

However, it is a political organization known as the Bharatiya Janata Party, or BJP, that has used religion most effectively as a tool to leverage its way into high office. To do this, the BJP reached back into history and twisted what it found into a national campaign of occasional violence and thinly disguised hatred. The party's leaders exploited the longstanding dispute over the Babri mosque, a sixteenth-century Muslim place of worship in northern India that activist Hindus claim is built on the foundations of an ancient temple to their god Ram. The notional temple is supposed to mark the place where Ram was born, so the site is viewed by the more fanatical Hindu believers as doubly holy. Muslims beg to differ, as does mainstream scholarship, which has found no evidence of a building of any sort beneath the mosque. Hindu groups, nonetheless, have long wanted to "rebuild" the Ram temple. The disagreement simmered for decades, resulting in court orders closing down the mosque and prohibiting any attempt to raze it or build a Hindu structure nearby.

The matter was, at worst, a troubling standoff until the Hindu nationalist politician Lal Krishna Advani invoked myth and brimstone in a cross-country political campaign in the early 1990s. As he rode in a Toyota van kitted up like a Hindu god's chariot, Advani's speeches inflamed grievances and passions, and implicitly told Hindus that it was all right to hate their Muslim fellow citizens. His journey culminated in a big rally near the disputed structure. Advani may be able to claim that he did not explicitly call for the destruction of the mosque that day, but his incendiary, provocative rhetoric set off a firestorm. Hordes of his followers swarmed over the stone walls and domes of the old mosque and ripped it to pieces with hammers, crowbars and their bare hands. The day of the attack, December 6, 1992, lives in infamy in India. An intact if worn structure was reduced to a pile of stones by saffron-clad militants who howled and screamed triumphal slogans as they went about their work of destruction. Around the country, Hindu mobs went on the rampage and Muslims sought revenge. When the dust settled, weeks later, thousands were dead, injured, widowed, raped or forced from their homes. And not just in India. Riots and pogroms against Hindus broke out in India's two Muslim-dominated neighboring nations, Pakistan and Bangladesh. Dozens were killed in both countries.

Even after the rioting was over, sporadic outrages continued to occur. Bomb explosions that killed hundreds in Mumbai a few months later were blamed on Muslim gangsters responding to the destruction of the Babri mosque. In July 2007, a court in Mumbai sentenced more than a hundred people to jail terms for their roles in that wretched attack. It was a terrible, destructive time. But in the end, despite many fearful moments and countless challenges to the authority of the state, the center held. A democratically elected government continued to preside over the vast, if sometimes troubled, land. Public debates and newspaper editorials took over from hot-blooded confrontation. Outrage subsided, at least as a potent destabilizing force. However, there was no doubt that the context of Indian politics had undergone a seismic shift. It was now all right to use hate as a political weapon.

The man charged with instigating the mosque-destroying mob, L. K. Advani, had managed to intensify a Hindu nationalist political movement that had rarely asserted its political power. Less than seven years after Hindu mobs tore down the Babri mosque, Advani's party, the BJP, would lead the government in New Delhi and preside over a series of attempts to undermine India's constitutional dedication to secularism. Before the mosque came down, the BJP and its allies had appealed only to a small, hard-line group of aggrieved Hindu nationalists, but after the sixteenth-century building fell, the party gained popularity with a troubling new constituency. This included educated city dwellers, young middle-class voters and others who had previously been taken for granted by more secular and liberal political parties. These were swelling ranks of people who felt that India's secular traditions had relegated Hindus to a form of second-class status in their own country. This message and the support it attracted helped the BJP win the most seats in elections in 1996, 1998 and 1999: never a parliamentary majority, but enough to lead various and disparate coalition governments. Although it lost the election of 2004, the BJP remains India's official opposition. Its leaders continue to debate the future course of ideology and policy, but the party is not about to disassociate itself from the imagery that grew out of the cynical attack on the Babri mosque and won the support of millions of Indian voters.

The successes of the Hindu right aside, there are even bigger changes rumbling through Indian politics. National political parties—Congress and the BJP—are losing support to smaller groups based on caste, language and geography. India's veteran left was quick to realize that this was happening. The country's Communists, who have enjoyed sustained but limited success at the state and national levels, made pacts with socialists and regional parties. Alliance-building among smaller parties became a legitimate path to political power in India. One or another of the two main national parties had to be courted to give any coalition the numbers it needed to win parliamentary votes, but, as events proved, the lure of power and its perks was enough to overcome decades of distrust and competition among political forces that were more used to fighting than cooperating. In the past, the electoral and parliamentary system rewarded majorities with power and government formation. Since the late 1990s, it has been coalition-building that achieves power. This is a crucial addition to the Indian political equation.

What was probably the country's most inconclusive election result ever, in 1996, gave coalition government its first real chance. The

BJP won the largest number of seats and formed a minority administration that lasted barely two weeks. Other parties were wary of the BJP's Hindu extremism and most stayed aloof from appeals to ally themselves with the new administration. It collapsed without ever taking a vote in parliament. Amid anguished commentary about a system in crisis, a most unlikely alternative presented itself. A thirteen-party alliance calling itself the United Front put forward a candidate for prime minister and was given its chance. With Communists, socialists, regional parties and malcontents forming its core, the Front seemed far from united. What it did have was the support of the Congress Party's MPs, the second largest bloc in parliament. This was extended without overt Congress participation in government, a fudge that allowed the party to avoid the taint of unpopular government decisions while not subjecting itself to another bruising election campaign that might just have seen its parliamentary totals reduced even further. Indian newspapers referred to the practice of voting for government legislation without participating in cabinet as "support from outside." The country was being governed by what was in effect an administration constructed to deny power to the BJP but that was no less legitimate for that.

Many expected a repeat of the folly and stasis of earlier failed attempts at coalition building, but this time the circumstances were different. Now there were no towering political personalities to shape the political agenda in or out of power. Nor was the country recovering from a traumatic crisis, as it had been so often during previous elections. If anything, India in the mid-1990s was starting to wake up, starting to realize its potential. The economic reform measures taken in 1991 were bearing fruit and Indian business was beginning to boom. Even the wider world seemed more stable and predictable than usual. There was no single crisis or conflict gripping the post–Cold War world. The Clinton administration in Washington seemed relatively benign and worldly compared with many of its predecessors. India's new government may have seemed inexperienced and fragile, but it came to power at a provident time.

The real achievement of this unwieldy political regime was not to be found in policy or even in its survival for nearly two years. It was that coalition governments came to be seen as viable by Indian voters. They could make decisions, handle crises and run the country.

India's cacophonous free media seethed with criticism of the United Front and its component parts. The prime minister, H. D. Deve Gowda, was routinely dismissed as either a "humble farmer" (his chosen phrase) or—the deliberately mangled version—a "fumble harmer." Yet the Indian economy was coming to life. It was becoming obvious to many that government no longer needed to be at the forefront of all forms of economic and social development; that markets, demographics and urbanization, among other things, all played a leading role in giving the country direction. Business leaders became role models in the absence of strong men and women in politics. India's middle class—then two hundred million strong and growing—had become the most potent force for change the country had ever produced. The next two elections, in 1998 and 1999, resulted in Hindu-nationalist–led coalitions that turned out to be no less centrist and compromise-oriented than the United Front. Attempts by hard-line Hindu ministers in these governments to introduce avowedly sectarian changes in law, such as banning religious conversion or the slaughter of cows and reworking school texts to glorify Hinduism, failed. The most popular achievements of these particular governments involved economic expansion, nuclear weapons tests, victory in a border war with Pakistan in 1999 and other matters that were largely nonpartisan by nature and widely supported in parliament and among the electorate. In 2004, Indian voters again chose an array of parties and candidates, but the result gave the Congress Party a chance to lead a governing alliance under the behind-the-scenes leadership of Sonia Gandhi. It seems likely that future elections will produce similarly mixed results.

The ability of coalition government to survive and even flourish in India—at least so far—is more than just a testament to the political flexibility and resilience of alliance-building politicians. It's a form of de facto devolution of central authority in a country that has struggled for most of its independent existence with the balance of power between levels of government. India's constitution was drawn up at a time when the trauma of partition and its aftermath fueled fears that the new country was fragile, too large and diverse to exist without a powerful central administration. There were very real fears that India could break into separate entities defined by language, ethnicity and religion. Over the years, separatist movements in Kashmir, Punjab and the remote northeastern states of India seemed to confirm these fears. At the same time, the constitution allowed for the devolution of power when possible. But politicians rarely give up authority willingly, so New Delhi remained at the commanding heights of political power, just as British colonial administrations had been when India was an imperial possession.

Eventually, pressure for change intensified. It came at first from the country's state governments. The changing nature of the economy and the demands of the electorate meant that Indian states found themselves with more services to deliver but no way of raising the money to do so. Taxation is largely a central power in India. At the local level, town and village councils were also expected to be more active, but they lacked resources, dependent as they were on central government. There is immense pressure in India for power to be devolved from New Delhi to state and local governments. In part, the splintering of support for national political parties and the growth of coalition government is a response to this pressure. But the process has been largely ad hoc, a result of changing voting patterns and demographic shifts that have been going on for more than a generation. These shifts include the growth of the middle class, urbanization and access to information through media and the Internet. The explosion in effectively unregulated satellite television news channels has enhanced the notion that power is no longer a prerogative of central government. Politicians and activists use the dozens of news channels, each with insatiable demands for content and sensation, to push their agendas independently of government. India is being forced to become more of a federal state, while its leaders often refuse to acknowledge or discuss the process.

There are concerns. Many political scientists argue that de facto devolution—having a group of MPs in a governing coalition in New Delhi that answers to regional or linguistic imperatives—is no substitute for a policy that actually devolves federal authority. Voters and opinion-formers in India are now beginning to ask the hard questions about the viability of centrally concentrated political power and government in the modern, market-driven age. Why does a massive, unwieldy Indian state get to exercise so much authority? Does the—at best—mixed record of the state justify its theoretically commanding role in the lives of people, business and the economy? As India's private sector begins to provide more and more jobs and economic growth, the tone of these questions is bound to become more strident and calls for restructuring more pressing.

Much is changing as the country becomes more urban, more open to global trade and trends and more sure of itself in international affairs and commerce. Most reputable Indian media outlets are hugely modern in outlook and rarely miss an opportunity to expose and vilify political patronage and corruption. The explosion in white-collar businesses and employment opportunities has given voice to a new collective interest group—one that demands rational outcomes from policymaking, sewers, roads, schools and health care. This is a group that rejects old-style neo-feudal politics, and it's growing in size and influence. There are versions of this voice around the country, even outside of major cities and the educated middle class. It is united by the perception that the role of politics is to provide stability and enable economic opportunity, to ensure that future generations don't face the same struggles as their ancestors. India is a young country, and increasingly the needs of children for education, health care and security are driving the politically active citizenry to change the power structure and make politics a force for good, rather than an opportunity for corruption and patronage, as it has been so often in the past.

7

THE NEW FREEDOM STRUGGLE

India's Activists in Action

INDIA'S VASTNESS, ITS COMPLEXITY, its sheer chaotic momentum, can overwhelm efforts at understanding. Here is a country with twenty-two official languages, not including English, which is widely spoken and increasingly important. All of the world's major deities are worshipped by communities that are often more populous than many Western countries. India's twenty-five million Christians, for example, outnumber Australians, the Irish and Greeks. More than 30 percent of the world's poorest people are Indian, more than half of them children, and yet the middle class—as measured by family consumption and income—is the largest and most expansive in the world. There are nearly six hundred thousand villages, hamlets and small towns in India, and some of them are among the fastest growing on the planet. Three of the world's largest urban areas—Delhi, Mumbai and Calcutta—are in India; the last Indian census, in 2001, showed their combined population to be in excess of forty million. Some 80 percent of Indians are said to live in rural areas, but that figure is suspect. Unlike China, which monitors its huge population closely, Indians move where, when and how they please, and their government has little to do with it. Fifteen million Indians go to the cinema every day. Almost the same number take passenger trains on the world's most extensive rail network. More than a million new private cars are licensed every year. There are more than fifty million motor vehicles on the road at any one time, and a hundred thousand people die in traffic accidents each year. That rate is expected to double every five years or so until driving skills and road conditions improve. About 25 percent of the cattle on earth are in India, and the country is by far the world's largest producer of milk. Most Indians do not eat beef because, as Hindus, they consider cows sacred. India has the second-largest Muslim population in the world, just after Indonesia but ahead of Pakistan. Three decades ago, Indians could not leave their country with more than US$100 in their pockets, so strict were the government's foreign exchange controls. Now Indian-based multinationals, such as the computer and software firms Infosys and Wipro, are listed on American stock exchanges and have branches in dozens of countries. An Indian citizen, Lakshmi Mittal, owns the world's largest steel-producing group and is listed by *Forbes* magazine as the world's third-richest man. Back in his homeland, nearly three hundred million people live on less than two dollars a day.

That perhaps is the source of the most striking of India's complexities and contrasts: the persistence and ubiquity of poverty alongside often extraordinary prosperity and growth of the knowledge-based economy. In Bangalore, the shacks of Shaktivail Nagar are just a few miles from Electronic City's modern campuses. Mumbai's office towers and high-rise condominiums are as costly as their counterparts on Manhattan's Upper East Side, while below them a hundred thousand pavement dwellers shelter under cardboard and wash at public taps. In the countryside, subsistence agriculture is fast giving way to agrobusiness, even as growing numbers of deeply indebted small farmers kill themselves by swallowing pesticides in the mistaken belief that their children will not have to pay back the moneylender. In the first three months of 2006, the Indian media reported that more than 350 heavily indebted farmers had committed suicide in a single district (Vidarbha) of the western state of Maharashtra. In parts of wealthy agricultural regions, such as Punjab, in the north, vast fields of strawberries and tomatoes destined for the country's jam and ketchup factories have replaced family crops of rice and wheat. The fruit is harvested each year by legions of ragged pickers from the impoverished

state of Bihar, where uncertain monsoon rains have perversely combined with floods to destroy local agriculture, transforming tillers of
the soil into migrant laborers, some three million of them from one
area of the state alone.

The disparities and the poverty do not go unnoticed. The difficult
lives and diminished prospects of the country's poorest citizens vex
many Indians. Do a Google search for the words *India* and *poverty*
and hundreds of websites come up. There are news reports, government studies and pleas for funds from charities. In addition, as always on the web, there is a mass of contrary opinion arguing that the
whole issue is part of a conspiracy concocted by people who want to
besmirch the country's reputation. What becomes clear when one
sifts through this material is that most Indians, at least those who are
computer literate and have Internet access, are struggling mightily to
come to terms with the same contrasts that present themselves so
starkly to a foreign visitor. And not just come to terms: many Indians
have fought for social and economic justice for their deprived fellow
citizens, compellingly and effectively. This is a process that is not without its successes. In the past twenty years, there have been significant
improvements in many of the baseline measures of human development: infant mortality has decreased while literacy has soared, access
to health care and clean water is better now than it ever was, and the
status of women advances every year.

In 2003, the Indian government made much of the fact that it was
no longer a net recipient of foreign aid but actually donated more in development assistance to other countries than it received from abroad.
In future, media reports suggested at the time, India would no longer require aid programs from small donors such as Canada, the Netherlands
or Finland but would avail itself only of market-oriented assistance and
structural reform loans from multilateral agencies such as the World
Bank, all aimed at improving its free market economic policies. In reality, aid has continued to flow from all of these sources to various projects and organizations in India. The ceremony was largely a sham, aimed
at the media and at stoking middle-class pride. The small organizations
that benefit from small countries' aid programs play a key role in antipoverty efforts in India. Indeed, they share much of the credit for the
improvement in poverty statistics over the past generation. Governments have achieved much, but they have not done so alone.

Aside from the aid community, India has many, many concerned citizens and activists who make the battle against poverty, discrimination and injustice their lives' work. These are almost always people who take exception to the philosophy of modernization and market economics that is widely espoused by India's middle classes. Some of these individuals are politically engaged. Others are artists, authors, filmmakers, trade unionists, environmentalists, medical doctors and lawyers who look at India's soaring economic growth and burgeoning IT sector and ask, So how has it helped the poor? Often, but not always, these are people on the left of the political spectrum; some are Communists, either party members or nonpartisan Marxists. Many are also middle class or even from wealthy backgrounds. A few live among the people whose lot they struggle to improve, while others enjoy the urban lifestyle of the modern, global elite. What they share is a commitment to the notion that rising tides do not automatically lift all boats. They believe that struggle and advocacy on behalf of the excluded will always be necessary, even as India acquires global political and economic influence befitting its population and economy.

India's great tradition of social and political activism probably began with Mohandas Gandhi, known as the mahatma, or great soul. He remains the acknowledged inspiration for many activists. Even those modern campaigners who count themselves among his detractors would admit that Gandhi's tactics and ideas have informed their own activities. Gandhi was born in 1869 when India was firmly under unchallenged British hegemony. At the age of nineteen, he traveled to London to train as a lawyer and felt the stirrings of his social conscience. He went on to practice law in South Africa—like India, a British colony—and found himself fighting against the pernicious racism of that society. It was here that he developed the tactics of nonviolent civil disobedience that would later serve the Indian freedom struggle so well. Gandhi returned to India in 1915 and became a powerful figure in his homeland. His was a political and spiritual voice that argued a convincingly moral and ultimately irresistible case against imperialism and foreign rule. He led many campaigns against British hegemony. Perhaps the most galvanizing among them was the Great Salt March of 1930. More than any other, this event inspired India's modern-day dissidents to take on great opponents and work optimistically in seemingly hopeless causes.

The Indian freedom struggle was itself struggling in the first few months of that year. There had been a powerful declaration by leading freedom fighters on January 26 that nothing short of total independence from British rule would do, but for the vast majority of poor Indians, sovereignty and nationhood were less urgent imperatives than was freedom from want. Gandhi understood this and realized that the big idea of independence was not taking root as he had hoped. He cast about for some gesture that would energize the farmer, the laborer, the landless and the landed alike. After all, Gandhi himself was from the Hindu caste of business families known as *banias*— people renowned for their market skills and savvy understanding of human behavior but not at the upper echelons of the caste hierarchy. As a bania, Gandhi understood the importance of symbolism and found the symbol he needed in the salt tax.

Salt was one of life's necessities. The toiling masses of India work in all weather. Often they sweat profusely. Salt helps to keep them alive, productive and healthy as it replaces the electrolytes lost to perspiration. Britain taxed every grain of salt used in every meal in every hut and household in the land. Whether it came in crystal chunks from mines near the northwest frontier with Afghanistan or from evaporating sea water along the coastal flats, salt generated revenue for the treasury of British India. Think of it, if you will, as taxing the sweat of the laborer's brow.

Gandhi announced in March 1930 that he intended to defy the tax. He did so in a letter to the viceroy of the day, Lord Irwin. The words of that note remain a classic of the genre: righteous protest speaking to power about its coming demise, though power doesn't know it yet.

"Dear Friend," Gandhi began, employing a familiar form of address that British viceroys were not known to encourage.

> *Before embarking on civil disobedience and taking the risk that I have dreaded to take all these years, I would fain approach you and find a way out. If India is to live as a nation, if the slow death by starvation of her people is to stop, some remedy must be found for immediate relief. I respectfully invite you to pave the way for immediate removal of those evils, and thus open a way for a real conference between equals. But if you cannot see your way to deal with these evils and my letter makes no appeal to your heart, on the 12th day of this month I shall*

*proceed with such co-workers of the Ashram as I can take, to disregard
the provisions of the salt laws.*[1]

Irwin's reply was noncommittal and the salt march began just as
Gandhi had promised. He set out followed by about eighty people.
That number soon swelled to hundreds and thousands and then tens
of thousands as the protest wound its way from the city of Ahmadabad toward the village of Dandi, several hundred miles to the west
on the shores of the Arabian Sea. At every hamlet or collection of
huts, Gandhi would speak and attract followers. Reporters, photographers and filmmakers, including many from the British and international media, were fascinated by the protest. Descriptions of the
scrawny charismatic man at the head of a procession of equally thin
and defiant Indians appeared in newspapers around the world. Film
cameras whirred and recorded Gandhi as he walked, staff in hand,
ever onward. It was probably the first deliberately staged mass media
event, and it worked.

The authorities had attempted to blunt the impact of the gesture
by scraping up all the salt from the drying pans around Dandi, but the
Mahatma was not to be stymied. On his arrival by the sea, he found
a clump of drying mud streaked with white. He bent over, while photographers snapped pictures and journalists scribbled furiously, and
picked up a handful of muddy salt. Theoretically, this small act was a
breach of the law. Salt could not simply be gathered in its raw state in
a quarry or on the beach. It had to be purchased from an outlet where
tax could be collected. The image of this frail bespectacled man waving a handful of mud on a Gujarat beach was the beginning of the
end for the British Raj. Across India, anger flared and protests intensified. Other leaders of the freedom struggle made salt marches of
their own and the arrests began, tens of thousands of them.

Another image was indelibly imprinted on the world's con-
sciousness from the front lines of the salt protests, and it, too, helped
speed Britain's departure from its grandest colony. When he was informed by Gandhi that another protest was to be staged—nonviolent, of course—outside a British government salt works, Lord Irwin
panicked and ordered that the Mahatma be included in the next wave
of arrests. The police seemed to take this as license to be even more
brutal in their attempts to put down the uprising.

At the Dharasana salt factory, hundreds of Gandhi's supporters marched toward the gates, their arms by their sides, singing Hindu hymns and chanting slogans. Police officers responded with inordinate savagery, laying into the protesters with metal-tipped bamboo canes, lashing them and splattering their blood. On Gandhi's instructions, the marchers did nothing to defend themselves and were dragged away bleeding and singing, many with big grins on their bloody faces. A more vivid picture of British repression faced down by moral force was not to be imagined. Four protesters died of their injuries; hundreds were grievously hurt. Gandhi himself was arrested as he meditated in his tent, but his detention only helped his cause.

That spirit of dissidence and courage in the face of brutal authority is alive and well in India. There have been countless protests modeled on the Great Salt March of 1930. In the capital, New Delhi, an entire street and park are set aside for demonstrations, hunger strikes and activism. The use of journeys and distances to make political points is common to all sides of the political spectrum, from the Hindu right and its procession of chariots calling for the destruction of the Babri mosque to symbolic long marches and road demonstrations by the left. Campaigners against big dam projects chain themselves to immovable objects and say they'll drown in the rising waters, forcing police to drag them away, an echo of Gandhi's followers at the salt factory. Hunger strikers threaten to fast until death if a particular piece of legislation isn't passed or is scuttled. Slum dwellers hurl themselves in front of bulldozers poised to destroy their homes, daring the operators to kill them even as they obey the government's writ. Matching personal risk of injury or death with nonviolent resistance lends moral authority to Indian activism even today.

Not every campaigner has the same flair and public profile as Gandhi, though. Many contemporary dissidents work quietly and directly with those in need of their help, shunning the media spotlight or the grand gesture. Dr. Achal Bhagat, a young psychiatrist and social worker, is one of these quiet ones. Through his practice and an organization that offers counseling and psychotherapy, Bhagat has come to a real understanding of the stresses and strains of modern Indian life. He has translated that insight into a passionate critique of India's aspirations to global and economic grandeur. These aspirations are spreading across every level of society. "Even the poor think they must get rich now," he says. "They see the lifestyle they want on TV and they hear of rags-to-riches [stories] or lottery wins and they wonder why they're still laboring for a few rupees an hour. They think it's their problem that they're still poor.

"Then there are the middle classes who stretch themselves to the limit, two incomes, raising kids, putting them through school, buying new consumer goods, worrying about falling ill, losing one's place in the structure. It's a ridiculous way to live but it's what we've chosen, what we're stuck with. I have to help people around their stress problems every single day."

Bhagat holds strong views about the free market and its role in India's development. He admits that the country needs economic growth and jobs, but he questions the coercive nature of market economics, the sense that if you're not getting anywhere, it's because there's something wrong with you; you're not working hard enough. You need to make more sacrifices. "It's all so unnecessary and so damaging to stress ourselves like this," he says. "My critique of economic reform, or whatever you call what's been going on here for more than a decade, is based on the human cost of it all, not politics or economics. Surely we can grow and develop as a society without leaving so many victims along the way." Stress-related mental illness is becoming commonplace, he says. Divorce, substance abuse, family violence and depression are all on the increase as Indians work harder to achieve goals that never used to be attainable. "Before we had this belief that we can all be Bill Gates or Narayana Murthy, people were largely happy with what they had. . . . They took delight in the passing of the seasons, festivals, neighbors and family. Now they all want everything right away, now. And it all begins in school."

It's beyond debate that a big part of India's success in the knowledge and service economies can be traced to education. Not the underfunded public system—even poor parents take out loans and go deeply into debt to send their sons and daughters to private schools that charge high fees, in order to give their children a chance at a decent education. Private schools in India are proliferating everywhere and, at their best, they are as good as any in the world. But this version of success, Bhagat contends, comes at a considerable cost. At the age of seven, a young student in one of India's better schools will begin to take a series of examinations. In many schools, each year

there will be at least three sets of exams that continue until matriculation. These exams are crucial in determining a student's future.
Good marks come from the regurgitation of information, vast quantities of it, learned by rote. The process of preparing for these exams
is hugely stressful. Bhagat has known stressed, frustrated students to
commit suicide, mutilate themselves, resort to drug and alcohol abuse
and suffer from clinical depression, all because of exam stress. His organization offers its most intense counseling services at exam times.
He and his staff talk to and treat thousands of young Indians who
find themselves under intense parental and societal pressure to pass
their tests and become a success.

"I have seen fourteen-year-old kids whose parents are yelling at
them about medical school and keeping up a high grade point average, kids with all the usual challenges of being teenagers forced to behave like they're studying for a post grad. It puts them off education
and alienates them from the outcome of their work. And that's the
least worst thing that can happen. It's this ridiculous system of want-
ing the moon and believing there's something wrong with you if you
fall short."

The boom in call-center jobs in India is producing more work for
Bhagat and his counselors, too. Call centers and similar businesses
have received a huge amount of positive publicity, and they are now
widely regarded as highly desirable places to work. Many undergrad-
uate students now strive for such jobs, Bhagat says, believing them to
be lucrative and relatively easy. The call-center employee lifestyle is
also played up, he says. The supposedly easy camaraderie of an
avowedly coeducational office; the escape from hierarchy so prevalent
in family, school and other walks of life; and the generous (by Indian
standards) salaries combine to make the jobs attractive. Some jobs in
call centers pay wages equivalent to $10,000 per year, far more than a
senior civil servant or even a government doctor would earn. But
again, Bhagat says, there is a cost. He sees evidence of the price in the
procession of suffering workers and students that come to his clinics.

"What do you do in a call center?" he asks. "You sit in a cubicle
in India and are confronted with problems generated thousands of
miles away. . . . Technology eliminates the distance and makes the
technical quality of communication near perfect. But you're inter-
facing with a different set of cultural norms and you're not equipped

for that, however much you learn the idioms of American English by watching movies and [taking] training courses. All night long on your shift, a parade of negatives marches by you. 'I can't access my account.' 'The bill is too high.' 'You people don't know what you're talking about.' Occasionally, you face overt racism and, more commonly, rudeness and hostility. Then you go home and try to live a normal life with your family. That means sleep deprivation or worse. You can't do that every night, week in and week out, burning the candle at both ends, without feeling the effects."

Call-center burnout has been noticed by the Indian media, too, though the press tends to play up the more lurid aspects of the phenomenon, the alcohol abuse and sexual promiscuity, rather than the less dramatic aspects, such as poor physical health, depression and anger.

Bhagat is too busy dealing directly with the victims of social and economic change to embark on a program of publicity-seeking protest. But Indians, he says, are learning what excessive aspirations are all about. "We want it all and we want it now. That's what we're told to do. It's attainable. Take out a loan, get a credit card, buy before it's too late. Work extra shifts to pay it off, burn that candle. . . . Raise families and work hard. But still be a dutiful son or daughter, observe your faith, be conventional while you're being unconventional. I look at all that and I don't see success, I don't see development. I see stress, burnout and trouble ahead. It's too much."

If Bhagat is understated in his activism, others wield publicity like a scythe. Arundhati Roy leapt to fame in 1997 with her Booker Prize–winning novel, *The God of Small Things*. The book, a global bestseller that has been translated into many languages, was a withering indictment of the Hindu caste system. In its pages Roy describes the doomed relationship between a man and a woman of different castes. There are constant scathing references to other aspects of modern Indian life that give a pretty good idea of what to expect from Arundhati Roy's muse, once it moved on from magic realism. Roy announced after her success that she no longer writes novels or fiction of any sort. She said she was giving up the genre because she distrusted her own reaction to the fame and wealth she was accruing, but also because India tested nuclear bombs, in May 1998.

That event shocked the entire world, but in India it was hugely popular. Indians were sending a message: "India has arrived at the

top table—get used to it." The consensus across the political spectrum was that India was right to test its nuclear weapons and now
the world had to treat the country with respect. Arundhati Roy
begged to differ.

In an opinion piece published in *Outlook* magazine in late July
1998, she addressed those who were celebrating the successful test:

> If there is a nuclear war, our foes will not be China or America or
> even each other. Our foe will be the earth herself.
>
> Our cities and forests, our fields and villages will burn for days.
> Rivers will turn to poison. The air will become fire. The wind will
> spread the flames. When everything there is to burn has burned
> and the fires die, smoke will rise and shut out the sun. The earth
> will be enveloped in darkness. There will be no day—only inter-
> minable night. What shall we do then, those of us who are still alive?
> Burned and blind and bald and ill, carrying the cancerous carcasses
> of our children in our arms, where shall we go? What shall we eat?
> What shall we drink? What shall we breathe?[2]

Roy was vilified for asking these pointed questions and for her outrage. "A chit of a girl" was one of the less offensive phrases heard in
middle-class discourse. But it didn't matter. Arundhati Roy had found
a new career among the social activists of India, the dissenters, con-
scientious objectors and troublemakers. She signaled as much later
in the piece when she wrote that the nuclear tests had actually liberated her, given her the freedom to do something that could change the
world, or at least change India:

> If protesting against having a nuclear bomb implanted in my brain
> is anti-Hindu and anti-national, then I secede. I hereby declare my-
> self an independent, mobile republic. I am a citizen of the earth. I
> own no territory. I have no flag. I'm female, but have nothing
> against eunuchs. My policies are simple. I'm willing to sign any nu-
> clear non-proliferation treaty or nuclear test ban treaty that's going.
> Immigrants are welcome. You can help me design our flag.
>
> My world has died. And I write to mourn its passing. India's
> nuclear tests, the manner in which they were conducted, the eu-
> phoria with which they have been greeted (by us) is indefensible. To
> me, it signifies dreadful things. The end of imagination.[3]

Roy has kept up her antinuclear stance but broadened her activism,
from opposing big dam projects to fighting the privatization of Indian

public companies. She's a ready commentator who looks good on television and can rattle off a quick denunciation at the drop of a clapperboard arm. But she's shown herself willing to put her body in the line of fire, too. Her participation in the campaign to prevent a series of dams being built along the mighty Narmada River in central India led to a Supreme Court citation for contempt and a day in prison. Roy had accused the court of being biased against the poor and in favor of vested interests. In most other countries following the British legal system, this comment, uttered outside the court, would be considered an expression of opinion and reported as such. In India, the high courts take their position very seriously, and criticism of judges, their rulings or the institution itself is not tolerated. Roy went to jail.

She is not alone in condemning the damage wrought by the construction of dams in India, and especially their effects on communities of indigenous tribal people, who most often seem to lose out when governments or corporations need land. Many Indian activists have drawn attention to the plight of people who have been displaced by big government projects and to the failure of the state to compensate or even acknowledge these injustices. The crusading journalist Palagummi Sainath, who uses only his first initial, P, in his byline, has traveled throughout India meeting those who have lost their land and livelihoods to dams and irrigation projects. In a collection of essays published in the late 1990s called *Everybody Loves a Good Drought,* Sainath takes to task the government, media, middle classes and activists themselves for, in his view, aiding and abetting in the plight of the displaced. Almost always, he writes, those who lose everything are those who we think had nothing to begin with. The indigenous peoples who live along the river systems to be dammed are thought to be uplifted by their relocation. This false notion causes more death, alienation, disease and poverty than any other. In fact, such people have much, he tells us, and it is not a hut full of possessions but an ancient culture, family and community mingled with deep ties to the land and an awareness of the earth and its rhythms. These intangible assets of the soon-to-be-dispossessed are easily disregarded by government and corporate forces that believe in only the narrowest possible definitions of progress.

Sainath has moved on to write about caste and water issues in other contexts, but his relentless energy and commitment remain undiminished. He is an unabashed critic of what is happening in India. He sees pitfalls and injustices everywhere. Nor are his criticisms vague, theoretical or ill formed. On the contrary, they are usually written in spare, painstaking prose and based on the hard graft of honest journalism. Invariably, a meeting with this focused and tireless campaigner begins and ends with a discussion of starvation, poverty and what he sees as the blind arrogance of India's middle classes.

"What do any of these people know?" he asks, gesturing at his fellow diners in a Mumbai restaurant. "Increasingly, they live in their cars and apartments, and it might as well be Paris or New York. Their media tell them about the stock market, cricket, Bollywood films. The poor play no part in their lives, save as cheap labor and something to tut-tut about when a poignant documentary comes on the BBC. We're building dams, yes, and this is damaging and problematic, but we're also building walls between us and the countryside, fostering unequal development and exploitation. This is worse. We are bringing in apartheid."

The campaign against the Narmada project is inspired by bitter experience elsewhere in the country. Famously—some would argue infamously—India's first prime minister regarded dams as "temples of modern science." A rationalist through and through, Jawaharlal Nehru believed that nature was a force to be harnessed or controlled by science for the benefit of mankind. In the early 1950s, Nehru's vision was realized in a network of barriers in river systems north of the sacred Ganges and west of Calcutta, to catastrophic and lasting effect. This led to the near-permanent inundation of vast tracts of Bihar, already one of the poorest, most backward states in the country. My guide to this disaster was Ram Chandra Khan, a police officer by profession but by inclination a Gandhi-inspired activist of the front rank.

In his home behind the main bazaar in the Bihari state capital city of Patna, Khan and I laid plans for a visit to his ancestral village. As local grandees, his family had a large landholding in what for centuries had been one of the more feudal parts of the country. Even the zeal to introduce land reforms after independence in 1947 had not had much effect in Khan's district. He was still, technically, the feudal lord of his area. Now, after the floods, there wasn't much above water that he could rule. "Just my island," he said with black humor. He promised to show me some of the worst misery in India. "You will see millions of people living like animals, farmers who have never learned to catch fish but whose fields are under water all year round. You will see how man's tendency to behave like God can devastate our lives." Khan explained that Nehru was initially to blame for the inundation that lay ahead of us. We were in Khan's car, driving on Bihar's dreadful roads, some seven hours from our destination. "He was, in many ways, a great man," said the policeman. "No one can criticize his passion or commitment to democracy, freedom and so on. Unfortunately, he was also devoted to science."

In 1955, Nehru's government launched an ambitious program to build interconnected webs of earthen dams known as "embankments." These were intended to control the often disastrous annual flooding of the many rivers that cross the flat landscape of northern Bihar and empty into the Ganges. Local people had largely learned to cope with these yearly deluges caused by a combination of monsoon rains and melting snow in the Himalayas in Nepal. Sometimes lives were lost and people displaced, but the rising waters were at least predictable, and they left behind rich silt deposits that renewed the fertility of an overcultivated land. It was part of the rhythm of life. But every decade or so, a long monsoon or sudden thaw in the mountains caused a catastrophic flood. Thousands, even tens of thousands, of villagers and farmers would be swept away, and countless livelihoods and communities inundated. The embankments were meant to end that cycle of disaster once and for all. Or so Indian scientists told Nehru.

The project took place despite the experience of the British who, precisely one hundred years earlier, had built similar barriers along the Damodar River farther to the east. Within a year, this project had been a disaster far worse than the annual floods. The British-built embankments kept the floodwaters of the Damodar from dispersing. This in turn led to the land becoming waterlogged. People were kept away from their farms far longer than had been usual when floods had disrupted the seasonal patterns of farming. Local food stocks were depleted. And soon the once lush fields in the flood plain of the Damodar became malarial swamps. Starvation and disease set in, and disaster relief efforts took over from productive agriculture.

This, in modern times, is what has happened on a much larger scale across northern Bihar. Embankment construction continued in the state throughout the 1960s, 1970s and 1980s. A web of earthen ridges created by bulldozers crisscrossed the countryside. Even as the flood barriers went up, there were ominous signs of what was to come. It took longer and longer for the annual floodwaters of the tributaries of the Ganges to dissipate. Most disastrous of all, the rivers began to flood all the way to the Ganges itself, which was in full flow. Water from the main river actually flowed backward into its tributaries. This phenomenon is repeated yearly to this day. Activists, Ram Chandra Khan among them, say this is a man-made environmental disaster comparable to the diversion of rivers in Central Asia by the Soviet Union and the near disappearance of the once mighty Aral Sea.

We were in a boat now, floating on the greasy brown waters that flowed between the road and Khan's "island." Khan began to expound yet again on the catastrophe around us. "The embankments are a disaster . . . folly . . . human arrogance on an unimaginable scale," and so began another heartrending soliloquy against Nehru, science and the recalcitrance of Big Government in India. We were between two major tributaries of the Ganges, the Kamala and the Kosi rivers. It was late April, more than a month before the annual monsoon was scheduled to arrive. In most other parts of North India, it was still dry, hot, a dusty hell. Here, however, was a vast sheet of water over the fields stretching as far as the eye could see. On either side of the narrow embankment from where we had launched our flat-bottomed boat, waterlogged land stretched out to the watery horizon. Boats, dying trees and the tops of submerged buildings dotted the dun-colored expanse. Yet, these were not the life-giving waters of other riverscapes in India. Instead, the air was thick with the smell of decay. The water was stagnant and mosquitoes buzzed in furious clouds.

Khan's mood grew steadily darker. As the boatmen poled us across to the bit of high ground where the Khan family stables had been converted into a small house, he mumbled to himself and furrowed his brow. The men in the boat quietly told us how the big family house had been torn down when its foundations were undermined by the water. Khan, they said, had ordered the stables be fixed up for those few family servants who stayed behind. No one else came to visit the farm anymore, save Ram Chandra Khan in his more melancholy moments.

"It's not for me, it's not for my family that I do this, campaign, come here, meet people like you," he announced as we set foot on the muddy landing next to the stable. "It's for the three million who've had to leave this place. Three million! I'm a policeman, I've got a pension, I'm okay. What about them? Most of them are the living dead." Khan says the people who've left their submerged farms in north Bihar are rickshaw pedalers and pullers in Calcutta, factory workers in Delhi and "probably prostitutes. Don't forget the women."

Later he took me on a trip over his fields. The boatmen had to use paddles when the water became too deep for bamboo poles to propel the craft. It was obvious that the paddlers were not natural boatmen of the sort you find in the watery landscapes of Kerala or the Vale of Kashmir. We often wallowed in one place or went round in circles as the Khan family servants flailed their paddles ineffectually in the turbid water. In many places people were throwing hand-knotted nets into the water. We watched them pull out a few small fish with each cast and then drop their catch into the baskets by their feet. "We were rice farmers," Khan said, "not fishermen. We grew vegetables and millet, later maize and potato. We had cattle and made butter from the milk. We don't even like the taste of fish."

Khan continues his lonely battle. For nearly a generation, governments have admitted the folly of the embankment program, and yet no solution has been proposed beyond giving small amounts of money to people who have had to move or, with cruel irony, teaching them to operate fish farms. Khan calls up Indian journalists and takes them on tours of the region, and he stays in touch with exile communities in other parts of the country. Environmental groups campaign for the embankments to be destroyed or modified, but this is one of the most neglected, poor and thus politically insignificant parts of the country. There's little reason for a venal, opportunistic political elite to take the hard, expensive decisions that might alleviate the problem. Ram Chandra Khan says he won't stop campaigning until he, too, is just another entry on the death registry of people from his district.

Gandhi's legacy consists of more than nonviolent and morally based campaigns against injustice. Gandhi also believed that the outcome of the freedom struggle should be a society that paid attention to its strengths in village life and local agriculture. He was wary of industrialization and the growth of cities. Such wariness may seem futile today, but a good Gandhian never gives up. Kishan Babujrao "Anna" Hazare has spent more than thirty years implementing his ideas and campaigning for social justice on the rocky plains beyond the city of Pune in India's western hills. Hazare, a former soldier, was almost killed when his vehicle was struck by a shell in India's disastrous border war with China in 1962. He says the incident gave him a lasting sense of his own mortality, and the growing realization that he had but a limited time on the planet. When Hazare left the army in 1975, he returned to his home village, Ralegan Siddhi, where he hoped to settle down. What he found horrified him. There were dozens of illegal distilleries producing home-brewed liquor. People were poor, and drunkenness and domestic violence were rife. This situation gave the burly farmer's son his first cause. Hazare either convinced or coerced the male villagers to stop brewing hooch, before moving on to campaign against tobacco and gambling. As his next cause, he encouraged small-scale irrigation based on the harvesting and preservation of rainwater instead of expensive drilled wells. All of these measures eased the burden of debt on families by increasing productivity and eliminating vice. At the same time, he urged village councils to respect and pay attention to the needs and views of women, and subtly set about moving women villagers into decision-making roles.

To meet Anna Hazare, it's best to travel to his home and headquarters at Ralegan Siddhi, a place he refers to as the model village for all his ideas. My guide and host at Ralegan was another former soldier, Colonel P. P. Phatak, who told me that working for Anna Hazare was a bit like being in the army. "You do your duty every day, and you soon learn the ropes, but sleep in late one morning and see what happens to you," he said with a laugh. We were rumbling through the countryside beyond Pune in an old Indian-made SUV. The colonel flicked his hand dismissively at alcohol shops along the way. Drunkenness remains a huge problem in India, especially among the very poor. Indian manufacturers produce a full range of bottled spirits for the middle-class consumer, including an ersatz "scotch whisky" flavored with concentrates made in the glens of Scotland. But for the poor the same distillers make a truly insidious and wretched alcohol from the dregs of the sugarcane crop. It is known variously as "arrack" or "country liquor" and comes in two-cup plastic pouches that cost less than a dollar each. In some more bibulous parts of the country, the roads are littered with torn liquor pouches, each one a binge, a beaten wife, a day's work missed and a nasty hangover—misery strewn across a landscape devoid of hope. This is the sort of drinking that Anna Hazare fought to eradicate from Ralegan Siddhi, as Colonel Phatak explained, after I joked about an army man needing his evening peg of whisky before dinner.

"Alcohol is the bane of India's poor," the colonel said. "There's nothing funny about it. The whole society would be better off if we'd never learned about alcohol."

Later, as I was meeting people in the village, I wondered if they were all as abstemious as the pamphlets about Anna Hazare suggest. Certainly, the very impressive women who ran the credit unions and child health clinics would adhere to the social reformers' rules. So, most likely, would the idealistic young doctors and engineers who had come from other parts of India to be part of a modern Gandhian experience. But I found it hard to imagine that the men who led cattle through the village square or bought snacks from the tea shop would easily turn down a drink. It was impossible to know for sure.

Meeting Anna Hazare is like being ushered into the presence of a pop star, such is the adulation of those around him. He's a squat man with broad shoulders and a tenacious gaze. He lives simply in a single room and dresses in homespun cotton and the wedge-shaped white cap favored by the men who led India's freedom struggle. Those who don't speak Hazare's native tongue, Marathi, have to communicate with him in Hindi. English is out of the question, though I sense that he can understand more than he lets on. I listen to him reel off statistics about Ralegan Siddhi, which I decided to stop regarding as a village when Hazare informs me that some thirty thousand people have been affected by his work in that area alone.

"When India was first independent," he says, "we had to choose between two approaches to development. Well, the government went for Nehru's top-down [approach]: the authorities doing everything for the people, whether they wanted it or not, whether it was logical or not. There were lots of disasters, and who can look around India today and say this approach has worked, that the poor are moving out of slavery? No, the other approach, Gandhi's, was the proper one, and that's what we do here. Bottom up. People organizing themselves to discuss and solve their problems, and politicians doing what they're told."

Hazare hasn't waited for politicians to help out Ralegan. He has organized the local people to help themselves, and it appears to have worked. When he first began campaigning and organizing among the villagers, he says, no women were literate. Now the district boasts almost full female literacy, an achievement that's almost unknown among the poor of India. All Ralegan schoolchildren attend classes for at least twelve years and achieve full matriculation, and their parents participate actively in the services and institutions of their community. They take part, Hazare says, because they helped build and pay for them.

"We raised money and built the school, the hospital, clinics, the temples and this compound where I work. All built and maintained locally by local people. We have sports programs, and two of our students are on the Indian track-and-field team for the Olympics. We have billions of rupees in our family savings accounts that women have accumulated through micro-credit–financed businesses and other investments. Girl students are encouraged to go to medical school or train as engineers, and, quite often, they bring those skills back here to help their neighbors." Hazare says local people make all the decisions on what to build, or whether to send students to college. Ralegan accepts no government or outside help and, he says, there's "no waiting, no kickbacks, no frustration with things taking too long."

India, in Anna Hazare's view, is the sum of its rural and semirural communities, and the way to end poverty in the country is to make every last one of them into another Ralegan Siddhi. "You spread this philosophy of ours, empowering women, micro-credit, doing things for yourself at a local level, and you see how quickly poverty ceases to matter. Take caste. If people are working together to raise money for school improvements or to harvest rainwater for irrigation, then they cease caring about such things. Certainly in a generation or so, it's no longer relevant or no longer a barrier to development."

Like Gandhi, Hazare thinks Indian democracy is too centralized and that governments in New Delhi and the state capitals have too much authority over people's lives. He believes that citizens should directly hold almost all power, making the important decisions by consensus in village and neighborhood assemblies called *gram sabhas.* Asked if India's huge population might make such a scheme unwieldy, he waves his hand in a circle and says that proof of the viability of the idea is all around us, in the success of Ralegan Siddhi. "People here meet and discuss everything, and their decisions are taken carefully and by consensus. It works here. It would work elsewhere."

Where Hazare's ideas become slightly more controversial is on the matter of cities and their role in development. Hazare is against urbanization. He wants city dwellers to move back to the countryside to rediscover the Gandhian ideal of cooperative village life. While there can be little dispute about what has been accomplished in Ralegan Siddhi, it is apparent that the sheer force of Hazare's personality has had a bearing on its success. His presence is a factor in keeping the project going: replicating his success elsewhere has proven difficult. People leave their villages because they are economically stagnant or socially backward. They flee poverty and discrimination, or they set off in search of new opportunities. The city or large town needs laborers, vendors and tea-shop waiters. As dreary as these jobs can be, they offer hope that lives can be changed. Hazare's belief in the sanctity of village life may be at odds with human ambition. As I wandered around Ralegan Siddhi, meeting women's groups in the temple, looking in on a reading class, visiting the bank and meeting its female president, something seemed amiss. No coercion was in evidence, but I sensed that those who didn't fully support the project weren't welcome. How could they be? It was a busy, active life, being a resident of this model village, and everyone had a role to play. No one lazed around. No one slept in the shade of a tree or gossiped over glasses of sweet tea—common sights in other Indian villages. Here, there was work to do.

"We are the best village in India," a young woman and community leader said aloud during a meeting at the local Hindu temple. "Nowhere else is like this."

Anna Hazare and his followers are not the only Indians to draw attention to the evils of corruption in Indian governance. Many former civil servants have become reformers after retirement, men such as Harsh Mander, who left government in 2002 to protest official connivance in the anti-Muslim pogroms and riots in the western state of Gujarat. Mander wrote articles in the news magazine *Outlook* in which he described refugee camps full of Muslim families in fear for their lives, and police who shot at the victims of brutality, rather than at those who had attacked them:

> The unconscionable failures and active connivance of the state police and administrative machinery is also now widely acknowledged. The police is [*sic*] known to have misguided people straight into the hands of rioting mobs. They provided protective shields to crowds bent on pillage, arson, rape and murder, and were deaf to the pleas of the desperate Muslim victims, many of them women and children. There have been many reports of police firing directly mostly at the minority community, which was the target of most of the mob violence. The large majority of arrests are also from the same community which was the main victim of the pogrom.[4]

Mander has also written a bestselling book, *Unheard Voices*—a collection of true stories about the lives of twenty Indians, including prostitutes, Hindus from the lowest castes, HIV-positive women, street children and others who are among the millions who have not shared in the country's prosperity. Mander observes that the poorest 10 to 20 percent of Indians are often left out of government- and aid-funded antipoverty activities because they are seen as unfit to be active participants. At best, he says, the very poor are looked on as passive welfare recipients and then only in very specific, targeted schemes that are few in number. Most of the worst-off get overlooked. This practice of "imposed invisibility," Mander argues, only increases their marginalization. "It completely misses what their most fundamental need is, which is self-respect and the chance to be heard." The book has been widely praised, in large part because Mander is not content merely to give a sad account of misery and wasted potential. Instead, he shows that the poor are resilient and creative and full of ideas for addressing their plight. His work has inspired documentary films and international news coverage, and he continues to write and advocate on behalf of those in India he sees as the victims of a callous and corrupt system.

About two decades ago, the world's aid donors, including UN agencies, overseas development departments in wealthy countries, and big private charities, decided that sending money to the recipient countries' governments wasn't working. They wanted to provide assistance directly to people who needed it. So they encouraged the growth of independent activist groups at village, regional and national levels. These were to be privately run organizations that could receive funds and spend them on their stated goal, be it ending poverty, helping women, treating disease or modifying behavior. In theory, they would be more accountable than governments, which have other sources of funds and can afford to be cavalier about donors' intentions. Thus was born, in India and elsewhere, the nongovernmental organization, or NGO.

To travel the Indian countryside is to move through an NGO bazaar. Instead of the calls of touts and hawkers, though, one encounters a succession of signs and slogans. Pictures of condoms adorn HIV/AIDS billboards. A truck roars by advertising the virtues of family planning. Atop a cartoon of two smiling children and their parents are the Hindi words *Hum do, humari do*—We two, our two. NGOs get women together to pool their meager savings to buy sewing machines or cattle. They start cooperative dairies and encourage sustainable irrigation and water harvesting. They restore old temples and try to change attitudes toward people suffering from debilitating diseases. Often someone from the Indian elite will found an NGO when he or she retires from a top job in the civil service or the business world. Sometimes the NGO has one employee, sometimes thousands. In neighboring Bangladesh, the NGO known as BRAC employs about one hundred thousand people in banking, retail shops, cell phone networks and, of course, programs to help end rural poverty. It has branches in other countries. In India and elsewhere, the NGO business is booming.

It's also changing the world in many subtle and unusual ways. The marriage between the NGO movement and the Indian propensity to social activism has had a real impact on poverty, inequality and other challenges. Examples abound. One of the more innovative is the M. R. Morarka foundation. This NGO was established by a wealthy business family from Jaipur as an act of philanthropy. The Morarkas come from a Hindu community known for hard work, success in business and clannishness. Before starting their NGO, they made their money in construction. The thrust of the foundation's work over many years has been improving the lot of the farmer and enhancing agricultural output. In India, and especially in arid Rajasthan, that means irrigation projects and cheap fertilizer. It means sustainable and inexpensive farming methods and crops that produce maximum yields. Fairly mundane but necessary work, it would seem. But several years ago, Mukesh Gupta became the executive director of the foundation and things changed radically. A new building was constructed, the number of projects increased and, most strikingly, the Morarka foundation started breeding earthworms.

Worms—millions of them, small and large, slimy and pink— ooze in gelatinous masses in fields and in breeder boxes outside Morarka headquarters, just south of Jaipur. Millions more are raised in similar conditions at the organization's field office, a four-hour drive away. That's where Mukesh Gupta has his office. He is a tall and dignified fellow, and he exudes confidence and enthusiasm. Gupta is a man who wears many hats: He is the head of a major Indian philanthropic venture, a philosopher, a scientist. He is also a self-described "worm rancher," though Gupta prefers to describe his latest project as "vermiculture, because, you know, people get a little funny about the word *worm*." He is as eloquent as a preacher on the Southern U.S. gospel circuit, whether he's talking about how women have taken over village credit arrangements in Indian villages or how Indian worms will take over the world.

"So-called organic agriculture is the future, the very near future," he says. "We are poisoning the earth with our inputs—chemical fertilizers and pesticides—and this is true in every country." Indian governments have subsidized fertilizers and other agricultural chemicals for decades, Gupta says, largely because of the success of the Green Revolution in the 1960s, when the country was able to produce its first food grain surplus. Part of that success was achieved by the extensive use of fertilizers and pesticides. Government factories produce the fertilizer and sell it cheaply to farmers, a practice that Gupta calls "a dangerous fraud."

The fertilizers "are almost unnecessary," he says, if farmers take the right steps. But since the 1960s, they've been urged to saturate the soil with sacks and sacks of chemicals. These are produced in government plants, where thousands of people work, and those jobs are politically important, just as the factories are to their communities. No politician ever does anything without calculating the cost and the advantages to his chances of reelection. The environment be damned.

"What we're finding out here with our worms, our vermiculture, is that we can invest the merest fraction of what it costs to make chemical fertilizer and breed enough worms to help all of India manage the soil properly. All of India!" Gupta says, with a flourish of his ever-present yellow pencil.

Worms are natural regenerators of soil, but they have been killed off in most agricultural areas by chemical inputs that were, in a sense, meant to augment their work. Worms move through the soil digesting some nutrients and excreting the rest. What comes out is known as a casting, worm waste. It is rich in nitrogen and other nutrients essential for crops. As well, the worm tunnels help aerate the ground, increasing its productivity. Concentrate many worms in a patch of land and it will become fertile without chemicals within a year. Gupta's zeal is backed by scientific evidence and plenty of economic indicators. "Crop yields improve in the short, medium and long term," he says, and the costs drop as the worms breed. All you need to get started is cow manure, and, says Gupta with a flourish, it's not even necessary to have your own cattle. Here he proposes a uniquely Indian solution to the problem of feeding the worms.

"Go to almost any Indian city and what do you see? Cows. Our sacred cows wandering the streets. Look down and see the result of this. Manure everywhere. Now, that manure is considered unsightly garbage by many, especially the middle classes, and much of it is left to dry up and blow away, or it's thrown into the rubbish to rot uselessly in a landfill somewhere. I've estimated there is a million tons of cow manure on Indian streets. A million tons! We should pay the unemployed youth of our cities to collect it and bring it to gathering points, from where it could be conveyed to worm farms and to farmers themselves. Use some of the money now spent on subsidizing poisonous chemicals to employ people and clean up the cities. I challenge anyone to tell me what's wrong with that idea."

Gupta's success in his worm-breeding operation is attracting international attention. Outside his office is a laboratory where British scientific advisers are helping Morarka upgrade the organic standards that Indian farmers learn from the foundation. One of these advisers, Dr. Tim Hunter, says that the idea is to turn India into a major producer of off-season organic produce for "British, European, even American supermarkets. It's a perfect fit and not as far away as South America, where a lot of the produce currently comes from." He adds that Indian organic produce will be much, much cheaper than the same products from California or Chile, the present sources of most organics in Western supermarkets. Near Morarka's worm-breeding fields outside Jaipur is a two-story house where an Indian-American man heads up the only overseas branch of the organization that certifies farming as "organic" for retailers in the United States. There are people working on marketing strategies for Indian worms, too, hoping to sell breeding stock in other countries. It's all Mukesh Gupta's doing.

"Our worms are tough," Gupta says. "They can withstand extremes of temperature and climate. Arid dried soil and mucky post-monsoon mud —they munch their way through it all. We might even have enough cow manure to export, too." India, according to Gupta, is now producing roughly 40 percent of the worms used in vermiculture worldwide. "And we've only just started. There are five thousand farm families now working with our worms and many more to come. We want them all to think of this as a business so they can spread the word about worms and make some money besides. Our wildest dreams seem achievable now."

India's activists and social entrepreneurs may seem like dissidents, but they actually augment the country's expanding economic prowess. Instilling a social conscience in newly affluent people might be the least of their concerns, but it's a crucial step in India's awakening. The plague of poverty will never go away without all Indians playing some part in its alleviation. Government has a role, but there is a limit to what it can achieve by itself. The private sector is providing millions of jobs, but these are largely for the better-off and well educated, rather than for the dirt-poor people of northern Bihar and of the drought-stricken plains of the Deccan plateau in central India. Only social activism on a grand scale, combined with charitable giving by individuals and corporations, can take the battle against poverty in India to victory: equity, equality of opportunity and social justice. Even if the Indian economy continues to grow, as forecast, by as much as 9 percent a year, poverty will remain deeply entrenched because of social exclusion and denial of access to health and education services in the poorest areas. Short of mass migration to the cities, with all the environmental and social challenges that would result, the ranks of the fortunate in India must start doing more to help their fellow citizens in poverty. The work of the activists is a step in the right direction, but it's only the beginning of the journey.

8

EDUCATING INDIA
THEN AND NOW

A Journey from Light to Darkness

APRIL IS THE BEGINNING of the intense heat of summer across much of India. It's also a time when more than a quarter of a million young men and women, backed fiercely by families, friends and teachers, take part in a rarified competition. Even to compete is a mark of honor and achievement. Only one in ten will succeed in what is thought by some to be the toughest intellectual challenge on the planet. This is the entrance exam for India's most elite engineering schools, the Indian Institutes of Technology, or IITs. (Spoken aloud, the letters should trip effortlessly off the tongue as "aye aye tee.")

The test is also known by a mellifluous acronym, the JEE, or joint entrance exam. It takes place in conditions of the utmost security. Armed police guard copies of the test paper and stand watch outside the examination venues. Inside, the invigilators stop short of carrying weapons, but their alertness to cheating would shame the U.S. Department of Homeland Security. A panel of leading university professors sets the questions each year. The professors meet in secret locations, their identities carefully concealed from those who might be tempted into bribery, coercion or worse.

There's a reason for this level of vigilance and the intense logistics: The Indian education system is plagued by cheating and fraud.

Students routinely buy copies of test papers in advance of the test. Usually these are stolen, but not infrequently they are supplied by cash-strapped or morally bankrupt teachers. Crib notes, smuggled cell phones, even sophisticated Secret Service–style radio sets have all been found inside exam halls. Test monitors may face both threats and bribes if they spot a scam in progress and attempt to deal with it. But the corruption that infects India's run-of-the-mill institutes of higher learning exists in a world apart from the Indian Institutes of Technology. No one is known to have fooled the ever-alert men and women who maintain the integrity of the JEE. So far.

There are just seven IITs, with a combined student population of around twenty-eight thousand. Three of the schools are located in India's great cities: Delhi, Chennai and Mumbai. The others are in distant towns that few outside India have heard of: Roorkee, Kharagpur, Guwahati, Kanpur. Among those foreign nationals who do know about the IITs of India are some of the top businesspeople and scientists on the planet—such is the reach of the IIT alumni and their presence in the global elite. But the rest of the world is beginning to wake up. When the CBS news program *60 Minutes* presented a report on the IITs in 2003, the host described them as "the most important universities you've never heard of. Put Harvard, MIT and Princeton together and you begin to get an idea of this school in India." IIT graduates are among the pillars of Silicon Valley but, beyond information technology, they can be found in practically every major corporation in the United States. When two giant airlines, United and U.S. Air, were attempting to merge in 2000, the deal-makers were classmates from IIT Kharagpur. The cofounder of Sun Microsystems, the head of the cell-phone giant Vodafone, the chief scientists of Bell Laboratories—all graduated from an Indian Institute of Technology. IIT alumni have also fetched up at organizations such as American Express, the International Monetary Fund, McKinsey and Company, Hartford Financial Services, Proctor and Gamble and the University of Cambridge.

It used to be that half of all IIT graduates went abroad in search of career opportunities and wealth. At least twenty-five thousand of them are in the United States, and a slightly smaller number live and work in other countries. These days, as India booms, a new trend is emerging. More and more of the men and women who get their degree from an IIT stay at home, or return after further study abroad to take up a job in India. The heads of Infosys and Tata Consultancy Services, two of the largest information technology firms, come from IIT. So do senior managers and executives of India's top chemical, pharmaceutical, financial and transportation firms. Regardless of where the institutes' alumni end up, though, their degree is nothing less than a winning lottery ticket. As IIT graduate and Netscape co-founder Pavan Nigam puts it, "Anybody who makes it into an IIT is . . . set for life."

On a misty, cool morning in November, I set out from Calcutta to visit the most venerable of the Indian Institutes of Technology, IIT Kharagpur. In 1951, when the school accepted its first students, there were no major roads between eastern India's largest city and the fertile hinterland around the new institution. Trains bound from Calcutta to Delhi stopped in Kharagpur, an important rail junction and a district administrative headquarters. It's not entirely clear why this particular town was chosen as the site for the first IIT. Official histories of the college say it may have been because many of the school's founders were members of the same linguistic and ethnic group. They were Bengalis, a people renowned as intellectuals, intense, thoughtful and obsessed with education. India's first prime minister, Jawaharlal Nehru, wasn't Bengali, but he appointed people from Bengal to be his advisers on education and science; they, supposedly, convinced him that the first IIT should be set up in their home state. Nevertheless, the choice of Kharagpur, rather than Calcutta or one of Bengal's other important cities, remains somewhat of a mystery.

Even today, Kharagpur is nothing special. It has a few factories with rusty smokestacks and a chaotic bazaar, but little else. On the outskirts of town, a sign points down a side road to Donald Duck English Medium School. The surrounding fields are lush and pretty, but the town itself is an unlovely urban intrusion on an otherwise sylvan setting. If there were a Michelin guide to India, it would probably say of Kharagpur, "Not worth a detour." My driver was from Calcutta and had never been to Kharagpur before. Thanks to a lack of signs and the brand-new highway petering out at the edge of town, we quickly got lost in the warren of streets that was Kharagpur's small downtown. We were met with blank looks when we asked for directions until a man on a cycle rickshaw, who must have taken students from the train station to the campus, pedaled up with a knowing look on his face. He gave my driver a long, rambling set of instructions in Bengali and we set off. Soon, shoppers with carrier bags gave way to young men and women with backpacks. We were close. Then, abruptly, the car was moving along shaded lanes with the unmistakable feel of a university campus. Bicycles outnumbered motor vehicles. Everyone was carrying books or other trappings of academia. We glimpsed distant administration buildings through the canopy of trees and soon found ourselves at a crowded tea shop where students bought breakfast and gossiped over steaming cups at outdoor tables. Not quite the dreaming spires of Oxford, but close.

In its early years, IIT Kharagpur held classes in a building that had once been used by India's colonial rulers for something quite other from molding and training young minds. In fact, there was a very deliberate symbolism in the choice of the former Hijli district jail as a place to begin teaching science and engineering skills. During the struggle for independence, British officials interred dozens of Indian freedom fighters at the jail, two of whom were killed in a prison uprising in 1931, shot dead by their British guards. The incident is commemorated every year at IIT Kharagpur as Martyrs' Day, and it is one of the most important occasions on the campus calendar. The old jail is a museum now, full of musty newspaper pictures of the freedom struggle and the early days of the school. Those stirring memories sit alongside clunky bits of analog equipment and machinery, either developed by IIT students or used by the college decades ago, before anyone had put together the words *digital* and *technology*. A clock tower that must once have dwarfed the surrounding trees now stands in their shade atop the graceful arches of the museum building. In a nearby grove is a small square structure that was once a solitary confinement cell for the most troublesome advocates of Indian independence. It has been left intact as a shrine to those who sacrificed their freedom for their country.

After paying homage to the past, it was time to glimpse the future. Down the road from the old jail was the institute's biotechnology department, one of the newest faculties at the college. Nevertheless, the state-of-the-art laboratories and classrooms were housed in a weathered Soviet-style office block. Only an exterior sign gave any hint that cutting-edge work was being done within the moldy walls. Inside, graduate students milled about, preparing for a day's research in the lab. My guide handed me over to Professor S. K. Kundu, one of the school's leading researchers and teachers. A slight, bespectacled man, he told me the person I really had to meet was Chitrangada Acharya, a slim woman in her mid-twenties who was completing doctoral research on the genome of the wild Indian silkworm moth. Kundu was her mentor and thesis supervisor. He suggested she take me on a tour of the facility. "Take your time," he said. "I think you'll be surprised."

There was an elaborate ritual to go through first. The integrity of the lab's hermetically sealed atmosphere had to be maintained. We pulled on sterile booties and long white coats, and scrubbed our hands as thoroughly as if we were about to perform surgery. Inside the lab, signs everywhere warned of the dangers of contamination and urged us to "be clean, green and as sterile as possible." People walked around holding their hands in the air to avoid incidental contact with walls, furniture or clothing.

Standing in her lab coat in front of a rack of test tubes and beakers of colored liquid, Acharya told me she was a little bemused by my interest. I said I had asked to meet the best and brightest and she had been chosen. That produced an embarrassed laugh.

"I'm no genius," she said. "So you had better not build me up too much. It's all about the work we're doing here." She and Professor Kundu were silkworm enthusiasts and thought they were on the verge of a breakthrough. They said the Indian worm produced the toughest, most resilient strands of silk but had never been domesticated. Their research was aimed at leaping over the necessity for that.

"We'll replicate the genome in the lab and then use silkworm stem cells to do all sorts of amazing things," she said, her excitement palpable. Possible applications include growing artificial skin to help burn victims, creating microscopic membranes for use in nanotechnology and producing extremely lightweight fabrics with the tensile strength of steel. The research was a joint project with Tufts University in Boston, and both Acharya and Kundu traveled between India and the American eastern seaboard several times a year with microscopic silkworm genes in their carry-on luggage. "Or at least the slides and culture dishes," she said. "I wonder if the customs agents know what they're looking at when they search our bags," she laughed as we headed for the office of the head of biotechnology, Dr. Satyahari Dey.

Here was a man whose work was somewhat less lofty than that of the students and teachers bent over their microscopes. Dey was an unabashed booster of the IIT system and he could launch his latest spiel at the drop of a laboratory hair net. His dream, he said, was to build a biotechnology park alongside the campus, and he had a model in mind.

"Look how important Stanford University is for Silicon Valley," Dey said, "and look how the business environment enables so much by cashing in on the spin-offs from pure academic research."

This was clearly a pitch he made on a regular basis and he slipped into it easily. "We collaborate with industry," he said. "We use our alumni connections and we build a biotech park here in Kharagpur with links to the institute. [Industry] provides the money, we provide brainpower and research viability. This will be so good for the town. Good jobs, schools and opportunities for local people." Dey pointed out the window as he spoke. Unlike in India's big cities, he said, there was no air pollution here. There was hardly any crime, and new schools were being built all the time. It was the perfect location for families, and the new highway and high-speed rail connections meant that Calcutta was just an hour or two away. Suddenly Kharagpur began to make sense as the site of a lofty seat of scientific research and learning.

"Eventually, there'll be an airport with international connections. This will bring global talent to the companies that set up shop here. Everyone will benefit." He spoke with the enthusiasm of a natural salesman. So many projects, he said, had industrial, medical or scientific relevance to major companies. It wasn't hard to share his passion, and I left his office for another tour of laboratories convinced that he was on to a winner of an idea. Biotech Valley in eastern India.

It turned out that IIT's graduate students were specialists in finding creative new ways of using common Indian species of plants, insects and animals. Students in the lab next to Dey's office were minutely examining the genes of Indian strains of pineapple and the sandalwood tree. A soft-spoken woman from Calcutta, Ratna Chitturvedi, was the sandalwood specialist. We found her standing in front of a machine that was shaking a glass container of murky, brown liquid. She explained that certain substances found in sandalwood oil, extracted at the molecular level, could be used to grow

human proteins, and this had applications in all sorts of medical research, including slowing skin aging and coping with HIV/AIDS.
That sort of work was very well funded in other countries, she explained, so she'd probably aim for a job with an American pharmaceutical company or research institution when her studies were over.
But not for long.

"I don't want to settle in the U.S., not at all," she said. "It's a means
to an end." Chitturvedi's immediate goal was to spend more time on
her research while receiving a decent salary. India's biotechnology sector did not yet provide the opportunity to do this. She talked of saving some money and being exposed to the new ideas that are
constantly being generated in U.S. research, funded by both private
and public money. But her plans were clear: "After America, I'll come
back to India, to my home state, Bengal, and do my work here," she
said, emphatically. "I'll start my own company if I have to. This is the
dream we all have in this lab."

IIT offered its students more than science and engineering degrees. At the Vinod Gupta School of Management, housed in a striking building based on the hanging gardens of Babylon and named
for a wealthy benefactor and alumnus who now made his home in
Lincoln, Nebraska, I met Professor Kalyan Guin. Jovial and bearded,
he said he had trained as an engineer, "but not at IIT. I wasn't smart
enough to get in." He worked for several years at a huge government-
run steel mill in the Indian state of Orissa before deciding on a change
of career. He looked around and then persuaded the board of IIT
Kharagpur to hire him as a lecturer in management. "Because I decided that managers run things, not engineers. If you want to make
any changes on this planet, you have to have management skills. And
we Indians have huge potential to be great managers."

I asked him why. To a casual observer, India was chaotic and confused, and definitely not the most well-managed country in the world.
He laughed. "You're right. Many things are not well managed at all.
But don't judge us by our governments or our public behavior. Consider our private lives. We're more than one billion people. We have
hundreds of thousands of enterprises, from one-man shops to steel
mills employing a *lakh* [one hundred thousand], and our daily life is
a constant struggle to navigate crowds, crises and family matters.
India is so diverse that it's no exaggeration to say that management is

in our blood." This, Guin said, gave Indians innate management skills that only needed to be drawn out and developed in the classroom and on the job.

That night as I relaxed in an austere room at the Technology Guest House, I pondered what I'd seen. The IIT Kharagpur campus was not particularly impressive in any physical sense. Take my living quarters for the night. Could I get the Internet to work in the Technology Guest House? I could not. Was there hot water in the shower? There was not. Was there a computerized reservation system for the visiting scholars, officials and others who bedded down here for the night? No, there was not. Aside from the Vinod Gupta hanging gardens building and the venerable former jail that served as the museum, the campus architecture was unexceptional. Exteriors were weathered and streaked with moss. Inside, the offices were dingy and small, and the corridors of the administration block exuded a slight pong of mildew. This could be blamed either on the intensely humid climate of Bengal or the less-than-diligent attention paid to maintenance by the Communist Party–affiliated unionized workers who ran campus services. The staff in the public relations department who handled my visit were friendly and helpful but had no clue what features of IIT Kharagpur would be of interest to a visitor. In the end, though fiercely protective of academic autonomy, the Indian Institutes of Technology were government bodies and suffered from many of the same drawbacks that afflicted other bureaucratic institutions, whatever the rapturous rhetoric that framed Indian discussion of them.

So far, so bad. But then there were the people. They were remarkable. Students and professors alike were focused and intelligent. This was undoubtedly the best and brightest among more than a billion people. The IIT entrance exam was a tiny, almost impenetrable valve at the top of a deep well of human potential. The few who squeezed through were as good a group of intellects and business talent as could be found anywhere. It was only natural that such high fliers would go on to be titans of business, banking, biotech and the computer industry. The image the IIT graduates convey conflicts with the conventional view of India. A country that is home to 40 percent of the illiterate people in the world, where fewer than half of the females over eighteen can read or write, at the same time contributes hundreds of highly motivated graduates every year to the global elite.

I could see how top talent could be filtered from such a mass of potential. But now it was time to explore the contrasts, the extremes of Indian life—to delve into history to see what precedents there were for Indian excellence on such a scale. I left Kharagpur the next morning bound for a place that was both a modern heart of darkness—deprived, poor and violent—and the seat of an ancient culture that had produced its own version of an IIT, an institute of higher learning that spread revolutionary thinking around the world more than a millennium ago.

Bihar is about an hour's journey by air from Calcutta. Any Indian will tell you that it's the poorest, most backward, corruption-riddled and poorly administered state in the country. It is the "Bi" in Ashish Bose's BIMARU, the first of the four sickly states. I boarded my flight at what used to be called Dum Dum Airport, after the suburb where the dumdum bullet was invented. Now it's named after a local hero, Subhas Chandra Bose, reviled in Britain to this day for his support for Japanese forces that attempted to take over India during World War II. We flew west on a spectacularly clear day, and I divided my time between peering out at the lush, green land below and leafing through a book about the poisonous politics of Bihar written by the journalist and native Bihari Sankarshan Thakur.

In the opening chapter, Thakur paraphrases British writer Jeanette Winterson:

> What of Bihar then? What do we say of Bihar? What do we say of a state itself so punched and blown it is not even supposed to feel pain? What do we say of a state so inured to wretchedness it refuses now to convey it or complain? How do we tell the story of a people who have stopped telling, who think there is no point anymore? *Yeh bihar hai, yahan sab kuchh chalta hai.* This is Bihar, everything goes. Nothing shocks.[1]

Bihar occupies an area about the size of Indiana. More than eighty-three million people live within its boundaries. The state is bisected by the River Ganges, and further subdivided by tributaries that flow down from the Himalayas, making the land among India's most well watered—and flood-prone. It's one of those places where, proverbially, a stick thrust into the ground will take root and become a tree, so fertile is the soil. It has a big sugar industry and one of the country's largest oil refineries. Over the years, Bihar has been something of a cauldron for new political ideas and movements. The fertile soil along the banks of the Ganges has nurtured political campaigns that have destabilized and toppled national governments. It has given birth to gritty, often violence-prone movements by low-caste Hindus demanding social justice. Bihari people seem to have a talent for organization and agitation. All things considered, this should be one of India's richest, most highly developed states, but the opposite is true. Most people in Bihar are grotesquely poor, and the quality of governance has long been among the worst in India.

Until 2005, much of the blame for these dire conditions had settled on the shoulders of Lalu Prasad Yadav, who governed the state for more than a decade as both chief minister and, as mentioned earlier, as the power behind a throne occupied by his wife. For all his faults, Lalu Prasad is an interesting man. He is from a caste of traditional cattle herders often spoken of derisively, by those who occupy loftier positions in the Hindu hierarchy, as "milkmen." He entered politics as an unapologetic caste warrior and parlayed his humble upbringing into an alliance of traditionally deprived communities, a powerbase second to none in contemporary India. Lalu's earthy demeanor and rabble-rousing style appealed to members of his own caste, but also to Bihar's downtrodden Muslim population and other excluded communities. His first election victory, in 1990, was seen by many in India as a ray of hope. His campaign mantra was "social justice," and he moved quickly to appoint his own people to government posts, displacing Brahmins and other upper-caste officials. But Lalu's various terms in office showed him to be capricious and concerned more with consolidating his power than with governing his people. Bihar slipped badly on his watch, and Lalu's defeat in a state election in November 2005 was greeted by many as a welcome opportunity for the state to make a fresh start. What can never be overlooked in India is the local belief in rebirth, in new opportunities arising from disaster or loss. These are central concepts in the Hindu philosophy most Indians follow. In this instance, both Lalu and Bihar were reincarnated. The state became more peaceful and seems to be better governed. Lalu Prasad was rehabilitated after becoming India's railways minister and running the country's perpetually loss-making rail network at a profit. That unexpected success has propelled him to a visiting professorship at the business school equivalent of the IITs, the Indian Institute of Management, in the western city of Ahmadabad. He remains one of the country's most important—and colorful—power brokers and political leaders.

I drove south from the airport at Patna, Bihar's sprawling and chaotic capital, as people were voting in that 2005 election to the state assembly. At the start of the journey, hardly any vehicles were on the road. Almost all motor traffic had been banned by election authorities because cars, trucks and motorcycles were too often used by vote-rigging gangs to escape from the police. A special permit got me a car and ensured passage through the numerous police checkpoints. Patna's nightmarish urban sprawl, quiet for once in the absence of vehicles, soon gave way to the fecund riverine landscape of central Bihar, richly green but pockmarked by the modern-day misery of its people. Poverty seemed even more acute in Bihari villages, where the poorest of the poor washed themselves under roadside water taps, oblivious to the dust raised by passing vehicles. My car rumbled through Jehanabad, a fly-blown town an hour outside Patna. A few days before, the local jail had been attacked by about a thousand armed Maoist guerrillas whose movement had supposedly sprung up to rectify the vast inequities of Bihari society. The Maoists freed hundreds of prisoners, including many of their comrades, and killed seven people, mostly police and prison guards. Now Jehanabad was an armed camp, with soldiers deployed everywhere and the gaping wound in the wall of the prison a reminder that revolutionary groups were out there, and capable of doing serious damage.

My destination that night was the temple town of Bodh Gaya, where the Buddha is said to have had his revelation that human suffering can be overcome by meditation and the practice of focused compassion. Among my companions on the road that day were Buddhist monks from Tibet and pilgrims from Sri Lanka. From its beginnings in India, Buddhism spread to Tibet, China, Japan, Burma, Siam (now Thailand) and Ceylon (Sri Lanka). Buddhist ideas appear in Greek and Roman writing and are thought to have inspired other key thinkers of the age. At the time of Buddha's preaching, the area south of the Ganges in what is today Bihar was home to some of the more advanced nation-states in Asia. There were philosopher-kings and wandering mendicants, and a flourishing market economy that traded in goods from all across the known world. There was also a university called Nalanda that was nothing less than the IIT of its time.

Remarkably, all of these achievements disappeared from the historical record for nearly seven hundred years. Buddhism effectively vanished from India in about the eleventh century. New conquerors took over, more tenacious forms of Hinduism reasserted themselves, and earlier religious practices were eclipsed. Languages were lost as well, the flowing scripts of early Buddhist civilizations becoming cryptic codes that kept their secrets locked tight. Those temples that weren't converted for Hindu worship were slowly buried under the dust and detritus of daily life. Where once there had been thousands of stupas—conical spired shrines housing Buddha statues—there now were anonymous mounds, mined for stone and brick whenever a local dynast needed building materials. It was only through the stubborn detective work of eighteenth- and nineteenth-century British archaeologists and scholars that Buddhism's Indian origins were rediscovered.

Before the archaeologists' and scholars' work, Bodh Gaya was believed to be a Hindu temple town. Until those mostly amateur and self-trained British scholars deciphered the inscriptions they uncovered at the site, only a few pilgrims from Buddhist lands such as Burma and Sri Lanka knew the significance of the towering structure at the heart of Bodh Gaya. It was believed by most that the building was yet another Hindu temple in a landscape of gods, demons and places of worship. Today, Bodh Gaya is a bustling, well-developed place of bespoke places of worship and guesthouses catering to people from across Asia with rituals and food familiar to them from home.

The central bazaar was dark when I arrived: power cuts were a routine occurrence in Bihar. Gossip in the tea shops was all about the election and how smoothly the voting had gone. One man told me that dozens had been killed the last time Bihar went to the polls, so he was going to the main Maha Bodha temple tomorrow to give thanks for a peaceful voting day. I drank my lemon tea and wandered out into the night, wondering whether to visit the main temple right then or wait until dawn, when waves of the devout would come to pray and prostrate themselves. In the distance, I heard the slow, rhythmic thunder of Japanese *taiko* drums and sat and listened to them instead. It was a magical moment. Perched on an abandoned wooden cart by the roadside, I let my mind drift as dark-robed Zen monks inside the Japanese compound led worshippers in their nightly rituals. There were few other sounds to disturb my reverie. Back at my hotel, the drumming lulled me to sleep and I dreamt of ancient processions across a landscape without concrete, cars or clouds of urban pollution.

I awoke at first light and meandered, sleepy but intrigued, over to the place where a world religion had been founded. A group of Sri Lankan Buddhists on their way to morning prayers filed out of a *dharamsala,* a pilgrims' place of rest. It was bitterly cold, just a few degrees above freezing, and the Sri Lankans were shivering despite their woolen hats, leggings, scarves, long coats and mittens. They were obviously used to more tropical climes. By contrast, Burmese monks wandered by wearing only sarongs and saffron scarves across their bare chests. Murmuring Buddhist texts, they were perhaps kept oblivious to the cold by the intensity of their ritualistic devotion. There were also plenty of Indian pilgrims and a group of schoolchildren who I later discovered had once been beggars. Dressed in red and gray tunics, the youngsters lined up outside the temple. A few had twisted limbs, or walked on all fours with backs arched high. Their teacher called them to order. A remarkable French woman who called herself Mummy-ji, she told me that these were children who'd been deliberately maimed by beggar-pimps, eager to exploit the revulsion and guilt of the able-bodied.

Many Indians consider the giving of alms at a place of worship a holy act that can result in a better life in the next incarnation. Working beggars know that piety offers rich pickings, so they turn up in droves at every Indian temple and pilgrimage site. It can be rather disturbing to have to run the beggars' gauntlet—past the armless, the legless, the fingerless, the blind, the disfigured and the pathetic—to get inside the temple. They are fiercely competitive and to give can be a perilous exercise. A one-rupee coin in a tin cup or a child's grubby fingers leads to a scrum of beggars with leprous faces and dirty hands demanding the same. "Saar, please, rupee saar, rupee for bay-bee . . ." Women waved infants at passing pilgrims, and men without legs approached at speed, traveling on stumps wrapped in rags and gnarled, calloused hands. They could easily outpace able-bodied temple visitors and were experts at extracting donations. It was, after all, how they earned their precarious living. Ahead was supposed to lie a spiritual, contemplative experience, but all too often one arrived at the temple unsettled by a range of conflicting feelings—guilt, annoyance, sadness, anger, irritation and pity.

The night before, I had hired Mukesh Sinha to be my guide. He was about thirty years old, slight and handsome. He had taught himself English and spent time trying to figure out what tourists wanted from their travels in India. He was also a bit of an expert in the ways of beggars, and he helped spread the alms around so as to cause the least unpleasant scene. Inside the temple, Mummy-ji's kids, on a day trip from their school in a nearby village, walked and crawled in long straight lines past the Buddha statues and the multi-national swirl of the pilgrims. In their crisp school uniforms, they were orderly and quiet but couldn't help gaping at some of the more exotic worshippers. Korean devotees in black robes and white sashes were of particular interest to the kids. So were Nepali Newars in tawny orange from Kathmandu and shaven-headed nuns from Tibet who looked like Mummy-ji, save for their Mongol features. All around the main spire of the temple, in a garden strewn with small shrines and pagodas, dozens of men and women perched on polished wooden boards, their hands wrapped with cloth so that they could easily perform the ten or twelve thousand full-length prostrations that devout practitioners do to acquire merit. One man mumbled his count in English: "nine thousand, seven hundred and two; nine thousand, seven hundred and three; nine . . ." Behind the temple, a throne of cut glass under the spreading limbs of a fig tree marked the spot where the Buddha gained his insight about human suffering. Many visitors to the shrine believe that this is the same tree that sheltered Buddha from the sun through his forty days of meditation, but that would make it at least twenty-five hundred years old, a rather unlikely lifespan for that particularly species of fig. The Sri Lankans whom I'd earlier seen shivering by their guest-house were sitting near the tree, listening to a prayer leader preach a sermon about the route to Nirvana, the escape from suffering and rebirth.

Later that day, Mukesh and I set out for Nalanda via the town of Rajgir, the former capital of the kingdom that controlled Bodh Gaya when Buddha began to preach his new religion. We rumbled away in a white Tata Sumo, an Indian version of a sport-utility vehicle, but without an SUV's suspension, power steering or drive train. It was largely flat in this part of Bihar. In fact, across the Gangetic plains of North India, there was little variation in the landscape. Aside from the odd protrusion of Paleolithic granite, the land was as flat as the Great Plains of North America. It was dusty now in the dry season; the monsoon rains would bring thick mud and occasional flooding, but by mid-morning you could see for miles. Mukesh pointed out a range of hills ahead and told me that was Rajgir. "Magadha in Buddha's time," he added, referring to the town's name when it was the seat of a vast empire. He had read the tourist pamphlets and could recite the story of Buddha's journeys from memory. I asked him if he was a Buddhist and he looked puzzled. No, he explained, he was a Hindu. "Only foreigners are Buddhists," he said, and we launched into a theological discussion. Interestingly, to many Indian Hindus, Buddhism is a religion practiced by people from other lands who have converted from their original faiths. Hinduism, by contrast, does not countenance converts. Only people born into Hindu lineages from India, Nepal and the Indonesian island of Bali can be Hindus themselves, or so goes the belief.

From bare, flat fields, the land suddenly reared up in a ring of high stone hills broken by gaps in only two or three places—a natural fortress and obvious site for the capital city of a martial empire, founded by a warrior king nearly three thousand years earlier. We arrived at a cleft in the rocks and drove through a somewhat tacky gate welcoming us to the "Land of Buddha." Buddhism may not have been much practiced by the locals down here in south central Bihar, but it was a thriving business. There were signs in English and Japanese for visitors, as well as in Hindi for those Indian pilgrims who considered Buddhism a part of their own pantheon of beliefs. Mukesh took me to several of the archaeological sites inside the rampart of hills: to hand-carved caves where Buddha had supposedly meditated; to the ruins of a prison where the founder of Magadha, King Bimisara, had been held captive and was deliberately starved to death by his son; and to a couple of partially excavated temples built nearly a thousand years before the birth of Christ. Atop one of the ridges was a brand-new Japanese-built "peace pagoda," a white concrete dome with a golden spire at the summit. Outside, a priest argued fruitlessly with armed policemen who insisted on carrying their weapons as they went in to pray.

From such a high vantage point, the boundaries of the ancient Magadha, later known as Rajagriha, now Rajgir, were obvious. A muscular rampart of boulders and dried mud cut through the grassy plain north of the rocky hills, protecting what had been the newer section of the city from bandits and marauding armies. The seat of the old kingdom, now little more than clusters of ruins and tourist signboards, had lain within the cliffs and their granite redoubt. Roads extended into the hazy middle distance. Important trade routes once converged here. Magadha had been one of the richest nation-states of its day. It was also where the first council of Buddhism met not long after Buddha's death to begin codifying the teachings of the faith.

The king, Bimisara, whose son had grotesquely murdered him by denying him food, had been an important patron to Buddha. The monarch's growing interest in the new, nonviolent faith was probably the death of him. While King Bimisara dabbled in religion, his enemies, largely bastard sons born of a series of courtesans and women of royal blood, ganged up and dislodged him from the throne. Important and powerful as it was, Rajgir had one big disadvantage. It lacked a steady water supply. One of Bimisara's descendants, who himself went on to found a major Hindu dynasty, moved the capital of Magadha to what is today Patna, on the banks of the Ganges. The old city withered to the village that still stands. With the rediscovery of Buddhism's roots by British savants and scholars two centuries ago, the community slowly revived from a sleepy farming hamlet to a place of pilgrimage and, latterly, a tourist destination.

I was walking slowly down the winding path from the hilltop peace pagoda, contemplating ancient goings-on, when I realized I was hungry. It was lunchtime and there was an ulterior motive for coming to Rajgir. My guidebook had promised that the best sushi in central India was to be found here.

Not long ago, this was something unheard of in India: the cuisine of Japan outside a big city. Usually, to travel in the hinterland of India is to eat only curry, rice and occasionally naan or roti. But Japanese

Buddhists and businesses have been investing in Indian Buddhism for years. They give money for the restoration of temples and historic sites and build monasteries at places such as Bodh Gaya. Japanese tourists in large numbers visit both Buddhist sites and the more usual Indian tourist destinations. They are notoriously fussy about food, preferring their national dishes to anyone else's, and they insist on the highest standards of hygiene and freshness. Thus, the existence of the Indo Hokke Hotel at Rajgir can be easily explained, even though it is a long way over rough and occasionally dangerous roads from the sort of urban comforts and attractions that usually draw middle-class foreign tourists.

The exterior of the hotel was unmistakably Japanese. A series of cylinders housed stairwells between the two stories and channeled fresh air into the hallways and sleeping areas. Most of the rooms at the hotel were Japanese-style as well, featuring tatami mats, low tables, and hip baths with a shower alongside so one can get clean before one bathes. A few Western-style rooms were on offer, just in case visitors didn't want to sit on the floor and sip their carefully prepared tea. Just off the lobby was a round, echoey chamber with a vaulted roof that was called the "temple," though it bore no mark or badge of any faith. I sat for a moment in its silence, but my stomach was grumbling too much for meditation. It was time to go to the Lotus restaurant.

My lunch of miso soup, prawns with white radish and sashimi, flown in that day by small plane from Calcutta, was splendid, as was the chilled Indian Kingfisher beer to wash it all down. My reflections since the trip to Kharagpur and IIT had turned often on the dramatic contrasts that are everywhere in India, and here was another: an incongruous yet wonderful meal amid the ruins of Bihar's past glory.

Just up the road from the Lotus was Nalanda, my final destination. The Chinese traveler Huang Tsang visited the university in the seventh century, about two hundred years after its founding, and his writings are the source of almost all our information about daily life within its hallowed halls. Huang wrote of a student body ten thousand strong, all of them men. A thousand teachers, all Buddhist monks, taught subjects such as mathematics, logic, grammar, languages, religion and medicine. As at IIT, there was a rigorous entrance exam at Nalanda, or so Huang wrote. The contents of the test remain a historical mystery. Buddhist tradition encouraged students to challenge accepted dogma, so Nalanda's students would have enjoyed real intellectual freedom. Iconoclastic thinking was encouraged. Some of the wilder, more esoteric forms of Buddhism practiced in Tibet and elsewhere are thought to have originated at Nalanda. But the school is also linked to other sects and aspects of the faith.

We drove for some time through Rajgir's outskirts—the low cubical concrete bazaars that are India's version of strip malls—before arriving at a long stone wall, lined as always with trinket sellers and more pilgrim-savvy beggars. Inside was the restored archaeological site of Nalanda. We were early, so we sat in chairs next to the security guard's hut and contemplated the place from a distance. Muslim invaders, fired by righteous fury at local religions that defied their monotheism, wrecked the buildings in the twelfth century. This was the event that effectively snuffed out Buddhism in India until modern times. There was one positive side effect: the scattered monks, students and seminarians journeyed far and wide to spread the latest Buddhist teachings through Asia.

Across the manicured landscape, red brick structures loomed over a low brownish wall. The British amateur historian and founder of the Archaeological Survey of India, Sir Alexander Cunningham, came here in 1862. Cunningham was one of the great figures of Indian archaeology and did much to uncover long-lost secrets of the country's Buddhist past. Nalanda was his greatest discovery. He traveled from Rajgir, following a translation of Huang Tsang's thousand-year-old account of the journey between Magadha and the Buddhist university half a day's walk to the north. When Cunningham came to a place known simply as Baragaon, "big village," he paused. There, across tilled earth and rice fields, he beheld something marvelous. According to his written account, there were "numerous masses of brick ruins, among which is a row of lofty conical mounds running north and south. These high mounds are the remains of gigantic temples attached to the famous monastery." In the footsteps of a Chinese monk from a millennium ago, the British scholar found one of the proudest sites of Indian archaeology.

For centuries, local people and passing armies had mined the bricks from the ruined temples to build roads and walls between fields. Statues and other artworks had either been destroyed or looted.

But carved foundations stones were still intact, and from these Cunningham and his successors lovingly restored Nalanda until it began to resemble the vast complex it had been in its day. Inside, numerous monks' cells and students' rooms opened onto courtyards that apparently served as open-air classrooms. There were kitchens and dining halls, and the whole institution was evidently divided into what might today be called colleges: group residences with their own teaching areas. The tall building most visible from outside was apparently a library. It was surrounded by painstakingly restored Buddha statues and stupas. All the books and most of the decorative art that once stood in the sculpture gardens and wall niches around the library had been destroyed when the monastery was sacked, but the oral knowledge had escaped with the monks who weren't put to the sword by righteous Muslim warriors. I sat on a low wall in one of the teaching compounds and tried to imagine what it would have been like more than a thousand years ago to attend the greatest university of the day. It's not hard to contemplate the academic side of life at Nalanda. At its more esoteric margins, Buddhism takes a view of the universe that's not far off the latest thinking in theoretical physics. Great Buddhist philosophers postulated centuries ago that matter was composed of small particles that couldn't be subdivided—probably the first reference to atoms. They taught that the universe had come into being through natural phenomena, not as a deliberate act of creation by a supernatural being—more big bang than Garden of Eden. Buddhist concepts of mindfulness and the beneficial effects of meditation are being verified by neuroscience and others who study the workings of the human brain. It's not much of a leap to compare this place to the biotechnology laboratory back in Kharagpur.

I had traveled far. Not so much in physical distance, but through time and levels of development. Bihar was modern India's shame, IIT Kharagpur its pride and joy. Yet Bihar had once been a glorious place, the intellectual and economic powerhouse of ancient India. The well-watered land along the River Ganges was still home to more than a third of all Indians, but the sacred waters flowed past misery, corruption and lives robbed of all dignity. Few people in the world lived with such reminders of history as the citizens of India. Those fortunate enough to study their country's past were aware that greatness had once existed here. The long-vanished monk-scholars of Nalanda no longer imparted wisdom and insight to the students of Asia. Bihar's main university, in Patna, was a politicized joke, a place of armed student unions and terrorized teachers who granted degrees through coercion as often as not. Beyond the IITs, there were few Nalandas.

It's undeniable that India's education system remains badly in need of attention. Primary schools are of inconsistent quality and standards. High schools are often crowded and lack resources; few have science laboratories or libraries that come close to meeting the needs of students following an advanced curriculum. Universities, especially the large, state-run institutions that offer a multitude of disciplines, are little better. Even those that have funds and decent facilities are often wracked by party politics. Indian political parties recruit heavily in colleges and universities, with the result that campus life is often paralyzed by clashes between student factions. The quality of education suffers accordingly. Not surprisingly, privately run institutions of learning are springing up to meet the demand from middle-class parents who want their children educated to the best standard available. In the capital, New Delhi, the best private high schools have waiting lists that are years long. School administrators have been accused of accepting bribes to give preference to particular students vying for a place, or giving in to threats of violence. The best of them have transparent, iron-clad admissions policies and take pride in their students and their achievements. Others are not so fussy, and India's lively press and television news channels frequently report on school scandals and parental outrage at shoddy standards and corruption.

Among the many challenges faced by policymakers is the growing demand for education and the stresses and strains this demand places on the public system. India's modern successes have much to do with the quality of education at its elite universities and the overall attitude toward education taken by parents and society as a whole. Families work toward a single goal: educating the children to the best standard possible. But the public sector hasn't kept its part of the bargain. The early idealism that led to the founding of IIT has not been replicated by more recent governments. If India's modern progress isn't to be an illusory phenomenon that flares briefly and then stalls amid continuing demographic and economic problems, getting education right is crucial. More attention and resources must be paid to primary and secondary schools, and a system of regulation put in place that both monitors and enables private-sector provision of education. More elite institutions such as IIT are needed, and existing universities need to be rescued from the debilitating effect of partisan politics as well. Both the pay and the accountability of the teaching staff need to be improved. Again, the private sector needs to be given the chance to invest in universities, either as profit-making ventures or philanthropy. If IIT Kharagpur, and not Bihar, is to be the model for the future, then much needs to be done, and urgently.

9

HINDUISM AND
ITS DISCONTENTS

Strength amid Weakness

ACCORDING TO ITS CONSTITUTION, India is a secular country, but religion is omnipresent. Everywhere there are Hindu temples, Muslim mosques, Buddhist stupas, Christian churches, Jewish synagogues, towers of silence where the Parsee community leaves its dead to be devoured by vultures, and countless shrines to holy men and women of uncertain provenance. On festival days, cars and computers are honored with religious ceremonies. Cows amble freely in the streets, their bovine foreheads streaked with red vermillion paste as a mark of their holy status. On the sacred Shia Muslim day of Ashura, the most intense devotees flail their bare skin with barbed hooks, splattering blood and bits of flesh everywhere. Others pound their chests with their hands and wail, tears streaming from their eyes. In the mountainous vale of Kashmir, a small cult believes that Jesus Christ survived his crucifixion and traveled east before his death. A compact white marble building in Kashmir's summer capital, Srinagar, is said to be the tomb of Jesus. Elsewhere, people believe that the gods walk the earth. Living deities such as the elaborately coiffed South Indian mystic Sai Baba, who uses his holy powers to produce sacred ash, something called ectoplasm and expensive watches from mid-air, has

tens of millions of devotees. The Gnostic, Syrian and Nestorian variations of Christianity are followed avidly in South India. Believers claim
that Thomas the Apostle brought Christianity to Indian shores in AD
42, before Greek and Roman scribes began writing down the gospel.

Official statistics offer a somewhat drier picture of India's spiritual landscape. About 82 percent of the population, more than 800
million people, is said to be Hindu. India is proud of having the
world's second-largest population of Muslims. At around 160 to 170
million, they supposedly outnumber adherents of Islam in neighboring Pakistan. There are around 26 million Christians and 25 million
Sikhs. Buddhism is a small but growing faith with some 12 million
followers, a number that swells as low-caste Hindus convert to escape
their status on the caste ladder. There are countless other small religious communities in India. Zoroastrianism, an ancient monotheistic
faith that originated in Iran, is now mostly found in India, with its
prosperous, well-educated and worldly Parsee community. There are
fewer than a hundred thousand Zoroastrians in India these days, as
intermarriage and a low birth rate threaten them with demographic
extinction. In the remote northeastern state of Mizoram, there are
people who say they are Jews, and rabbis in Jerusalem have recognized
their claim to being one of the ten lost tribes of Israel.

India's official policy of secularism is meant to promote communal harmony among these many faiths and forms of worship. It
hasn't always been effective. Hindus and Muslims have clashed and
shed each other's blood on many occasions. The worst interfaith carnage took place at the time of the partition in 1947. All too often since
then, especially when tensions are high between India and Pakistan,
India's two largest religious groups have been at odds. The other non-
Hindu religious communities are much too small for even the most
militant Hindu radicals to consider them a threat, though conversion
to Christianity among the poor and low-caste remains controversial.
An Australian missionary and his two young sons were attacked and
burnt to death by a Hindu mob in eastern India in 1998, a crime that
some on the Hindu right still say was justified.

Another point of controversy is whether the ubiquity of religion
in India means that Indians are somehow more spiritual than other
peoples. Some in India believe that this is the case. They claim that the
ancient faith of Hinduism was long the most advanced form of wor-

ship and spirituality on the planet, not to mention deeply rooted in science and precise observation and analysis of the natural world. Commentators such as the diplomat and author Pavan K. Varma feel differently, at least on the matter of spiritualism. Varma's bestselling book from 2004, *Being Indian,* speculates that Hindus regard their faith as merely another tool to achieve material well-being and social status. Varma is nothing if not robust and unflinching when he looks at his own people. He says that Indians are acutely aware of the role of power in human relations. Hinduism helps place people in categories that give or deny them access to power, and Hindus adjust their behavior accordingly. The spiritual nature of the faith comes a distant second to these more practical applications. But there is one place in India where the living faith of most Indians seems deeply ensconced in the realm of the spirit, a place where any devout Hindu, given the opportunity, would go to die.

The holy city of Varanasi is one of the oldest continually inhabited urban areas on earth. Scholars think people have been living there for five thousand years or more. On one of his periodic jaunts around the world, Mark Twain passed through Varanasi and commented that the city was "older than history, older than tradition, older even than legend, and looks twice as old as all of them put together." It still does. There are some outward signs of modernity: neon lights, a billboard advertising cell phones tacked onto the side of a temple. There are cars, electronics shops and computers, but they seem not to count for much here. They may all soon be forgotten while the piety and devotion that surrounded them grows ever more intense. In the teeming bazaars behind the ghats, or bathing platforms, that line the banks of the sacred River Ganges, all these temporal matters seem largely irrelevant. Time itself doesn't seem to matter. Here you might witness a funeral procession, with the corpse shrouded in silk and marigold garlands, borne on the shoulders of men chanting "God is truth." There, a Hindu holy man with fingernails almost a yard long, standing stark naked and blissful amid the chaos. Clouds of cannabis smoke billow from government-run hashish shops. Cows, thought by Hindus to be the reincarnated souls of men and women who have lived the purest lives, wander unmolested through the vegetable market, munching as they go on carrots, potatoes and bunches of spinach. They may be sacred, but the vendors shoo them away when they can, occasionally with a rather powerful shove and an obscene word or two.

Indians have many different names for Varanasi. Each reveals a facet of its religious and historical significance. Devout Hindus speak of Kashi, one of the original temple towns mentioned in ancient scriptures. The British, chronically unable to pronounce any words that came from beyond their sceptered isle, called the place Benares or Banaras. Well-read Hindus might say Anandavana, the forest of bliss. They may also mention that the Hindu deity Shiva is believed to be a resident, hence the name Rudravasa, the place where Shiva lives. The modern name, Varanasi, is the simplest and least poetic of the city's titles. It merely refers to two small Gangetic tributaries that define the urban area, the Varun and the Nasi.

It was one of those magical days of early summer in North India's most intensely spiritual city. The sun was just above the horizon but already the crowded banks of the River Ganges were flooded with golden light. The merest wisp of a breeze was blowing. It would soon die off in the mid-morning heat. All around me I could hear the chants, murmurs and general noise of devout Hindus intent on cleansing themselves of sin in the sacred waters of the Ganges. Riverside loudspeakers mounted on rough wooden poles crackled into life. Some broadcast Hindu hymns, others the latest falsetto hits from the Bollywood film and dream machine. The pilgrims carried on regardless.

A man dressed in white robes sat at a metal table outside the temple that his family has helped run for generations. As he spoke, he gestured with his hands, drawing patterns on the table top, stopping occasionally to ponder before resuming his discourse. Veer Badra Mishra is one of India's leading environmentalists when he's not carrying out his official duties as *mahant,* or head priest, of the Tulsi Ghat temple. People come from all over India—indeed, from around the world—to call on him and listen to his ideas for cleaning up the holy river that runs through Varanasi. A trained engineer and scientist, Veer Badra Mishra often finds himself telling foreign callers about his Hindu faith.

"You see, it's not right to think of it as a religion," he said. "It's so much more. It's a way of life, yes, so say many people in India who try to be nationalist about Hinduism and say that even the Muslims and

Christians are Hindus still, no matter how they worship. But that's not what I mean, no. It's not a way of life either, as many will tell you. It's a way to pass through life and see what's on the other side. It's a million, million ways to do that. It's infinite."

There are, Mishra explains, some twenty-five branches of Hindu belief that he has managed to identify through his research. Many of them, he says, are exclusive of each other, let alone of other forms of belief. Ten or twelve are overtly atheist: they reject the existence of supernatural deities. Others allow for the existence of billions of gods and goddesses. A few are monotheistic or so deeply esoteric that it's hard to ascribe any dogmatic beliefs or ritual sense to them.

"It's as if various sects of Christians didn't agree on the divinity of Christ or even his existence but went on calling themselves Christians anyway, in huge numbers. It's unthinkable. This is no religion. This is no way of life. This is India and this is how we do things."

As a priest who basically inherited his vocation, Mishra is clearly a devout believer himself. Asked what particular strand of Hinduism he follows or believes in, he smiles and avoids giving a firm answer. He explains that dogma matters less than intent and practice. That morning had begun for him as every day does, with a cleansing bath in the sacred River Ganges. That had taken place from a ghat, a flight of stairs on the riverbank, leading from street level down into the water, which also doubled as a bathing platform. As it flows through Varanasi, the Ganges is entirely contained by ghats. At festival times, the ghats are lined by hundreds of thousands of devotees, men, women and children. Many popular temple ghats are crowded year round. Those people offering prayers often sit crossed legged, murmuring verses from Hindu scripture. Others bathe or prepare elaborate arrays of flowers, food and candles to set on a lotus leaf and float down the current. At night the river is dotted with glowing, bobbing lights as these tiny boats drift downstream.

Mishra's bathing place was quieter than most public ghats. It is inside the temple that he and his family run, though it is open to the visitors who wander in and out as they please. Hinduism is nothing if not casual and accommodating. Mishra, then a spry man in his early seventies, slipped off his white robes, stepped knee-deep into the flowing water and faced toward the rising sun. His lips moved through a series of hymns and Hindu couplets as he prayed and slowly shuffled down the underwater steps of the ghat. When the water reached his shoulders, he drew in a deep breath, clamped his eyes and mouth tightly closed and eased his head underwater. The river flowed by. Flower petals, leaves and less identifiable bits from the offerings of pilgrims upstream drifted over the ripples on the surface of the water where Mishra submerged himself. There was an almost constant hum of people mumbling prayers and quietly chanting on the ghats to either side. They, too, were cleansing themselves of sin in the sacred waters.

Mishra surfaced, his eyes and mouth still shut until the water flowed from his full head of white hair, then he drew in a breath and popped under water a second time. About fifteen seconds passed before he came up again to breathe. Two more total immersions later, he backed, bowing, up the steps of the ghat and went to dry himself. The current is fairly swift outside Mishra's temple, but the water smells unpleasant, stagnant with a chemical taint. It's barely translucent, greenish brown in the sunlight, turbid and dark at night. Some four hundred million people live along the Ganges in North India, and the sheer impact of their lives on the holy river has been immense and harmful. Industrial waste, sewage and, of course, the ashes from cremations, and intact dead bodies thrown into the river have turned these flowing waters into a sacred sewer. No one knows this better than Veer Badra Mishra. For years he has campaigned to clean it up.

"All strains of Hinduism tell us that water is sacred, that we must care for the resources of the earth," Mishra observes, "but what do we do to the Ganges? We dump our sewers into it, making our holy river a toilet. We allow sugar mills, distilleries and chemical factories to pour in waste without exception, so long as the owner is politically connected. We throw dead bodies in and urinate, spit and foul the waters every day. So many of us in North India, we disrespect the Ganges, we ignore our scriptures, and then we ask God to save us from sin with a sacred bath in poison. That's what Hinduism has become."

Mishra's passion is based on his faith. And science. Every morning, true to his faith, he takes a toxic holy dip, not only, he says, to cleanse his sins but to leverage his prayers for the health of the river that he loves—his own offering to the gods, or godhead, of his carefully guarded personal belief system. Mishra hopes fervently that people change their attitudes toward the pollution of India's rivers. "If I open my mouth underwater I could die," he says, "so I tighten up my lips and nose and allow none of this so-called holy water into my mouth. It could kill me if I swallowed it. Certainly, I'd fall ill."

What Veer Badra Mishra is doing, worshipping by the riverside and then trying to save the river through activism and teaching, is true to his Hindu beliefs. For Hinduism is nothing if it isn't constantly changing, syncretic, open. The twenty-five strands of belief that Mishra described are neither conclusive nor widely accepted. Other scholars offer a variety of approaches to Hinduism. Most accept that there are three or four main schools of worship, with dozens of others that can be either folded into the main categories or regarded as separate.

Although gods seem to be everywhere in Hinduism, and most devotees, no matter the school, believe in supernatural beings, others would say that Hindu deities are largely metaphorical aspects of an overall divinity—a single godhead, an overarching collective spirituality that is ever present in humankind, in all forms of life. The earliest references to what became the Hindu faith speak of two central characteristics of the divine: *Brahman,* or god, and *atman,* or self. But these are often seen as unified. God is within. The answers lie in the self. The essence of divinity is in humans themselves, not in some supernatural overlord that has powers of creation and destruction. There is no Cartesian duality at the beginning of Hinduism. Body and soul are one. Tales of the myriad gods so well known today came much later. Still, even if their stories were intended as metaphor, the stories of Krishna, Sita, Ram, Brahma, Shiva and Vishnu have caught on. Over the centuries, many of those supernatural beings have become objects of worship or ritual focus in various parts of the Indian subcontinent. Cults have sprung up. They have fought with one another, merged with others and taken in outside influences from other faiths such as Islam, Christianity and locally based animism.

The writer and critic Pankaj Mishra argues that what passes for modern Hinduism can be traced to British and European scholars who codified the practices and culture of India as history. These outside scholars applied their own familiar models and rules in the process of interpreting ancient writings that had been intended for a far different purpose. In an essay that ruffled more than a few feathers when it was published in London's *New Statesman* in 2004, Mishra writes that Indians didn't even have a single label for their faith before foreigners began to study the ways of the subcontinent a few hundred years ago. In other words, there was no Hinduism. Instead, Mishra says, there were many local cults and forms of worship all over India. Some were larger movements, others strictly confined to place or time. These mixed and melded as people traveled but without the overall intent of creating an overarching theology, an infrastructure of faith. Hinduism, in short, is a work in progress and a relatively recent one at that.

"In the 18th century," Mishra writes, "the British were both appalled and fascinated by the excess of gods, sects and cults they found in India. It was similar to the pagan chaos that a Christian from the eastern provinces might have encountered in the west just before Constantine's conversion to Christianity. Like the powerful Christians in Rome, the British in India sought and imposed uniformity."[1]

Hinduism as it is defined today, both by Hindus and others, is marked by a series of vivid images of divine beings, largely drawn from two epics written between two and three thousand years ago, the *Ramayana* and the *Mahabharata*. These are tales of battle and intrigue that bear more than a little resemblance to Greek and Norse mythology. Gods have divine powers and supernatural stature, but their morals are anything but pure. They get drunk and cheat on their spouses. They kidnap, rape, murder and steal. They tell lies and urge their followers to take questionable courses of action. They use magic and guile by turns to defeat their enemies. These epic tales have entranced generations of Indians for millennia and their imagery has been the stuff of poetry, prose and, more recently, movies and television. In fact, TV versions of the two epics, made in the 1980s, became the world's most popular television programs, according to the *Guinness Book of World Records*. Each series had more than ninety episodes, about sixty hours of programming in total. The programs were made before computer-generated special effects became available, and some of the battle scenes and godly miracles can seem rather cheesy, but there can be no doubting the high drama and mass appeal of both series. They have been shown around the world and are still widely circulated on DVD and VHS tapes.

Whether on television or in text, the *Ramayana* and *Mahabharata* can best be described as religious instruction combined with entertainment. Scholars see them as deliberately authored oral histories intended to enrapture listeners and fill them with awe, while simultaneously amusing them. The *Bhagavad Gita,* one of Hinduism's most important religious texts, is disguised in the narrative of the *Mahabharata* as a long discourse by the god Krishna to the hero Arjun. Other ancient writings regarded as articles of faith by Hindus include the Puranas, Brahmanas and the ancient Vedas, which are widely believed to be the world's oldest surviving religious texts. These are more recognizably didactic than some of the other texts, less easily seen as thinly disguised entertainments. They consist mostly of hymns to various deities that provide instruction on methods of worship, animal sacrifice and evoking divine intervention in earthly matters. Again, it could all be metaphorical, indicators to the devout of the relevance of the simple pillars that prop up Hinduism at its deep, almost impenetrable core. These are the notions of brahman, the all pervasive force that can be thought of as god, and atman, the self, and their essential unity.

These linked ideas come from the Vedas, but in one form or another they pervade the myriad versions of the Indian creed as fully as the idea of salvation informs all Christianity, and submission to the will of Allah defines the various sects of Islam. Hinduism is a deeply personal faith, where the individual, through tradition, contemplation, ritual and deep respect for family and social position, forges a definition of the divine. Worship of gods and goddesses is not an act of subordination but an attempt to bargain with a powerful, yet often fallible, spiritual force. At Hindu temples and shrines, offerings are proffered to the resident deity in exchange for some boon: a son, a good marriage, an end to illness. Whether Hindus actually believe that the stick of incense they burn or the sweetmeat they leave for the god is a bribe or an appeasement is another matter. Some will tell you that the offering represents respect for the mystical and unknowable infinite and at very least a ray of hope that circumstances will change, whatever or whoever gets the credit.

India's explosive growth in recent years—its burgeoning middle classes—hasn't made it any less religious, any less Hindu. Surveys of public attitudes toward faith consistently show that modern, white-collar, highly educated Indians remain as devoted as ever to their faith.

Temples everywhere are crowded and hectic. Many have had to install parking lots for the massed vehicles of their newly affluent worshippers. Pilgrimages to remote temples and mountain aeries where wise men dispense spiritual advice are so popular that holy men are begging the devout to come in shifts, not all at once. There are even rituals to thank the divine for a new car, a computer or a child's admission to a distant American college. Rich Indian families have traditionally endowed temples, or built new ones. Indeed, many of the most elaborate places of worship in booming cities such as Delhi or Mumbai have sprung up in the past decade or so, as a generation of entrepreneurs and businesspeople retire and seek a place in the infinite to call their own.

Hinduism is an essential, all-pervasive component of the fabric of India. Someone born in India, to Indian parents, is in some way Hindu, even if he or she follows the Christian, Muslim or Buddhist faith, or so it is believed by many on the subcontinent. Like Judaism, Hinduism is a religion of blood, not of revelation. It is a gene pool as much as a creed. Unlike the faith of the Jews, though, Hinduism is not tribal. Its adherents do not spring from a single geographic or ethnic source. More than 3,500 years ago the nomads that some call Aryans arrived in the subcontinent from Central Asia. The admittedly sparse historical record indicates that they found local people following many different forms of worship. Aryan oral tradition was distilled into the written works known as the Vedas, but not before indigenous traditions were incorporated as well. Subsequent centuries saw faiths and practices whirled together into an amalgam of ideas that took deep root and became modern Hinduism.

It can be a challenge to be a devout Hindu. There is a great deal to remember: rituals, complex networks of divinity, family and caste duties. In fact, not many Hindus pay close attention to the demands of their faith. I was at a wedding once in New Delhi where the bride was Indian and the bridegroom was from Europe. To please the woman's family, the groom had studied the rituals that would be used by the pandit, or Hindu priest, who presided over their vows. The ceremony was held out of doors, but an altar of flowers and sandalwood had been constructed, with a sacred fire burning in a copper pot. The couple sat side by side, facing the pandit across the flames. As the holy man intoned ancient words in Sanskrit, and looked expectantly at his charges, giving them cues to respond verbally or to throw flower petals into the fire, he soon got a puzzled expression on his kindly face. For the only one of the two to respond in a timely and confident manner was the non-Hindu groom, who had done his homework. The thoroughly secular, probably agnostic, bride often looked puzzled, even impatient, as the old priest sat waiting for his fellow Hindu to play her part in the marriage ceremony. Her family was no more clued in and spent the entire ceremony gossiping and playing with several children, occasionally casting their eyes on the groaning table of curries and sweets that awaited the happy conclusion of the ritual.

By and large, Hindus don't measure each other by degrees of devotion to faith. Religious practice is personal, shared only with close family, if at all. But there are broad patterns from the scriptures and traditions that devotees can choose to follow. A refrain often heard from Hindus while describing their creed is (even as Veer Badra Mishra had told me) "It's not a religion, it's a way of life." That observation is largely based on the way sacred texts instruct Hindu men to behave in the four broad phases of their unfolding lives. These commit the devotee first to learning, being a student. That's followed by a time as a householder, raising a family. Then comes mixing contemplation of the infinite into the demands of daily life, being still involved in family, business affairs and so on, but with increasing amounts of time spent studying religious texts and meditating. Finally, the last few decades of life are thought to be best spent as a fully committed religious contemplative, a wandering holy man or hermit with no contact whatsoever with the mundane.

Defenders of tradition argue that such a structure has social utility, or perhaps it did in quieter, less economically demanding times. Another, crucial observation about Hindu practice as outlined in scripture is that it applies almost entirely to the lives of men. India's lively feminist movement has long rejected what's seen as the exclusion of women from playing a central role in their faith. Even women of the highest caste, Brahmins, are seen largely in context of their male relations, as wives, daughters and widows. This is a stubborn attitude that still excites passions. Canadian filmmaker Deepa Mehta's 2005 movie *Water*, about the sorry treatment of Hindu women whose husbands have died, took years to produce. This was because the initial shoots in India had to be abandoned amid a right-wing backlash against the portrayal of a faith that was unkind to women. About all that can be said in defense of this scriptural gender inequity is that it was conceived thousands of years ago, when society was overwhelmingly patriarchal. The changing reality of India today—now urban, middle class, and cosmopolitan—will doubtless force changes that will in turn be absorbed into Hinduism. That, it's argued, is the definition of syncretism.

Far more troubling is the issue of caste. For as open and flexible as Hinduism may be, the social hierarchy that lies at its heart is almost intolerably rigid. A discussion of caste and its origins can be extremely contentious. Much depends on the point of view of someone explaining the issue. Apologists for a system that by its very nature divides and discriminates say the caste structure is a time-honored method of social organization based on the need for different paths and professions. It created a pool of skilled labor and specialized expertise, they say, that helped society stay intact through millennia of war and conquest. Opponents of caste say it is a racist and exploitative method of entrenching power and privilege.

The origins of the caste system apparently lie in the attitudes of the Aryan nomads who regarded the indigenous people of India, who were darker-skinned and unable to speak their language, as *mleccha,* outsiders. Over the centuries, that word has come to imply impurity; the implication is that someone who is *mleccha* is less worthy. There is ample evidence in the Rig Veda, the earliest Hindu text, that caste hierarchies became more complicated and entrenched as a nomadic life gave way to farming and settlement. One particular verse from that text is often cited by those who believe that caste was intended as a discriminatory system from the very beginning. It describes how the various castes were born from the body parts of a god:

> The *Brahmin* was his mouth,
> Of both his arms was the *Kshatriya* made.
> His thighs became the *Vaishya,*
> From his feet the *Sudra* was produced.

From this come the four main categories of caste that still exist today. The Brahmin is the priest and custodian of knowledge, the Kshatriya is the warrior and ruler, the Vaishya is the merchant and businessperson and the Sudra and all others are the laborers, those who work with their hands. Within these four classifications are thousands of other classifications known as *jati,* which are based even more specifically on occupation and skill set. The different castes have sprung up over centuries and even millennia as new technologies created new tasks. But what has not changed is that the whole system rests on the notion of purity. The upper castes are regarded as more pure than the lower. This arises from belief in reincarnation, that death brings rebirth in a different form. Thus people from a high caste are believed to have earned their status by virtuous behavior in an earlier life. Conversely, the lower rungs of the caste ladder are thought to be occupied by those who have sinned in a previous existence. This is karma, one's fate or the divine rhythm of the universe, which is eternal and has relevance far beyond the problems and pleasures of daily life.

In modern India, discrimination because of caste is illegal but widespread. Awareness of caste, especially in rural areas, remains acute. People outside the urban middle classes are regularly ostracized, beaten or even lynched for inter-caste love affairs. Those from the low end of the hierarchy often draw their water from different wells and drink from different cups in the tea shop. In the cities, such practices are generally deplored and reported in the media with disapproval and demands for redress. But even among urbanites, modern middle-class life has its own forms of caste discrimination. Many people are sensitive to one another's origins and caste. In the introduction to his play *Pygmalion,* George Bernard Shaw wrote: "It is impossible for an Englishman to open his mouth without making some other Englishman hate or despise him." Those Indians for whom caste is relevant may have a similar response to their compatriots. Even those who have discarded the old ideas often find themselves hardwired to react in certain ways. One can do business with people of different castes, even socialize with them, but it's unthinkable for a son or daughter to marry someone from a lower or unsuitable caste.

In fact, caste is often the most important criterion for choosing a spouse. On websites and in classified ads, prospective brides and grooms are categorized by caste. The website www.shaadi.com, which calls itself "the world's largest matrimonial service," offers more than a hundred caste categories for young men and women in search of married bliss. Reflecting modern ways and the influence of the wider world, there are also brides and grooms who advertise their charms under the categories "born again," "Protestant" and even "caste no bar." Mostly, though, the lists are organized according to the familiar categories. The caste system may be vilified by its critics, but it remains as relevant as it ever was in the households and temples of India.

Caste discrimination persists despite the long-standing commitment by political parties and leaders to end its pernicious and discriminatory role. Statistics relating to caste are hugely controversial, and it may be overly reductive to cite rough statistics based on the four broad categories of caste, but there is no doubt that the downtrodden far outnumber the hierarchically privileged. Brahmins are relatively few in number compared with Sudras and Vaishyas. But numerical disadvantage has not prevented the higher castes from utterly dominating positions of power throughout Indian history, guarding knowledge and making war while the bulk of the population traded and labored. Attempts to rectify this historical injustice began in the second half of the twentieth century. From its inception as an independent state, India has applied progressive and far-reaching policies of positive discrimination in an effort to become more inclusive. Long lists of castes and communities that traditionally suffered from exclusion were drawn up and attached to the constitution. Those lists, known as schedules, have grown and expanded in the ensuing decades, even though the original intent of the policy was to provide a leg up to the downtrodden and usher in a new era of meritocracy and equality of opportunity.

The schedules provide for reserved places in universities, the civil service and government for those from low or deprived castes. To be from a scheduled caste or tribe in today's India is to theoretically enjoy a series of privileges and advantages that outweigh discrimination. When the schedules were drawn up, it was hoped they would soon become irrelevant and be phased out as a more merit-based, equitable society evolved. Instead, democracy has combined with demography to give birth to caste-based politics. Political leaders from traditionally disadvantaged castes have used their community as a voting bloc at election time, paying for support between trips to the polls with jobs and pork-barrel projects that benefit only their particular group. Other side effects of caste politics include the paralysis of hopelessly politicized university campuses and government ministries by hiring policies that emphasize blood over ability.

The cauldron of casteism, as it's become known in the Indian media, seethes and bubbles with the aspirations of the majority of the Indian population, people born into disadvantage but favored and encouraged by the world's largest and most comprehensive policy of affirmative action. Few low-caste leaders find lasting common cause with people from other backgrounds because the system empowers them just enough to attain office and gain access to resources on their own, enabling their continuity of power. In India's two largest and poorest states, Uttar Pradesh and Bihar, large blocs of what are euphemistically known as "backward" castes are courted by competing political parties that ostensibly rail against hierarchy but have an entrenched interest in its perpetuation. And at the lowest, most excluded levels of caste, by some estimates, up to 20 percent of the Indian population have, until very recently, been largely excluded from political life, despite generations of activism on their behalf.

A person from the lowest castes, whose daily duties deepened the impurity already instilled by humble birth, was regarded in British colonial times as untouchable. That was a literal concept. A person of higher caste who came into physical contact with an untouchable was soiled and could be "purified" only by ritual cleansing. Author and social reformer Mulk Raj Anand's novel *Untouchable,* published in 1935, presents a powerful portrait of the daily humiliations of life at the bottom. In one memorable passage, the protagonist, an eighteen-year-old named Bakha, calls out, "*posh posh,* sweeper coming," as he walks through his town. This, Anand writes, was to give higher-caste folk a chance to get out of the way, lest Bakha's garment brush the hem of a passing lady's sari, or dust from his footfalls waft onto the sandals of a Brahmin. The plight of the untouchables so troubled Mohandas Gandhi that he proposed a new name for them: *harijans,* or children of God. He also urged Hindus who benefited from low-caste labor to do such work themselves. Curiously, the very people who were supposed to be liberated by the new terminology objected to it. Untouchables themselves took issue with the term *harijan.* Just because someone was known as a child of God didn't make him or her any less impure to those on higher rungs of the brutally inequitable ladder of caste.

Among those who found Gandhi's proposal pointless, even unhelpful, was a crusading lawyer named Dr. Bhim Rao Ambedkar. He himself was an untouchable. Today, thanks in large part to his own activism, he would be known as a *dalit*. This is a highly politicized word. In English it means "those who have been broken," or "the oppressed people." The word is intended to convey the glaring injustice of the caste system each time it is uttered, whether by a *dalit* or someone farther up the hierarchy. Ambedkar was a giant on the stage of the Indian freedom struggle, but he receives far less attention from historians than Nehru, Gandhi or Mohammed Ali Jinnah. In part, this is because of a long-standing historical bias toward narratives of nation-building and statecraft. Those three men founded countries, while Ambedkar fought for social justice. Ambedkar believed passionately that a new state that failed to offer equality to castes, communities and the sexes was not worth fighting for. But more than anything else, Ambedkar remains a controversial figure in modern India because he explicitly rejected Hinduism, and urged his followers to do the same.

He was born in humble circumstances but went to good schools because his father had been in the British Indian army and could afford to educate his son. After graduating from high school, Ambedkar worked for the administration of one of colonial India's native states, whose liberal ruler, the maharajah of Baroda, sent him to Columbia University in New York City. America's openness and legal system impressed him, while, in the classroom, he absorbed lessons on the need for economic and social justice.

The guarantees of freedom and equality in the American constitution seemed to Ambedkar the basis of a civilized society. He subsequently completed a doctorate at the London School of Economics and went on to the Inner Temple to study law. He was called to the bar, becoming yet another Indian freedom fighter who learned the ropes of British jurisprudence and put them to use in India. His qualifications and international experience should have helped him prosper in his native land, yet each time Ambedkar went back to India, his caste status would grate on him. In America or Britain, he was just another Indian student or lawyer to be judged by his grades and the quality of his conversation. In his own country, he was shunned as impure, untouchable.

Ambedkar distrusted Gandhi's calls for a revitalized Hindu faith, even as the Mahatma reached out to the lowest castes and promised them liberation from servitude and humiliation. From the 1920s onward, Ambedkar worked as an activist lawyer and publisher of tracts denouncing caste and Hinduism both. As a democrat and staunch opponent of fascism, he urged *dalits* to join the British Indian army to fight Nazi and Japanese imperialism. He regarded both as racist ideologies that threatened to impose on the world a version of the Hindu caste system. This put him in direct conflict with Nehru and other leaders of the freedom struggle, who were calling for a boycott of the British war effort unless London granted colonial India greater autonomy. It was neither the first nor the last time that Ambedkar would clash with the men destined to lead a free and sovereign India.

After Indian independence in 1947, and despite his differences with Gandhi, Nehru and other stalwarts of the freedom struggle, Ambedkar was named as his country's first law minister. He was put in charge of drafting a constitution for the new nation. Newly liberated from colonial rule, free India was to be a beacon of hope, democracy and equality on the world stage. The constitution that emerged from the process that Ambedkar led was promulgated in 1950. It explicitly abolished the practice of untouchability and made all forms of discrimination illegal. But Ambedkar's reforming zeal—and, unfortunately, his low-caste status—made him many enemies. In 1951, he proposed legislation that would expand the rights of women. It failed in parliament and Ambedkar resigned from the government in disgust. Increasingly angry that caste and inequality remained powerful forces in newly independent India, Ambedkar began an explicit campaign to urge his fellow *dalits* to renounce Hinduism entirely. He had opposed his country's majority religion for decades but was now publicly denouncing Hindu beliefs and practice. In 1956 he embraced Buddhism, a faith that he had come to believe explicitly rejected caste. More than three hundred thousand of his low-caste supporters joined him in the largest mass conversion ceremony ever seen in India. It should have been a moment of triumph for him, but he was suffering from diabetes and chronic depression. Ambedkar grew increasingly frail and died in 1956, at age sixty-five.

Ambedkar's legacy in today's India is a radicalized *dalit* movement that is growing in political clout and effectiveness. There are *dalit* writers, painters, poets, playwrights and, of course, politicians. A *dalit* middle class has sprung up, largely based around academia and, to a lesser extent, the arts. But there are still those born at the bottom of Indian society whose plight lies beyond the activism inspired by Dr. Ambedkar.

At the lowest echelon of caste—even today—are people such as Bakha from Anand's novel, people who still call themselves sweepers. The term doesn't refer to the men and women who wield bundled twig and straw brooms to brush dust and leaves from sidewalks and roadsides across India every morning. A sweeper—the word is said with a certain intonation, even a significant look—is someone who collects human waste from homes without flush toilets. Once, in the days before Indian cities offered at least limited piped water and municipal sewage, there were millions of them. Toilets were made of wood and had removable drawers that were accessible from the street, where the sweeper could scoop out the contents each morning and cart them away. It was the lowest, most impure form of labor. Gandhi urged higher-caste Hindus to be more judicious in their daily bowel movements, to adopt practices that didn't require sweepers to bear away the result. People should clean up their own messes, he said; but his words had little effect. These admonitions are seen today as an example of how obsessive and cranky Gandhi became in his later years. This is unfair. Hindu fastidiousness, which is manifest in the caste system, in eating habits and other aspects of daily life, applies only to the individual and his or her immediate vicinity, not to more remote surroundings or to society as a whole. As Veer Badra Mishra would argue, it is seen by many Hindus as acceptable to foul the environment, whether with human or industrial waste, so long as one washes and observes certain rituals afterward. In Gandhi's day, this meant having a sweeper push his stinking cart through the predawn streets, gathering feces along the way.

Such jobs still exist, even though they are in defiance of Indian law. There are still far too few toilets connected to sewage systems in India. Human excrement is found in many open or public areas in cities, along roadsides and railway tracks and in ditches. The poor and homeless have nowhere else to go. More than one thousand Indian children die every day from waterborne disease, due mainly to the absence of proper methods of human waste disposal. Now that Gandhi is long gone, it falls on a remarkable organization called Sulabh International to agitate for reform. I stumbled onto Sulabh by accident.

Driving away from New Delhi's Indira Gandhi International Airport, I noticed a gray, single-story building. It sat in a landscaped garden of shrubs and trimmed grass. Groomed gravel paths led through the grounds to two doors at either end of the building, with the universally recognized pictorial symbols for men and women mounted on the doors. There was not a stray bit of litter in sight. The whole thing gleamed. A blue sign with white painted letters on top of the building proclaimed "Sulabh International Public Toilet" in both English and Hindi. I stopped my car to investigate the place. There were, I discovered, toilets, as the sign said, and they were spotless. I also found bathing facilities for both men and women, and attendants to look after them. Those who could afford to pay were charged a nominal fee, equivalent to a few cents; for those who couldn't, access was free. A young man showed me around. He took pains to take me into the open tracts of land nearby, pointing at the ground to show me that no one had been going to the toilet there. "No shit, no shit," he kept saying, and I agreed.

In Sanskrit, *sulabh* is the word for "easy." The name of the organization, and the thinking behind it, are the work of its founder, Dr. Bindeshwar Pathak. Pathak is an upright, handsome man in his sixties who looks far younger. Persuading all Indians to make proper use of toilets, he believes, will resolve many of the country's health and social challenges. It's that easy, he repeats, many times during our conversation. His goal is nothing less than safe, hygienic sanitation for all of India's billion-plus population and liberation for the remaining 250,000 sweepers.

"A toilet in every home, and ample public toilets for travelers and the homeless, would make everything easier," he said. We were sitting in an office decorated with photos of him with popes, the Dalai Lama, UN agency chiefs, European and Asian leaders and a succession of Indian cabinet ministers. "This would, of course, end waterborne disease. Dysentery and diarrhea cannot exist without human waste to spread them, and if [the waste is] put in a toilet and a sewer, not on the ground or in public, then where's the disease? Do you have any dysentery in America? In Europe? Of course you don't.

"We would eliminate the need for scavengers, the people who still collect the waste in this country in defiance of our laws. There are hundreds of thousands of them still, pulling wooden carts and picking up our waste. This is barbaric, the worst work imaginable, and people who do it are beyond untouchability. No one wants to know them. They are doomed and their children are doomed to illiteracy, alienation, outcast status."

Pathak prefers the word *scavenger* to *sweeper*. He's fond of pointing out that India's great successes, its self-sufficiency in food, its nuclear weapons, its space program and information technology companies, all exist alongside a quarter million men, women and children who work as collectors of human waste. It was their plight, he says, that drew him into the promotion of public toilets and sanitation—not some obsession with cleanliness, but concern for a group of people who are perhaps the worst-off in the country. He is a Brahmin, born in the caste-ridden eastern state of Bihar, and he shocked his rather orthodox family when he chose to do research that plumbed the most disgusting depths of the caste system. He lived with sweepers. He went out with them on their rounds and helped them in their odiferous work. He got to know all too intimately the challenges and daily humiliations that come their way. His PhD thesis, now published as a report by Sulabh, is a scathing indictment of an Indian society that could have afforded another system of waste disposal but chose to continue with sweepers and scavengers, with all its foul effects. "We [Hindus] have this idea that if we throw our garbage over the wall of our compound, it no longer exists. Similarly, if we move our bowels and the product is taken away by a scavenger, we have done nothing wrong. We have done, in effect, nothing at all. This is in gross defiance of the texts and scriptures of our faith," he says. Pathak is a devout Hindu, and he takes great umbrage at those within the creed who defend caste-based practices such as scavenging. "It's wrong, it's false, it's blasphemous to say there is any religious justification for this sort of behavior." In fact, he says, Hindu scripture specifically prohibits the handling of human waste by other humans.

Pathak also believes that human feces are wasted in India. They could be used as fertilizer or in the generation of electricity or the production of fuel for cooking. The challenge, he says, is to overcome the natural aversion people have to excreta. There are dozens of projects in India and around South Asia to turn human waste into cooking gas. Sulabh backs several of them. Waste is deposited into a sealed concrete container with a valve on top. As the waste material naturally degrades, it produces methane gas that can be pressurized and burnt as fuel. Although it burns cleanly and without odor, biogas, as it's known, is a hard sell in many communities. People remain dubious, not convinced that it won't contaminate food or their homes.

Sulabh encourages people to build toilets appropriate to their surroundings and using available materials. In arid climates, where water is at a premium, this might be a drop toilet, where the feces are allowed to dry on a platform well below the seat, to minimize odor. Where the climate is damper, the organization encourages people to dig septic fields and make use of plants to help process and purify waste water. Britain's Prince Charles has a natural sewage-processing pond on his estate in Dorset that uses common bulrushes to cleanse waste water. The prince is one of many well-known supporters of Sulabh's work. Some environments are more suitable for pit toilets. Others need running water and a connection to sewer pipes. Those who are willing can connect their toilets to a biogas generator. There are few kinds of loo that Sulabh doesn't design and build.

The organization also has a toilet museum, which includes a working model of the first flush mechanism, designed by the English engineer Thomas Crapper in the nineteenth century. But what's most impressive about Pathak is how, like Veer Badra Mishra, he remains a devout Hindu while acknowledging that his faith enables horrible forms of discrimination and unacceptable behavior. It is true that there is no scriptural justification for scavenging, but because it is a social practice that dates from ancient times, there is a belief in India that Hindu tradition condones it. Pathak rejects this. He urges fellow Brahmins and other members of higher castes to adopt scavenger families and oversee their education and development. He puts the touchables and untouchables in touch, if you will, and stresses how this is true Hindu practice. Some fifty thousand scavengers, he says, proudly, are no longer collecting human waste, thanks to his efforts. They work in offices, factories and at Sulabh itself, spreading the word about toilets. Their children attend an English medium school to learn about Shakespeare and sewing machines and, once they graduate, they need never take on the task undertaken by their parents and grandparents.

The work of Dr. Pathak and Sulabh is an example of something not all that common in India: Hindu philanthropy. There are few if any explicit requirements in Hindu scripture for the practice of charity. The hordes of beggars that surround temples take advantage of people's desire to acquire merit by giving alms, but nothing in Hindu texts requires such acts of giving. Hindu charity work among the poor is a fairly recent phenomenon. Rich Hindus have traditionally put their money into building temples or promoting the cause of their religion, not into alleviating the lot of the poor. Not that individual Hindus haven't been generous, compassionate and concerned with the eradication of social ills. Examples abound. But in the main, Hinduism is seen by most of its followers as a code that stresses the self and its place in a narrow group bound by family or caste.

Changes in Hindu practice have come in many different ways over the centuries. Lately, the upheaval wrought by economic change and contact with the rest of the world is reshaping Hindu thought. Hindus are having to reconsider traditional practices such as joint family living and the caste system. In the past, contact with other religions has led to change. Islam and Christianity both have had a powerful effect. Both are revealed religions, monotheistic and with strong requirements that followers put the needs of others—of all others, not just friends, family and community—ahead of their own. Both condemn selfish behavior and proclaim that divinity can be achieved only through kindness and compassion.

The fact that Islam and Christianity pick up adherents through conversion has also had a profound effect on Hinduism. Sikhism may have evolved as an amalgam of Islam and Hinduism. Sikhs worship a single god and are required to be charitable and compassionate, but their belief in divinely inspired gurus who dispense wisdom has Hindu overtones. Imperial Britain spread Christian compassion and charitable works through its churches and missions, making many converts among the lower castes by providing education and social services. Several Hindu reform movements have sprung up and now use the borrowed ideas of missionary work and of the use of schools to entrench faith. The principles of the European Enlightenment and the Protestant Reformation—accountability, rationalism, science—permeated nineteenth-century efforts to make Hinduism more modern and relevant.

Veer Badra Mishra puts it best. The Hindu priest who bathes in the polluted Ganges but spends his days trying to clean up the sacred river said, "Our faith must be relevant, not a bargain with the divine or with death or the unknown. It must be relevant. And to be this way it must directly encourage us to help people, to make real sacrifices for our fellow man and for our planet. To help our communities and others in need, to be moral and positive in our energies and work. These are words, and they can be empty words, just as the sacred texts can be [empty] when they are ignored or forgotten. I think most Hindus in India know this and choose to be superstitious or observe only the empty rituals of our faith, just as Christians in America seem to want only salvation, not the world of compassion foreseen by Christ, or Buddhists in Sri Lanka are chauvinist and violent, not compassionate. We're all in this together, really, and the Hindus can't ignore that much longer."

Hindu imagery and patterns are ubiquitous in India. It is the faith of the vast majority of the people, and it informs even those who seek other spiritual paths. Its negative features, its casteism, its lack of a moral message and the appearance of rank superstition fuel constant debate. Barely a day goes by without a story appearing in a newspaper or on television about caste discrimination. Philosophers and sociologists ponder how to instill better behavior and a civic conscience in Indians. The educated and liberal elite are sniffy about the garish temples and rituals of their country's religious faith. Yet the Indian character is imbued with the strengths and weaknesses of Hinduism itself, and even the march of modernization, materialism and globalism doesn't seem to be challenging this close adherence to one of the oldest ways of life on the planet, whatever the modern setting. People such as Bindeshwar Pathak work to alleviate, and eventually get rid of, the worst excesses of the caste system. Women are gradually forcing change in traditional patriarchal patterns of Hindu thought. A five-thousand-year-old faith is resurgent and influential, even as Indian society becomes more modern and recognizably Western in outlook.

10

NUKING THE SOFT STATE

How India Learned to Love the Bomb

MONSOON RAINS WERE pelting down on the sprawling suburbs and northern neighborhoods of Mumbai, India's commercial capital. It was July 11, 2006, and the heat was intense. Even when it rained, sweat oozed from people's pores, mingling with the torrent from above. Few enclosed spaces in the city are more uncomfortable than the train carriages that rattle along the Western Railway line from Churchgate and Victoria Terminus stations. More than five million people ride Mumbai's trains every day. Office workers, laborers and migrants are packed vertically, standing up, in the second- and third-class carriages. Business people sit shoulder to shoulder in first class. On that day, as every day, even vestibules between the cars would have been crammed with dozens of passengers, a few even hanging precariously from the open doors, a single foot and sweaty palm holding fast to the racing train. And on top of each carriage, on the ridged steel roof, a phalanx of men, sitting free and somewhat cool, spattered by the rain.

Inside the lower-class compartments, faces were slicked with sweat. A few people swigged water from plastic bottles. The clackety-clack of the wheels all but drowned out conversation. But this was the commute home from work. People were tired, just concentrating on getting through the journey to their suburban apartments and houses. If you want to work at a decent job in India's liveliest city, you learn to cope with discomfort. Only the rich can afford to live comfortably in downtown Mumbai. Everyone else either commutes or lives in a slum.

At 6:24 p.m., as the train was rolling through Khar-Santacruz station on the outskirts of the city, passengers in the second- and third-class carriages would first have felt, and then heard, the roar of a tremendous explosion. The train lurched and shuddered, and several carriages tumbled off the tracks. Passengers were thrown about violently, crashing into each other or flung against barred windows and metal luggage racks. Bones snapped and sharp edges ripped flesh. Howls of pain and horror filled the dark space inside the toppled carriages. Smells mingled: hot metal, spilt diesel fuel, blood and cordite. At the front of the train, the scene was much, much worse.

The bomb had been planted on a luggage rack in a first-class carriage. The shock wave and searing heat ripped through the air-conditioned interior, leaving no one unharmed and nothing undamaged. People sitting near what was apparently a paper-wrapped parcel, packed with Semtex industrial explosive, had simply vanished, blown into bits and a few smears of blood. Those farther away from the bomb were hideously injured by the shock wave, smashed into metal walls and seats, their bodies twisted and mutilated by the force of the blast. When the first rescuers arrived minutes later, dozens lay dead or dying, their screams and moans making a dreadful chorus in the wreckage. Even as the shattered carriages settled into the ground the rain continued to fall, washing streaks of blood from metal and turning rivulets of muddy water red. One newspaper account called it "the colour of human suffering."

Variations on this scene occurred almost simultaneously seven times that day in Mumbai. The incident was the worst train bombing ever in a city that has known more than its share of violence, terrorism and unrest. Although arrests were made and fingers of blame pointed in various directions, it may never be known for certain who planned and carried out the attacks. Indian police are poorly trained and barely equipped to carry out forensic investigations. Though they claim otherwise, they know little about the militant groups that operate on the fringes of society in South Asia. India unequivocally asserts that Pakistan's spy agency, the ISI, planned the carnage and instigated Islamist terror groups to carry out the bombing. Pictures of the alleged perpetrators, all described as Muslim, were released to the media. They look like many other men in South Asia, dark hair cut short, dark eyes, mustachioed, scowling. Several militant Muslim groups branded as terrorists by India and some Western countries have denied involvement and, in some cases, condemned the killings. Their assertions ring hollow given their own grisly records of death and destruction over the years. Indian media reports based on leaks from New Delhi's own spy agency, the Research and Analysis Wing (RAW), have named new cabals of Islamist fundamentalists that have mutated from earlier manifestations, and again fling blame—if not proof—toward Islamabad. Many innocent Muslim men have been arrested and tortured by the police in hopes that a few miserable words of confession can be wrung from them to please the politicians.

Survivors and the families of victims were promised compensation by government ministers, usually a few thousand dollars or, in really high-profile cases, ten thousand or more. The injured were taken to decent hospitals for difficult treatments but often found themselves stuck with the bill. In some cases, the promised compensation was not paid until families appeared on the TV news, telling heartrending tales of destitution and loss. Such outrages and their grim aftermath have been repeated several times across India in recent years. Bombs have exploded on trains and in crowded markets. People die or suffer injury and bereavement. The country moves on. The pain and loss within individual families remains.

There is no lack of aggravated grievance among India's citizens. And they have access to technology and outside help that can stoke hatred and encourage violence. Muslims are, of course, among the most aggrieved right now. In the past, those with grievances have included Sikhs, leftists and even failing university students who have turned to terror to protest their powerlessness and convey their loathing of the system. On September 11, 2001, I sat in an office in New Delhi and watched with the rest of the world as the attack on America unfolded. In common with everyone else who saw the second plane crash into the World Trade Center, I felt a wave of panic, followed by certainty that something had changed in the world I knew. I noticed that one of my colleagues was smiling at the images on the television screen. What was she feeling, I wondered, and her

answer still chills me to this day. "Now," she said, "the Americans will
know what it feels like."

Even though I reacted at the time with shock and sharp words, I
later felt some empathy for her point of view. Indians are grimly familiar with terror and its impact. They shared America's grief and
horror at the 9/11 attacks but found it hard to resist giving in to the
thought that U.S. citizens were getting just a taste of what Indians had
endured for years. India's right-wing Hindu nationalists like to say
that their country is a soft state. By this they mean that India has always been accommodating and tolerant toward even the most violent
manifestations of grievance and the assertion of rights by minorities.
The political sphere deals with such crises not with hard-edged una-
nimity of purpose, but with emotion, debate, fatalism and even resignation. The soft state is one that believes it exists on a moral footing
and that wants its interlocutors, neighbors and enemies to realize this.
If only everyone appreciates India's essential goodwill, then peace and
prosperity will be the inevitable result. Opponents of this point of
view argue that a nation as important and strong as India should be
confident and single-minded about its national interests. There has to
be political and public consensus when the country is slighted, chal-
lenged or attacked. The response must be quick, decisive, sharp and
effective. Israel (often) and the United States (occasionally) are cited
as models of such behavior. These are countries not to be trifled with,
and, it's believed, India should emulate them.

Invariably, terrorist attacks such as the Mumbai train bombings
provoke an anguished national debate. Should India continue to ap-
pease, as some see it, the sense of exclusion felt by more radical members of the Muslim community? Is it enough to take pride in the
country's long-standing traditions of tolerance and syncretism that
are supposed to absorb and accommodate the grievances of minority groups? Or should a more robust and confident India define its
interests more narrowly? The tone of the debate varies over time and
with the provocation that has sparked it. It remains unresolved. But
even as things are, it's possible to admire the Indian response to violence. The day after the Mumbai attacks in 2006, the rail line that
had been damaged in seven places was open again, and the trains
were on time. There was extra security, and passengers were understandably nervous. But very few people, apparently, avoided going

to work. Millions crowded the trains as usual, grimacing and gossiping as scenes of carnage passed by the carriage windows. Commuters showed, according to newspaper reports, a sort of defiance, a quiet pride in the restoration of routine that sent a firm message to those who tried to shatter it. Whatever had happened, it was business as usual in Mumbai.

In fact, India is well on its way to becoming less of a soft state and more of a superpower. There is growing agreement on this among the elite and middle classes, between even the most bitterly opposed political parties and in the upper, policymaking echelons of government. Since the late 1990s, only the old left in India, the still-influential Communist parties and some Gandhian traditionalists have clung to the belief that moral righteousness matters more than military strength. Elsewhere, it's widely assumed that the country's growing economic influence soon will command a commensurate degree of international respect. A global role in international security matters is also assured, it's believed. That attitude, entrenched in the middle classes but found throughout society, received its biggest boost on the day India tested a nuclear bomb.

In the sun-baked sandy wastes of Rajasthan's Thar Desert, at a place called Pokhran, the surface of the planet trembled visibly on the morning of May 11, 1998. On seismographs around the world, needles leapt and alarms were sounded. The indications from the instruments were clear: This was no earthquake. The shudders in the earth's crust were brief and there were no aftershocks. India's nuclear test explosions had been a success. Videos released by the Indian government showed officers and scientists in Pokhran punching the air in a very American expression of glee. In New Delhi, the normally taciturn prime minister, Atal Bihari Vajpayee, was said to have wiped away a tear at the thought of the fury unleashed below the desert sands. A lifetime's ambition, it later emerged, had been fulfilled for Mr. Vajpayee. He had led his country into the exclusive group of nations that openly possessed the capability to fight a nuclear war.

The news was sprung on an oblivious India and a largely unsuspecting world a few hours after the first series of tests. Vajpayee prepared to address a hastily convened news conference in the garden of his official residence. His staff had made doubly sure that the foreign media were there. They called the news bureaus several times to make it plain that something extraordinary was about to be announced. Most reporters assumed that the prime minister was about to call a snap election or make an appeal for support from his troublesome allies in the coalition government. They ambled along to the austere but highly secure bungalow near New Delhi's diplomatic enclave, unaware of the firestorm that was to follow the press conference.

The Indian flag fluttered from a small flagpole behind the lectern from which Prime Minister Vajpayee made his announcement. "Today, at 15:45 hours," he began, speaking in English to make sure that no one missed what he was saying, "India conducted three underground nuclear tests in the Pokhran range. The tests conducted were with a fission device, a low-yield device and a thermonuclear device. The measured yields are in line with expected values. Measurements have confirmed that there was no release of radioactivity into the atmosphere. These were contained explosions like in the experiment conducted in May 1974. I warmly congratulate the scientists and engineers who have carried out the successful tests. Thank you very much indeed."

For a few seconds, no one spoke. Reporters sat in stunned silence. The prime minister walked away from the lectern waving, refusing to take any of the babble of questions that eventually erupted. Journalists reached for their cell phones. No one had seen this coming. No one at all.

Perhaps the most embarrassed faces were those in Western intelligence agencies and foreign embassies whose job it was to keep track of nuclear proliferation issues. They all missed the signs. The CIA was especially embarrassed. The American intelligence agency supposedly had the best data, from spies, communications intercepts and satellite photography. Its main task in India was precisely to watch for nuclear test activity at Pokhran, where India had staged a test explosion once before, in 1974. Just three years before the 1998 tests, CIA satellites had picked up indications that India was preparing for a nuclear test, and the U.S. ambassador had persuaded the prime minister to call it off.

This time the Americans were clueless. Apparently, Indian scientists had figured out when American spy satellites were passing overhead and had arranged their work schedules so that any conspicuous activity took place only when the sky was clear of prying eyes. They dressed in military fatigues and moved components around at a measured pace to avoid attracting attention. It was a remarkable legerdemain. Strobe Talbott, then deputy secretary of state in the Clinton administration and the American point man on India, says his staff learned about the Indian tests from CNN, and he himself passed the information on to the CIA. "A bad government day" was how one of Talbott's State Department colleagues summed it up.

Frantic activity ensued as the international community sought to lock this particular barn door, even though the horse had well and truly escaped. The aim was to stop neighboring Pakistan, India's bitter military rival, from following the Indian lead. That Islamabad had access to nuclear technology was well known. The chief scientist of Pakistan's nuclear program was Dr. A. Q. Khan, who subsequently emerged as the man who had sold nuclear weapons know-how to Iran, Libya and probably North Korea. In 1998 that wasn't known, but Khan was wanted on an international arrest warrant for allegedly stealing nuclear centrifuge plans from a Dutch laboratory where he had worked in the 1970s. He'd done it for Pakistan, and his country knew him as the "father of the Islamic bomb." Pakistan, the world was sure, could build and test nuclear warheads. It just hadn't done so openly yet.

At first, U.S. President Bill Clinton tried bluster and the threat of crippling economic sanctions to deter Pakistan from undertaking nuclear tests. He warned of the dire consequences to global stability. And he offered inducements to make a nonnuclear policy attractive. Pakistani prime minister Nawaz Sharif was told he'd receive vast sums of money to pay off his country's debts. He was promised access to American intelligence about India's nuclear program. He was offered everything short of the proverbial kitchen sink, but no bribe on earth, no coercion at all, would have worked. For his own political survival, Sharif had to test his nuclear bombs, and he did, just two and a half weeks after the Indian explosions.

The global media and the chattering classes were horrified. It was pointed out time and again that these two countries had fought three all-out wars and countless border skirmishes in just fifty years. Hatreds and enmities dating from partition were alive and festering. The next conflict, we were assured, was bound to be a nuclear one. Economic sanctions were imposed on both nations. Foreign-aid flows

dried to a trickle, and access to international credit was severely limited. Military, scientific and even educational exchanges ceased. Japan,
one of the largest aid donors to both countries and the most viru-
lently antinuclear of all the rich nations, suspended almost all of its
assistance. Meanwhile, in the streets of the new nuclear powers, it was
party time. People at every level of society were overjoyed. It was one
in the eye for the sanctimonious West, and it showed that India had
arrived, and that Pakistan, too, was powerful. Nuclear test explosions
were celebrated with fizzing fireworks and the staccato bang of strings
of firecrackers.

India's progress toward a more focused sense of itself in the world
may not have actually begun with the dramatic tests in Pokhran but,
from that moment on, a more aggressive and self-confident foreign
and security policy was a sure thing. Of this, India had little doubt. C.
Raja Mohan, a journalist and policy analyst, argues in his book *Crossing the Rubicon: The Shaping of India's New Foreign Policy,* that his
country is finally finding the confidence it needs to gain global influence and make its point of view known in foreign capitals. Raja
Mohan is a pragmatist with a big idea: that India can become a serious global player if it behaves with wisdom and self-assurance and
builds a viable domestic consensus on troublesome issues. The 1998
nuclear tests, in his view, helped India forge a powerful sense of unity.
He sees the economic changes in India since 1991, and the country's
leading role in the global knowledge sector, as a key part of his country's transformation into a superpower.

"We began to cross this particular Rubicon when we decided to
ease restrictions on the marketplace in the nineties," he says. "It's more
of a swamp than a river, and we're still crossing it. We have decades of
accumulated mistakes in foreign and domestic policy behind us. Instead of choosing sides in the Cold War, we pretended to be above it
all when it was obvious that the West was where we had the most interests—democracy, liberalism, even free markets, all that. No, we had
to be nonaligned in company with all manner of Third World dicta-
tors. We had to lecture the Americans and the Brits about moral issues and social issues. It was terrible."

Now, Raja Mohan says, India sees the world as a source of investment and trade, a place to travel, and "as an opportunity, not as
a collection of foreigners out to get us. That was our earlier attitude,

you know. 'They just don't understand India,' we'd say when they would depict our poverty or religious violence in the media. We were far too prickly about how others thought of us." He laughs as he explains that American diplomats once called India the "Rodney Dangerfield of nations" because it didn't get any respect. India's founding fathers, he says, valued moral stature over military might and expected other countries to go along with that idea.

India learned over many decades that being right, or virtuous, wasn't what earned international respect, Raja Mohan says. The world beats a path to India's door, not because it's the global equivalent of the sage on the mountain, dispensing wisdom and advice to all comers, but because of the growing economy and the fact that a huge middle class is one of the world's most desirable markets for consumer goods and services. Then there's nuclear weapons. "The nuclear tests of 1998 were the turning point," Raja Mohan says. "Once they took place, and we turned out to be a responsible power, willing to cooperate with nonproliferation regimes but quietly insistent on our right to defend ourselves, then we earned some real respect." No more Rodney Dangerfield.

Privately, many foreign diplomats say India tested its nuclear capacity less for military purposes than to boost its self-esteem, to earn that global respect that Raja Mohan talks about. A retired military attaché who was stationed at a Western embassy in New Delhi at the time of the tests says India has no intention of ever using its atomic warheads. He accepts what India says, that the nuclear weapons are strictly for self-defense and lack the capacity to inflict significant damage on a major power. He points out that the country has no civil defense plan in case of nuclear attack by one of its enemies. It's clear that the tests were politically rather than militarily motivated, says the former attaché.

"They don't anticipate fighting a war with Pakistan with these things," he says, "nor do they really plan to fight China. So who else? The U.S.? France? Russia? No, there's no war plan, just a sense that they've arrived at the top table and everyone had better be nice to them. It's the strangest reason for a nuclear bomb I've ever encountered."

Brajesh Mishra was one of the key players in the 1998 decision to test nuclear weapons. He is a former career diplomat who became national security adviser to the governments led by Atal Bihari

Vajpayee between 1998 and 2004. When he was spending all his time
at the prime minister's side, Mishra was understandably reticent
and kept a low profile. But now that he is out of office, he finds himself with time on his hands and welcomes a chance to explain his
global vision. Mishra lives in a spacious flat in New Delhi's posh but
increasingly crowded Vasant Vihar neighborhood, not far from the
southwestern edge of the city. He receives visitors graciously and
gets straight to the business at hand. It's clear that he is proud of
the decision to stage the explosions, and he doesn't agree with the
suggestion that India tested nuclear weapons to enhance only its
global stature and not its military options in wartime. Mishra cat-
egorically refutes the notion that India's nuclear arsenal is a diplomatic lever, not a weapon of war, as the former attaché told me.
"The nuclear tests were about national security, first, last and totally," he says. "Any new respect or influence we gained from them
is merely a by-product of that. But, of course, we welcome it. When
[our government] came to office, India had spent nearly ten years
since the end of the Cold War trying to find a place in the world.
When we left, I think there were more people willing to listen to
what India had to say, to give our views some credence. We are
emerging as a fairly big player in international affairs, and if that
came about because of our nuclear tests, so be it. But make no mis-
take—we didn't detonate those explosions so we'd be allowed to
join any clubs or have our telephone calls returned in London and
Washington. That was happening anyway. We were establishing new
ways to defend ourselves in a dangerous world."

In the months before the tests, the government that Mishra was
part of was having political difficulties. A member of the governing
coalition—a former actress with a huge following in South India—
was threatening to pull out of the alliance and move a vote of no confidence. More than one Indian commentator has suggested that the
nuclear tests at Pokhran were motivated, at least in part, by the worsening situation within the government. Not so, says Mishra.

"No, no, you won't get me giving any credence to that wild idea.
We certainly didn't do something as momentous as test our nuclear
arsenal just to tame a wild political ally. And even if we had, it did-
n't work. Remember? That [ally] pulled out and forced an election,
which we won with an even better margin. So no, the nuclear tests

were what I say they were, matters of national security. Since they also, as it turns out, factor into the respect that India gets in the world, so be it. But mostly that respect is due to our restraint since the tests, our diplomacy, our economy, so many other things that we're doing to enhance this country's rightful place in the world. But politics . . . no way, no way at all." He continues to smile and shake his head, perhaps reflecting that the domestic political fallout of the nuclear tests belies his assertions that politics did not play a role in deciding to explode atomic devices. Both the immense popularity of the nuclear tests and the steadfast response of Vajpayee's government to a Pakistani incursion into Indian territory in May 1999 led to his government's reelection later that year, as Mishra pointed out. The nuclear option helped, even if it wasn't exercised solely with political gain in mind.

Mishra has always been in favor of India being more focused on its national interest. And yet, like Raja Mohan, he says he's no bellicose warmonger who wants his country to assert itself militarily whenever it gets the chance. Indeed, Mishra helped prepare India's diplomatic response to an international community concerned about nuclear proliferation in South Asia. This was to reassure allies and enemies alike that the explosions in the desert were not meant as an aggressive act aimed at any other country. He wrote statements pledging that India had no plans for any further tests and that it wanted talks with all its major allies on how best to proceed. The terms of the Nuclear Non-Proliferation Treaty, the NPT, might be observed, he told world leaders at the time, even if India was not a signatory. The NPT designates just five countries—the United States, Russia, France, Britain and China—as legitimate possessors of nuclear weapons and calls on all other signatories to renounce them. India rejects the treaty's premise outright.

"We respect the NPT, we have never and we will never proliferate, share or let our nuclear technology be used by others," Mishra says.

Both Pakistan and India survived the world's outrage. Indeed, it faded away rather quickly. Almost immediately after the tests, a high-level dialogue was launched between Strobe Talbott of the U.S. State Department and the Indian statesman and cabinet minister Jaswant Singh. The talks produced little of substance at first, but the countries indicated to each other and to the world that there was little appetite for hostility in either capital. American sanctions were gradually eased on India, more quickly than on Pakistan, which embarked on a mysteriously reckless military incursion a year later that plunged the region into a brief spasm of conventional war. It took President Clinton's intervention to force a Pakistani climb-down, and this led to even better relations between Washington and New Delhi. A military coup in Pakistan in October 1999 brought General Pervez Musharraf to power and forced Islamabad even farther into Washington's doghouse, a place it was to remain in until the 9/11 attacks sent America scrambling for allies in the Islamic world.

That's not to say there was not good reason for the world to be wary of the Indian and Pakistani nuclear tests. Relations between the two countries are plagued by mistrust, and the threat of war is ever present. Even after the tests in 1998, there was friction between them that could easily have led to all-out, even nuclear, war. The wounds of partition, when the subcontinent was ripped asunder by religious violence, have hardly begun to heal. There have been many rounds of peace talks, many agreements and fine words about building confidence and establishing mature, friendly relations. But no substantive or sustainable progress toward resolving major issues has been made. The contested status of the Himalayan territory of Jammu and Kashmir is the most serious of those issues. At the time of partition, Kashmir had a Hindu king and a Muslim majority population. It was the most glorious of the princely states of British India. As part of the terms of independence following partition, the maharajah was allowed to choose whether he would join India or Pakistan. The ruling Singh family had been given control over Kashmir by the British in the 1800s in appreciation for helping subdue the Sikh armies of the Punjab in a series of sharp, bloody little wars. Maharajah Hari Singh, the great grandson of the first ruler, dithered over which country to choose, and as he did so, destiny took a hand.

Pakistani tribesmen, encouraged and covertly supported by their government, invaded Kashmir in 1947 and raged through the upland valley that is the political and cultural heart of the state. There were many reports of atrocities, and the world—preoccupied with the aftermath of World War II, the rise of the Soviet Union and the looming threat of Communism in China—was powerless to intervene. India, however, acted quickly. Prime Minster Jawaharlal Nehru told the maharajah that if he joined India, the Indian army would expel the invaders. A controversial and still largely unclear sequence of events ensued that saw India take military control of the Kashmir valley and force the invaders back to slivers of territory they had captured early on. Battles and skirmishes were waged for months until the United Nations established a ceasefire line that is still the de facto frontier between Indian and Pakistani portions of Kashmir. UN Security Council resolutions were passed calling for the Kashmiri people themselves to decide their fate in a vote to be held after the two sides withdrew their military forces. This hasn't happened.

To this day, Pakistan insists that the dispute can be settled only by a UN-sponsored plebiscite, while India calls for bilateral talks. Around 1990, a bloody rebellion erupted in the Indian portion of Kashmir, with fierce fighting between Muslim militant groups and the Indian security forces. By some estimates, as many as sixty thousand people have died since then, and horrific human rights abuses and atrocities against civilians have been committed by both sides. India convincingly accuses Pakistan of arming, training and encouraging militant groups, along with international jihadist groups such as Al Qaeda. Pakistan says India occupies its part of Kashmir in defiance of the UN resolutions, and that the Indian army targets Muslim civilians in its anti-insurgency operations.

Apart from Kashmir, India and Pakistan actually have much that could potentially make them partners and allies. They speak nearly identical languages and share many of the colonial traditions that came from British rule. Other common features include cricket, obsessive tea drinking, the regimental organization of their armies and a certain type of English spoken by older generations of the elite. They share a passion for the classical music and literature of their mutual past, and for the pop culture of the present. There are many more shared attributes than differences, but the dynamic of the relationship is troubled. Both countries are prone to anger and quick to remember past wrongs. Even globalization has made little difference. There is, for example, comparatively little legal trade or travel between them.

Were India and Pakistan to reach some sort of settlement on Kashmir, all other points of contention would be easily dealt with. Various boundary issues, water sharing from Himalayan river systems, and other items on the long list of disputes could be settled through dialogue, compromise and public pressure. With the exception of Kashmir, the contentious matters are the usual stuff of state-to-state relations, the kinds of disputes that exist between the United States and Canada, or between France and Germany. Kashmir is different. It is a daily reminder—in both countries—of the horror and pain of partition. Survivors of that episode still bear the scars and nurse the hatreds of sixty years ago. Kashmir keeps the bitter memories alive.

One thing is certain. If India is to realize its potential as a global player on economic, diplomatic and military fronts, it will have to bring to an end to the recurrent conflict with Pakistan. The two countries spend over $23 billion a year on their armed forces. India accounts for four-fifths of that total. This expenditure robs both nations of resources that might better be devoted to health care, clean water and education. The time and energy consumed by managing the dispute might better go to strategic planning for the world's real challenges: environmental degradation, global warming, pandemics, economic inequalities, terrorism. Media on both sides of the border, deprived of the daily diet of rhetoric and violence from Kashmir, might better spend time exposing the government malfeasance and corruption that plague both states. Ordinary Indians and Pakistanis might welcome the chance to get to know each other better and to harness the synergies and commonalities of their shared geography and history.

In private, national leaders and politicians mostly despair at the grisly inertia that keeps the two countries locked in a state of perpetual tension. The late Benazir Bhutto once shared her real feelings on Kashmir when several journalists clustered around her desk at her house in Islamabad. She was out of political power at the time and so free to speak her mind, though no one dared to actually publish her words.

Kashmir, she told those around her, restricted the options of Pakistani leaders in relations with India and in global diplomacy. While she served as prime minister, she said, protocol and practice of Pakistani statecraft meant a daily litany of the sins of India in the Himalayan state, and reiteration of old UN resolutions that few other nations still remembered. "It's as if a few million people in a largely forgotten place, Kashmir, hold as hostage one and a half billion in our two countries," Bhutto said. Her views are shared by many in India, but there, too, such frankness remains rare.

At the heart of New Delhi, on top of Raisina Hill, one of the city's few heights of land, sits a pair of striking buildings with oddly prosaic names. North Block and South Block face each other across a broad, empty plaza. Each has an impressive dome, modeled on the cupolas atop St. Peter's Cathedral in Rome and St. Paul's in London. Behind them is a much larger edifice with a plain, almost austere dome, apparently inspired by Buddhist architecture. It caps a vast palace of many wings, porticos and windows. The men who designed New Delhi, Edwin Lutyens and Herbert Baker, put these three buildings at the heart of their masterwork on the assumption that Britain would hang onto India a little longer than it did. Commenting in the January 1931 edition of London's *Architectural Review,* the great traveler Robert Byron welcomed the grand opening of a new capital for British India with a lyrical flourish, steeped in imperial hubris. "It is expected," he wrote, "that the representatives of British sovereignty beyond the seas shall move in a setting of proper magnificence: and that in India, particularly, the temporal power shall be hedged with the divinity of earthly splendour."

In those days, North and South Block were the seat of the civil service, the "steel band" that bound Britain to India and the disparate pieces of the colony to each other. The palace behind was the home of the viceroy, the king's representative in Britain's proudest colonial possession. Pomp and pageantry took place in the vice-regal pile and its lush gardens. The real business of running government was carried on in the offices and meeting rooms of the two ancillary buildings. Below the humble heights of Raisina Hill is the Romanesque building that housed the parliament of India, a circular edifice with more than a hint about it of the Colosseum in Rome. Its situation by arch-imperialist architects—beneath the cluster of domed buildings that housed the administration and its overlord from London—was not accidental. Indians had some say in their government, but not much.

In contemporary times, everything has changed and yet little is different. Parliament is sovereign in the Republic of India, but civil servants in North and South Block still wield much practical authority. In part, this is because of political instability and the near impossibility of cabinet ministers finding enough time amid the chaos of public life to master their complex briefs. That's the charitable explanation. Another is that too many mediocrities make it into cabinet these days. Government by coalition means that the cabinet must accommodate representatives from the twenty or more political parties often required to assemble a parliamentary majority. Indian civil servants take it all in stride. It's no accident that one of the most popular British television comedies of all time, *Yes Minister,* has an Indian version that is said to be hugely popular with the denizens of Raisina Hill.

India's External Affairs ministry, often called simply "South Block," is headed by the country's most senior diplomat, the foreign secretary. Usually there is a minister in overall charge of the political aspects of foreign policy, defending the country's successes and explaining its failures in parliament. The secretary runs the practical aspects of India's relations with the world and supervises a team of diplomats in New Delhi and in foreign capitals. But in late November 2005, Foreign Secretary Shyam Saran was the man in sole charge of South Block. His boss, the external affairs minister, had been forced to resign because of a scandal over the Iraq oil-for-food program. Saran was on his own, a rare opportunity for the professionals to run the show while the amateurs bickered in parliament. This, at least, was how columnists depicted the situation. Ever the diplomat, the foreign secretary himself was far more circumspect, observing only that India was a democracy and he had no plans to assert civil service authority over the ministry. He did, however, have some thoughts and insights about India's foreign policy aspirations for the twenty-first century. Things were changing, he began, abroad and at home.

"We've always lived in a tough neighborhood," Saran said. "We've had wars with our two largest neighbors—Pakistan and China— military engagements in three others countries—Sri Lanka, Maldives and Bhutan—and occasionally troubled relations with Nepal. But this is not how we see India's role in Asia, as some of sort of big brother military power that's going to resort to force to settle disputes. India has so many tools at its disposal." Saran says these include access to India's vast market for foreign goods, diplomacy, foreign aid and a network of friendly countries that look to New Delhi to take a lead role in South Asia. It's an obvious question: Are nuclear weapons in the foreign policy tool kit that Saran refers to?

"Yes and no," he replies. "We are a nuclear weapons state now, but our interests lie in nonproliferation, in extending the *cordon sanitaire* that we erected around our own atomic research and weapons program, to others. We are broadly engaged in the world in so many areas that, in a sense, we are the most globalized nation in the neighborhood. We can bring the benefits of this to our allies and neighbors and everyone benefits, not just India, not just the neighboring state. So take Pakistan. Imagine a full-fledged trade and commercial relationship, some sort of free trade agreement perhaps, or just trade regimes that are mutually beneficial. Their software designers come here to work for Infosys or IBM India, our builders buy their cement and employ their laborers, we outsource work to Pakistani call centers, whatever. Who can imagine war if that's going on?"

Saran says he's a great believer in globalization, so much so that he had told his corps of diplomats to read Thomas L. Friedman's *The World Is Flat* so that they could use the book's bullishness on India as talking points at embassy cocktail parties. Saran said he read Friedman's columns in *The New York Times* every week. I asked him if he was aware of an idea that Friedman put forward in an earlier work, *The Lexus and the Olive Tree*. In that book, the author postulated what he called the Golden Arches theory of international relations. No two countries that have a McDonald's restaurant, he wrote, had ever or would ever go to war with each other. To Friedman, two globalized economies that were wealthy enough to interest foreign fast-food chains and other investors would solve their problems peacefully, with the least possible disruption to business or burger-flipping. But when India and Pakistan fought a small but intense border war in 1999 over a disputed bit of Himalayan territory, the Golden Arches loomed large in the shopping malls of both countries. Did that, in the foreign secretary's view, negate Friedman's idea?

Saran laughed but quickly grew serious and returned to his main theme. "No, that's a theory proven in the breach as well as by events. He [Friedman] may have been a bit overly specific linking McDonald's and war, but what he meant was something perfectly valid. Any country that is focused on doing global business, on expanding its economy, on creating jobs and funding services through bigger tax revenues, educating its people, all that, that country isn't going to start a war, and it's going to look long and hard at peaceful means to resolve disputes."

He cited China to illustrate his point. India had fought a disastrous war with China in 1962, an event that shattered decades of close relations between Beijing and New Delhi. It had taken a generation for the two countries to even talk to each other meaningfully again, and very little concrete progress had actually been made toward a formal peace treaty or agreement on the disputes that sparked the war. Yet trade and commerce had taken over the relationship between the two countries, and that was all that mattered.

India faces more than a few hurdles as it makes its way to the sort of greatness that Saran, Raja Mohan, Mishra and others long for. In that "tough neighborhood" that Saran spoke of, many smaller countries are ambivalent, if not downright hostile, to India. Most South Asian states profess to enjoy close relations and links with New Delhi but bristle in private at the way India treats them. In Nepal, for example, anti-Indian feelings have often boiled over into riots and unrest. When, in 2000, an Indian actor allegedly called Nepalis "stupid" during a television interview, mobs took to the streets in Kathmandu and wrecked Indian-owned businesses and shops. Several died, including a teenaged girl, shot by panicky police officers. When the dust subsided, it emerged that the actor had said nothing of the sort and was horrified by what had happened. And it's not just Nepal. So powerful is the anti-India sentiment in Bangladesh that vast reserves of natural gas are going unexploited because governments don't dare to propose selling it to the nearest and most viable customer, India. Bangladeshi gas, it's felt, is for Bangladeshis. Never mind that the country is too poor to build the pipelines and pumping stations needed to get the gas to market, and that most Bangladeshis couldn't afford to buy it anyway.

It's not entirely surprising that India's neighbors feel as they do. India has been known to throw around its considerable weight in the region. In 2000, a film factory the Indian branch of Kodak had set up in Nepal was forced to close by Indian bureaucrats who insisted on a strict interpretation of trade rules. The factory had been built in Nepal in the first place only because another layer of the Indian bureaucracy had assured Kodak it would be exempt from such rules, making production in Nepal cheaper and more attractive to the company. Hundreds of jobs were lost, and India's reputation for capriciousness was powerfully reinforced. Then there's the charge that Indian diplomats often treat their counterparts from neighboring countries paternalistically and expect them simply to fall in line with India's position on international affairs. "They are like annoying uncles to us," says a former Nepali official. Not only that, India has meddled in the internal affairs of its neighbors, encouraging separatists in Sri Lanka and Maoist rebels in Nepal, among others. Saran had served in most of India's neighboring states in one capacity or another, and he admits that the neighbors have a point. A country with dreams of global grandeur had better clean up its backyard and establish friendly relations with the people next door.

"It's true our regional partners may believe they have good historical reasons for not trusting us. But that's history, not the present, and I think again that our economic successes will take care of this attitude once and for all," says Saran. India's vast market will draw in business and goods from the neighboring states of South Asia, he says, and jobs will cross borders in both directions. He invokes Canada's relationship with the United States. It's not always ideal, but it is still the world's largest trading partnership, and neither country is inclined to let anything disrupt the two-way flow of business, people and ideas. "Nepal could be our Canada, so could Bangladesh, even Pakistan," he says. Saran agrees South Asia will be a test for India. If Indian diplomacy and trade can have an impact in the immediate vicinity, then it can be influential and effective elsewhere. Indian diplomats in South Asian capitals are aware of this, he says, and their work will be judged on how they improve the relationship between their host country and New Delhi.

I left Shyam Saran's office, my ears ringing with fine phrases. He and Raja Mohan were convincing on the subject of India's role in the world. Their argument that their country had already arrived, that it had earned international respect and influence through its software designers and nuclear test explosions, carried conviction. A recent meeting of the World Economic Forum in Davos, Switzerland, was given a wry subtitle by one participant: he called it the "love India" session. The "love" had been elicited through the earnest efforts of Finance Minister Palaniappan Chidambaram, who had led an impressive delegation to Davos to push the idea that India was the next go-to place for global business and culture. The pitch will be made even more convincing when India has changed the way it gets on with its neighbors. What India must not change is its tolerance and resilience when responding to troublesome, even horrific, events such as the Mumbai bombings of July 2006. Those people who rode those commuter trains to work the day after the bombings, looking out with defiance as they clattered past the twisted wreckage, those are the Indians who will shape the country's future, as much as any atomic bomb designer or tenacious diplomat.

11

BECOMING ASIA'S AMERICA

The Next Liberal Superpower?

THE YEAR IS 2040. At the United Nations, delegations are deeply divided over a troubling conflict. Two member states are fighting a border war over economic and immigration issues. The mass movement of people from poor to wealthy states continues to be one of the main challenges facing the world. The twenty-five permanent members of the UN Security Council are about to vote on whether to send in UN troops and technicians to establish and keep the peace. Then one of the most powerful members of the Security Council tells the closed session that it is prepared to fund the UN force by itself, and to provide the technicians, in return for a guarantee that its soldiers will not be directly involved in fighting. "We have a proud tradition of not interfering in other countries' affairs," says the ambassador from India, "and we consider that sacrosanct, even if mandated by this august council."

That's right, India. The most powerful country in the world and a permanent member of the Security Council is taking a lead role in resolving yet another crisis with potential to destabilize the globe. Indian troops are already evacuating Indian citizens from the trouble spot, the ambassador says, taking holiday-makers and dual-nationals to safety aboard the navy's largest aircraft carrier, the *Atal Bihari Vajpayee,* and airlifting others in Indian-designed helicopters and aircraft. The External Affairs ministry in New Delhi says there's no thought of intervening in the fighting, but India remains concerned that peaceful means cannot be found to resolve the dispute. The minister calls for a humanitarian truce and warns that Indian forces must not be fired on or subjected to any hacking by the opposing forces. UN technicians are busy erecting an impenetrable firewall around the Indian command and control structure.

This is a scenario that may seem fanciful in the unipolar world of today, but it's not much of a stretch to predict that there will be some new superpowers on the block by 2040, if not well before then. One of them is certain to be India. The United States of America will no longer have the high podium to itself. Indeed, it would be rash to guess what America's status will be, given its current military overreach, the parlous state of public finances and the poor outcomes that characterize the U.S. education and public health systems. The United States is the richest, most powerful society ever, but the world is changing. Asia is surging, and so are parts of Latin America. New petroleum finds in Africa and Russia's huge gas reserves are repositioning geopolitics. Many unpredictable forces challenge the economic and political certainties that have lain behind American power. India has its own challenges. Nevertheless, it is poised to move into the sort of global role that the United States has occupied for more than a hundred years—that of a liberal superpower.

A few centuries ago, there was nothing like the United States of America. The world's great powers were France, Britain and Spain. Russia, the German states and Austria-Hungary were on the rise; the Ottoman Empire was waning. In the New World, before European settlers started agitating for independence, the colonies supplied the raw materials for imperial economic expansion and military adventurism. There were no democracies. No country could boast of anything resembling a free press. Britain had a parliament but it was run by the traditional landed elite and an increasingly influential business community. Britain's ships ruled the waves and its armies enforced imperial writ in India, Africa, Southeast Asia, China and many smaller, more obscure corners of the globe. Britain was the superpower of its day. But it was no United States.

After the War of Independence, the United States became the first national society to be founded on a set of ideals, rather than on race or centuries of history. The American Constitution and Bill of Rights, although based on the European Enlightenment and French revolutionary thinking, laid the foundation for a nation that is essentially *liberal.* There is no other word for it. Human rights are more important than social consensus. Freedom is broadly defined and made sacrosanct. The underlying assumption is that people of goodwill and intelligence will carry out the letter and spirit of constitutional law to continue improving and, indeed, expanding freedom, human rights and the pursuit of happiness. That is exactly what has happened in the United States. There have been many setbacks and causes for concern, not least in recent years. A rising authoritarian trend has restricted rights and freedoms. In some cases, the courts have acted quickly to enforce the constitution. In others, the outcome has been more mixed. But it's not the case that the American constitution, with its liberal outlook, has in any way become less relevant, or lost its power to protect its citizens. Over time, American freedom has become almost inviolate. The media may not consistently perform their constitutional role, but their right to do so is vigorously defended. Dissenting voices may at times be obscured or ignored, but they thrive. Public debate can be ill informed and lack focus, but it's hard to imagine America without it. As a society, Americans have more freedom and more rights than many other citizens of democracies, even though it can be argued that they are neither sufficiently aware of those rights nor as quick as they might be to defend them. It's also true that practitioners of American democracy are often mediocre, venal or partisan. Not enough of the citizenry votes or participates in the political process. Big business has too much influence, as do other well-funded, highly motivated special interest groups, but at least it is possible to raise your voice and force changes, given enough money and time. The power and influence of money have often undermined the ideals of American democracy, but at least this is widely known and debated by well-informed, interested people. There are well-endowed groups and movements that work hard to mitigate the role of money in politics and government. Even at its worst, the system has mechanisms to correct the flaws that are built-in and well protected.

Add to these unique strengths the more traditional muscle and heft of the biggest, strongest and most advanced military the world has ever known and you have a "liberal superpower." Before America, this would have been a laughable concept. The world's dominant powers were traditionally brutal and self-interested, bristling with hubris, always ready to slap around a potential rival or put down a rebellion with extreme prejudice. Indeed, what were known as "punitive expeditions" against upstart Natives and potential regional rebels became a specialty of the British armed services in the nineteenth century, when the empire was at its height. In Ethiopia, India, Sumatra, China, South America, Albania, Greece and Turkey (and the list goes on), British ships, sailors and soldiers wreaked havoc by way of teaching local lessons, and it worked rather well. Other European imperial powers behaved in much the same way.

The debate over whether or not the United States is an empire is an old one. The question has been argued at least since 1898, when victory in the Spanish–American War gave Washington a few imperial possessions (Cuba, Puerto Rico, the Philippines) to administer. But even if there is an American empire, it is essentially a liberal one. It was acquired through influence and soft power as much as by military might, and it has been governed by a democracy that spends much time questioning its own motives and actions. Not enough, America's opponents would say, but that is a quibble. The United States is a liberal superpower, the first the world has ever known, but not the last.

Believers in the European Union have global pretensions. They may dream of replacing the United States as the most powerful force for good in the world, but the EU is perpetually constrained by internal contradictions and the differing views of member states on almost every issue. Brazil seems ready to start realizing its full economic and political potential but will likely remain a regional influence, rather than a global superpower. Were any of the oil-possessing states to take democracy seriously, they would have to be considered as potential liberal powers, at least on a regional scale. Nigeria and Saudi Arabia come to mind. But both are far from liberal, and thanks to ruling classes that are simultaneously corrupt and short-sighted, are unlikely to acquire visionary leadership anytime soon. China remains an authoritarian, rather brutal society that is opaque about its hopes and dreams for the rest of the world. Chinese leaders have long stayed out of other countries' affairs, but the country's economic surge and quest for sources of energy are at the center of Beijing's global political ambitions for now. China's new, more active role in Africa is certainly part of this strategy. Russia is emerging as a major supplier of energy to Europe and China, but no one would describe Moscow as being even remotely liberal. Countless smaller countries are liberal enough but lack either the potential or the ambition to reach superpower status. The list would include Canada, Australia, South Africa, Great Britain, France, Germany, South Korea and even Japan, unless it substantially rebuilds its military, something that's currently forbidden by its postwar, U.S.-imposed constitution.

No, only India stands out from the crowd of countries that could equal or even replace the United States. Admittedly, this is a possibility that will not be realized for many years, if it's to happen at all. But the raw materials are all there. The many challenges and difficulties are well known: poverty, inequity, corruption, environmental degradation and a rather fissiparous approach to politics lead the pack. But it can be argued that at least India knows where the pitfalls lie and understands that they must be overcome. Countless organizations and individuals work tirelessly to raise awareness and mitigate the country's problems. The media report on both the issues and on those who seek to resolve them. Indians use their freedoms of speech robustly and often. Nobel laureate Amartya Sen calls this India's "argumentative dialectic" and himself argues convincingly that public debate at every level of Indian society is a powerful force for stability and constructive change. Even the poorest and most powerless of the poor, Sen believes, have a voice and views on how their elite is governing and behaving. It's difficult if not impossible to keep misgovernance and crime out of public view. And literacy is soaring in India; it has increased by 20 percent over the past few decades, which means more media, more awareness, more pressure for accountability and good government. This is the underpinning of the liberal part of the equation.

The superpower potential is less obvious. For although the country has a large, well-funded military that is technically sophisticated and adequately equipped, it's hard to see how the armed forces of a poor country can project sufficient coercive force to claim even regional hegemony. More than three-quarters of the Indian military budget is spent on staff costs: wages, pensions, health care, housing, training and so on. The rest goes to equipment, weapons and technology, much of which is produced in India and not always of the highest caliber. The inevitable and almost universal corruption found in military procurement is even more of a challenge in India than elsewhere, costing the armed forces inestimable chunks of funding each year. Plus Indian forces and military planners have little or no battle experience beyond their own borders and immediate region. While Indian troops have been deployed to fight many times since independence, they have not been engaged in wider conflicts or in other continents, save as part of UN missions. Their capacity to project force effectively or to gather military intelligence in distant places remains largely theoretical. An aspiring liberal superpower must be capable of projecting its strength and influence.

As well, there have been problems with many of the Indian military's deployments within the country's borders. The Kashmir insurgency was brutally mishandled in the 1990s, with thousands of documented cases of wanton cruelty and atrocities committed against civilians. Actual progress in the fight against militant groups that were themselves guilty of human rights abuses was thin on the ground. To its credit, the Indian government did investigate and prosecute some of the more egregious cases involving its troops, albeit under heavy domestic and international pressure. Some of the northeastern tribal rebellions have raged for decades with no real progress on the military front. There, too, reports have emerged of human rights abuses. Only in the last ten years or so have sustained attempts been made by the armed forces to broaden their counterinsurgency approach to include hearts-and-minds campaigns, and to acquire a real understanding of the grievances that drive internal rebellion. Many feel this was long overdue.

Commodore Jasjit Singh, a retired air force officer who now works at a think tank in New Delhi called the Centre for Air Power Studies, argues that the entire military structure has long been held back by outdated thinking among defense planners, and by corruption in the procurement process. He says any country with ambitions of superpower status has to work on its air power, its naval platform for the projection of force and its ability to quickly deploy large numbers of military assets to distant theaters of conflict or need. He also believes in the use of civil affairs campaigns to win local support for military activities in a combat zone.

"We are army obsessed," he says. "We ignore the air force because it requires large sums of money spent outright, at the beginning of realizing your ambition, and that limits corruption potential, especially if you're buying from an incorruptible company. Also, few of our lawmakers have been military pilots, so they don't know what the air force can do, how quickly it can get in, deliver its payloads and get out."

Singh thinks the Indian navy is the cutting-edge military force in the country. He points to the refitted Russian aircraft carrier bought in 2005. This, he says, is important for both force projection and softer forms of global influence such as disaster relief and evacuating citizens from troubled foreign areas. "Our navy led the way in tsunami relief around the region as an example of what they can do. It also leads in new thinking, with the air force second and the army a distant, distant third."

As Singh and others convincingly point out, projection of hard military power is no longer the only requirement for a country that wants a global political role that matches its size and economic heft. The Asian tsunami of 2004 did indeed provide such an opportunity. Indian ships were sent to the Maldives, Sri Lanka and even Indonesia. Sailors and soldiers set up medical camps, provided food and water and participated in multinational relief efforts. They were among the first to be sent to nearby disaster zones. That was despite the impact on India itself from the tsunami. More than sixteen thousand Indian citizens died around the southern coastal areas, and millions were displaced and impoverished when the surging waters destroyed their homes, boats and livelihoods. The Indian armed forces led the relief effort, the army by land, the air force providing transport and damage assessment from above and the navy sending medics and disaster teams into remote or inaccessible areas.

A spate of catastrophes at home has helped make India's security forces highly skilled at disaster relief. Some would say they are among the most adroit and well organized in the world at mitigating the immediate effects of catastrophe. When the eastern state of Orissa was struck in 1998 by a monstrous cyclone that left at least thirty thousand dead, soldiers made their way through residual storms and hundreds of miles of blocked roads to reach stranded victims. An early priority was clearing space for air strips and helipads so casualties could be flown out to field hospitals. Soldiers also did distasteful but necessary work, such as collecting decaying bodies from waterlogged areas for mass cremation, all in an effort to minimize the contamination of water supplies and the spread of disease. They carried out their duties alongside the utter collapse of civil authority during the first weeks of the crisis. At some of the monstrous earthquakes that have rumbled along the Himalayan fault line and its tributaries, at the western village of Latur in 1993 and in Gujarat eight years later, the Indian armed forces provided the most immediate and effective relief in the early, most trying days of trauma and devastation. Later, in each case, a civilian-led effort built on the military's early successes.

Of course, the armed forces learned how to deliver medical care and to bring disaster relief during the wars fought with Pakistan, and in bitter insurgencies such as those in Kashmir and the northeast. As part of an effort to win hearts and minds, the army often sets up temporary medical camps for local people, where they treat eye problems, provide polio inoculations or even deal with women's health issues. In the distant, deprived heartland of India, where obscurantist Maoist groups hold sway, uniformed medics and doctors dispense care in remote villages where civilian government officials might be killed.

Projecting force and influence through military operations can take many forms. It's not just about killing the enemy. Since 2000, India has put considerable effort into developing its relationship with the United States. Traditionally, America was viewed by Indians with skepticism or downright hostility. The CIA was often accused of being behind mysterious bombings or other violent incidents. India's Communist parties were often at the forefront of the accusers in these cases, but mainstream politicians played the anti-America card when it suited them. The economic interests of American companies were always suspect, a feeling often encouraged by Indian manufacturers that felt threatened by their U.S. competitors. Famously, or infamously, the Coca-Cola company packed up and left India in 1977, ostensibly because it would have had to divulge its secret formula. In reality, it was driven out as much by the hostile attitude toward foreign business of a socialist industry minister and a coalition government that had never expected to be elected in the first place. IBM left at the same time, along with a host of other American companies. Their departure was cheered by many and seen as a sign of national success, though thousands of newly unemployed white-collar workers probably felt differently. In large part, the aversion to Washington was caused by America's marked tendency to ally itself with Pakistan in South Asia, while New Delhi looked to the USSR. The Americans viewed the Pakistanis as anti-Communist moderate Muslims and valued their participation in various military alliances and exercises. That closeness cost Washington its credibility with India, which viewed Islamabad— with some justification—as the source of military adventurism and terror tactics aimed at Indian interests in South Asia.

In 1971, India invaded what was then the eastern wing of the bifurcated country of Pakistan, as millions of refugees fled across the Indian border. Pakistani soldiers were carrying out veritable pogroms against the ethnic Bengalis, who outnumbered other Pakistani groups in the territory. The U.S. secretary of state at the time, Henry Kissinger, was a robust and unapologetic believer in gunboat diplomacy. He prevailed on then-president Nixon to order the dispatch of an American aircraft carrier, the USS *Enterprise,* to the Bay of Bengal to signal Washington's support for Pakistan over India. Ostensibly, there were fears that Soviet troops might support the Indians in their invasion of East Pakistan, and that China might also become involved. In reality, Kissinger was telling the Indian leader, Indira Gandhi, that Washington was displeased with the attack on a long-standing ally and that military operations needed to stop. Mrs. Gandhi ignored the warning and her troops eventually forced Pakistan to surrender, which led to the founding of the newly independent state of Bangladesh. It was a dangerous moment. When it passed, the two giant democracies remained at loggerheads for decades.

In the 1980s, India took its first cautious steps toward more market-friendly economics. Relations with America began to improve. The relatively young, Western-oriented prime minister, Rajiv Gandhi, had big ideas for making his country competitive and prosperous. The much vaunted economic reforms of 1991, though needed in the first instance to stave off a major loan default, had the added effect of making Washington happy. American companies were pleased as well.

Boeing began to do more deals with India's airlines. Coca-Cola, IBM and many other firms started the long process of reestablishing themselves in the world's largest democracy and fastest-growing middle-class market. The software and IT boom cemented the relationship. Young Indian computer programmers were needed in their hundreds of thousands in Silicon Valley, and powerful IT entrepreneurs such as Bill Gates were able to convince the U.S. Congress to greatly increase quotas for specialty work visas. At the same time, Indian-Americans showed a new interest in their homeland, its budding openness to investment and the enhanced prospects that came with that. They formed lobby groups and worked with lawmakers to improve attitudes in Washington toward India. Crucially, the Indo-American community raised funds for U.S. politicians and sponsored trips to India. They played the insiders' game in Washington and slowly broke down the old barriers. According to Strobe Talbott, then deputy secretary of state, President Bill Clinton was determined to form a close alliance with India and put relations with New Delhi at the center of his administration's goals in Asia.

India's nuclear tests of 1998 threatened to upset the apple cart, but Washington's quick recovery from its initial outrage helped usher in a whole new phase of amity, cooperation and respect. The change in climate and reality between New Delhi and Washington has continued apace. The administration of President George W. Bush even accelerated the process. In what was possibly the boldest nonmilitary foreign policy development of his presidency, Bush helped negotiate a deal to bring India back into the international nuclear community. During a visit to the United States by the Indian prime minister Manmohan Singh in 2005, Bush made the stunning announcement that America and India would henceforth be nuclear-armed allies that shared sensitive technology and cooperated on various issues, including nonproliferation. Skeptics in both countries were furious. The deal was seen as undermining efforts to prevent the spread of nuclear weapons. By accepting that India had nuclear arms, Bush had undercut the Nuclear Non-Proliferation Treaty, which specifically forbade any country but the permanent five Security Council members from legally possessing an atomic arsenal. The deal, it was argued, had chilling implications. Strobe Talbott, at the time serving as a senior fellow at Washington think tank the Brookings Institution, warned that the nuclear accord with India so undermined the NPT that countries that had respected it for years by not developing weapons, so-called nuclear have-nots such as South Africa or Brazil, might now conclude that a few test explosions were the best way to get respect and technology from the United States.

"Seeing the outcome of Singh's visit to Washington," Talbott wrote, "some—perhaps many—of those nuclear have-nots will be more inclined to regard the NPT as an anachronism, reconsider their self-restraint, and be tempted by the precedent that India has successfully established and that now, in effect, has an American blessing."[1]

In India, old suspicions about America resurfaced at the political extremes as well as in scientific circles. The deal was denounced as free entry for American spies into New Delhi's den of nuclear secrets. Indian detractors found fault with pledges to separate the country's civil and military nuclear programs. The former would be subject to international inspection. The latter would not. Yet not all in India were so sure that it was a bad thing. Younger voices hailed the understanding with Washington as a breakthrough, a way to get access to American science on an unprecedented scale. Most importantly for India, the deal gave impetus to its plans for an ambitious nuclear power program to provide much-needed electricity in the years ahead. India imports almost all of its oil and gas, and its coal reserves are not of high quality. There has long been a view that an extensive network of nuclear reactors was needed, but this was always impeded by Washington's suspicions. Now the United States is a supporter. Ironically, though, as this book went to press, India's Communist parties were threatening to force an election on the issue of the nuclear deal with America. Government ministers put the deal on the back-burner, and Washington got a lesson in the internecine politics of its emerging ally and potential successor.

Of course, growing closer to the world's lone superpower doesn't mean that a country is becoming more like the United States. But in the absence of vast petroleum reserves, open markets and close ties with Washington are very much a prerequisite for success in the post–Cold War world. A few countries, notably Iran, Cuba, Venezuela and North Korea, have demonstrated that opposition to Washington is a viable option as a central plank of foreign policy. But none of these countries has potential for superpower status.

Then there's China. Much is made in Washington and other capitals about New Delhi being a counterweight to Beijing, a liberal democracy with a booming economy offsetting an authoritarian state with even higher growth rates. It's true that China remains an enigma for policy planners in foreign ministries from Tokyo to Washington. Everyone wants trade with China, and access to its labor and manufacturing efficiencies. The appetite of the growing Chinese middle class for Western consumer goods and brand names is a major attraction. But Western strategic thinkers are vexed by China's military ambitions and its assumptions of a sort of Asian hegemony. They wonder whether the Chinese Communist Party will continue to exercise preeminent authority or whether the country will collapse into regional fiefdoms.

It's impossible to say with any certainty what lies in store. Negative outcomes seem less likely than a kind of muddling through, crisis after crisis, with mixed effects. But what is obvious is that the prospect of China becoming its own version of a liberal superpower is highly unlikely for the foreseeable future. So much thinking in the circles of power in China is either predicated on the grievances and setbacks of the past or driven by hard-edged economics. Accountability of the elite—crucial as we've seen, in a country with pretensions to be a liberal superpower—remains negligible. Which is why people resort to violence when they object to official behavior or decisions. In recent years, there have been hundreds of riots and attacks on government officials by members of the Chinese public fed up with local corruption or hubris. These events go largely unreported, but the world is becoming more aware of public discontent in the world's most populous country. China is totally committed to its economic course but has almost no capacity to change or even modify the arrangements. However much economic power has been diffused by the mix of government and private investment, such a massive centralized state doesn't make changes overnight. If it does alter course, the shift is bound to be slow and opaque, with none of the public discourse that accompanies change in a democracy. This is not America, and it is not India.

It can also be argued that India and China are moving closer together, that their economic and political strengths complement each other. As Professor Ashish Bose put it to me once, "China may be the

factory of the world, but we are the office, the technology people. Everyone agrees that we need to get better at manufacturing, and
the Chinese might start to work in areas where we excel now—call
centers, back-office services. But there's . . . enough work to go
around." In short, Bose and many others believe, it's a win-win situation. India–China trade has soared in recent years, from a few hundred million dollars annually less than a decade ago to nearly US$14
billion in 2005. The two countries have signed wide-ranging trade
agreements and are discussing new ones. They have flagged off a
road-construction project that should give them viable, year-round
land links within a few years. Increasingly, everyday purchases in India
carry the same "Made in China" label found in so many Western
countries. Indian Hindus have begun to notice that the special items
they buy each year to celebrate holy days such as Diwali or Dushera
were made by Chinese workers. An officially atheist, Communist republic is manufacturing images of gods for the world's most diversely
religious democracy. This is not the behavior of two countries that
hate each other and are destined to go to war. Nor do budding liberal
superpowers endanger their economies and their prospects for continued growth by picking fights with major trading partners.

Becoming Asia's America will make India less likely to fight wars,
even against Pakistan. The country will quite simply be too engaged
with trade and business and global affairs to assume the classic pos-
ture of the belligerent. The Indian military is likely to remain regionally dominant but focused on defense, with multilateral
deployments more likely than simple force projection in the region
and beyond. India has other fish to fry. It is likely to want to use its
military assets to win hearts and minds and keep global sea lanes free
for trade, to work with allies on joint exercises and antiterror operations, and to share its hard-won expertise in disaster relief.

Perhaps it does the subject a disservice to think of a future India
as "Asia's America." The label works to explain and elaborate on the
two words *liberal* and *superpower,* but it also restricts and confines
the potential of a nation and society immeasurably more vast and
complex even than the United States. The sheer heterogeneousness
of Indian society, with its languages, regions and arrays of interest
groups, is already giving rise to the sort of politics and problem solving that prepare the country for a future global role. That India lacks

the grand national consensus of the United States on a range of issues is a drawback now, but will be a strength in the future. Too often, Washington-led domestic agreement on external threats or strategic priorities has been accepted by an unquestioning congress and an indifferent public. Iraq is the most recent, and arguably most glaring, example, but there are many others. Think Vietnam, the war on drugs and Guantanamo Bay. When the consensus view has proven wrong or harmful to U.S. interests, the national self-doubt and sheer funk that grip America causes harm and disquiet around the world. If it gets things right, India has the opportunity be a new kind of superpower, one that hedges its bets and works politically all of the time to develop and hold a national consensus. But, ideally, India will also be flexible enough to accommodate changes in tone or direction when the situation warrants.

Even now, India sees itself as a consummate, if quiet, team player on the international stage—depending on the quality of the diplomats involved, of course. Shyam Saran insisted with some pride that the days when his country was known only as a prickly, easily offended, obsessive moralizer were over. India was playing in every field in town, he said. That included HIV/AIDS, antiterrorism, drug trafficking, international organized crime, efforts against sea piracy, intellectual property rights, trading rules, aid and development, harmonizing banking law, drug testing in sport and so on. "If you want to deal in any of these areas," he said, "you need India, and we are engaged. It means a lot of work for a fairly small corps of diplomats, but it also means we get better and better people, professionals and experts. We reach into our private sector and the diaspora all of the time, and it's working beyond our wildest dreams." Saran is a senior diplomat charged with representing his country's interests; he is not likely to understate the case for India's improving status. But the argument he makes is a strong one. Gone are the days of Cold War nostrums and nonalignment, of choosing your economics according to which side you're on. It's a big, bad world with many supranational challenges, and an aspiring liberal superpower needs to be ready for anything. India has the strengths and is acquiring the assets and the capability to take up this role, either alone or in concert with an array of other countries. The world's largest democracy is thinking big.

CONCLUSION

What It Takes to Be Great

NOTHING IS CERTAIN. India's progress could easily stall, or fall afoul of one of the many challenges that lurk along the way. In early 2007, *The Economist,* a magazine that's long been bullish about India's potential for prosperity and global political influence, carried on its front page a cartoon of a Royal Bengal tiger standing against a green jungle backdrop. Smoke and flame gushed from the tip of the tiger's tail and the headline proclaimed "India Overheats." It was a surprising and troubling editorial line from a respected and famously sober magazine. The accompanying article pointed out that many of India's fiscal and monetary indicators, the broad brushstrokes of its economic picture, were pointing toward a slowdown. Most companies were operating at or near their optimum capacity. Inflation was rising rapidly, with only a tepid response from the Central Bank. Consumer and commercial credit, newly liberated from years of tight regulation, was ballooning and, with it, debt. Indians were buying imported goods like never before, especially from China, and the imbalance between imports and exports had never been larger. There had been a stock market bubble throughout much of the past four years, with share prices rising fourfold, far faster than in Shanghai, New York or London.

Life for India's huge middle class is getting tougher and more expensive. House prices are at record highs. So is demand for housing in major cities. Mumbai, Delhi and Bangalore are all more expensive than their Western equivalents when salaries and other costs are factored in. People are moving to distant suburbs that require them to spend one or even two hours commuting. Crowded roads and air pollution from vehicle traffic are bad and getting worse. Family life in awakening India offers an array of consumer choices and benefits that previous generations never knew, but the cost is high in time and money. Children want the same video games and DVDs as their counterparts in the West, and they have to be sent to decent schools if they're to have a chance at passing the joint entrance exam and getting into an Indian Institute of Technology, or just about any other respected university or college. The country's best primary and secondary schools are vastly oversubscribed and incredibly costly—thousands of dollars a year for tuition and books. Even if a child is accepted on his or her academic qualifications, many schools require parental interviews before admission. Ostensibly, this is to make sure family support will be sufficient to help students meet the tough demands of the curriculum, but many suspect some schools of snobbishness or casteism. There's growing pressure to regulate or even ban such interviews, but they're unlikely to vanish so long as supply and demand for high-quality education remain mismatched on such a massive scale.

There's ample evidence in the booming IT and BPO industries that India might fall victim to its own success. Too much has been achieved too quickly. New businesses, fueled by venture capital and brimming with hot, marketable ideas, are not in short supply—but skilled, capable people are. The country's colleges and institutes gave India the early edge over the United States and other technology powers by producing more engineering and science graduates than any other country, several hundreds of thousands every year and growing. That gave companies such as Infosys and Wipro the capacity to hire the best graduates and to thrive accordingly. Each company still gets more than a hundred résumés for every job it has to offer. But other firms can't afford to be so choosy and, particularly in the burgeoning call-center and offshore services sector, good workers are increasingly hard to find.

Even with help from the private educational sector, the crunch continues. An abundance of jobs and opportunities is giving existing workers the ability to move around, cherry-picking opportunities and demanding higher pay. Wages are soaring at the reputable end of the BPO sector, putting pressure on the economies of scale that made India's companies attractive in the first place. An Indian call-center worker, employed by a large, well-known Western firm, no longer makes just a tenth of what his or her colleague in Europe or Canada would earn. Then there's burnout. The sheer burden of BPO work on individual workers has been well documented by counselors such as Dr. Achal Bhagat and by the Indian media. Many smaller or independent call-center firms—those that take on work from a wide range of clients, not just one big brand name like Microsoft or Canada's Scotiabank—put immense stress on their employees by constantly changing the nature of their duties. One day they're representing a credit company in Florida, the next a help desk for a software firm in Edinburgh, with all the confusion of changing accents and idioms that such a switch entails. There may not be the same stress at the entry level, or for those not quite good enough to crack the upper ranks, but it's still tough. Most call-center business plans now make allowances for the large number of employees who either burn out and lose their productive edge or move on quickly to better-paying jobs. Annual employee turnover at the lower end of the business can be in excess of 90 percent, according to industry insiders.

The face of the Bengal tiger on the cover of *The Economist* wears a troubled look. (Naturally enough, perhaps, since its tail is on fire.) But the magazine suggests that political and financial leaders alike are too caught up in their own rhetoric about their country's impending greatness to take the urgent action needed to cool things down. Surveys of investors and business executives show that confidence has never been higher. The government is predicting five more years of growth at an annual rate in excess of 9 percent, nearly at China's white-hot pace. Goldman Sachs recently forecast that this rate of growth could continue until 2020, and the news sparked euphoria. What didn't get reported, at least so prominently, was Goldman Sachs's proviso that such levels of growth were possible only if there was a significant investment in infrastructure and services. The investment firm also called for more, potentially controversial, economic reforms. Without them, the firm warned, growth could fizzle and the risk of fiscal crisis would grow.

Put simply, if economic expansion is to be sustained at its current rate, India needs to start by building better roads, ports and airports. Some 40 percent of Indian produce spoils before it reaches the market. This is largely because of the long periods it spends on battered, overcrowded highways that are often blocked for days by accidents. Moribund port services and achingly overburdened airports hinder the flow of trade and exports. This is especially damaging where high-value agricultural produce and manufactured goods are being moved. It's not just the business community that needs better services. Ordinary Indian people need substantial improvements in the provision of health care and public education. A recent study found that only half of government-appointed teachers showed up for work in rural and semirural schools. Public health posts suffer from similar understaffing and absenteeism. Doctors may draw their government salaries, but they're more likely to be found dispensing medical treatment for money at a nearby private clinic. Indian health care is publicly funded and cost-efficient on paper, but it is actually one of the world's most privatized systems. Government funding accounts for less than a quarter of total spending on medical services. Medical rights activists say the quality of care and treatment varies widely and the country is falling short of its own commitment to make sure every Indian can get proper health care when it's needed.

The entire country needs substantial improvements in electrical power provision. Blackouts and shortages plague most cities in times of peak demand, especially during the burning heat of high summer, when life (and commerce) without air-conditioning is almost unthinkable, at least for the more affluent sections of society. The shortages are not entirely due to a lack of power production. The country can, at least theoretically, meet its needs from existing capacity. The problem is that less than half of the electricity consumed in India is actually paid for. Much is stolen. The sight of bare copper cables slung by hand over high tension wires to bring power to informal slum colonies is far from uncommon. Many small and medium-sized businesses manage to steal their electricity as well, either by bribing power company officials or by simply not paying their bills. Consequently, most Indian government power companies and state electricity boards stagger along with huge deficits. Often the worst offenders, especially in northern states such as Bihar and Uttar Pradesh, are government agencies and state-owned factories, which can use political connections to avoid paying their power tariffs. Cutting off supply to such entities is rarely an option, again because of politics. Repeated attempts to reform the power sector in India have made limited progress. There are too many vested interests blocking reform: power workers' unions, government agencies, businesses that are substantial employers and contributors to political campaigns. The logic of markets and economics pale in the face of such factors.

So much for the classical economic analysis of the problems India faces. Then there's poverty. Between two hundred and three hundred million Indians earn less than US$1 a day. The number has slowly declined throughout the years of India's economic successes, but it remains a powerful indictment of a system that can't seem to spread the wealth around quickly enough. India has made statistical inroads against poverty in recent years. The percentage of the population that gets by on around two thousand calories of food intake per day—India's accepted measure of poverty—has been halved. But overall numbers remain roughly similar, and the fact that such a large bloc of citizens remains so profoundly deprived is emphasized by the explosion in middle-class affluence. Contrasts abound. Rat catcher Sadanand Palande plies his trade in Mumbai, where a penthouse apartment costs millions of dollars and film moguls drive by in BMWs and sleek Lexus limousines. In Bangalore, the people of Shaktivail Nagar move their bowels in their colony's burial ground a few miles away from the glittering office blocks at Infosys, Wipro and Hewlett-Packard. Hundreds of thousands of people who own nothing but the clothes on their backs live rough on the streets of Calcutta as the city transforms itself into another software, IT and BPO capital.

Reliable statistics are hard to come by. How many of India's poor are landless laborers who follow the work from farm to farm or toil on construction projects in cities and towns is hard to estimate. Workers from India's worst-off state, Bihar, can be found everywhere. They carry heavy loads as Himalayan porters and sweep the landscaped lawns of beach resorts in the southern state of Kerala. The migratory life leaves little time for family investments in health or education for children. Youngsters work alongside their parents: an extra pair of hands means a little more money, but schools require a settled life, so a degree of illiteracy stubbornly persists. Those considerable improvements in poverty and literacy statistics over the past twenty years have also served to emphasize the sheer intractability of the toughest forms of deprivation, those arising from caste, displacement from the land, acute or chronic catastrophe and health problems. These are poverty issues that can't be resolved through economic growth and an expanding job market. They require government and social intervention, policies that address root causes and offer relief from the worst excesses of exclusion.

HIV/AIDS is, and will continue to be, a significant burden on India's health system and growth potential in the coming generation. By some estimates, there are more people infected with HIV in India than in any other country. In fairness, official figures from China, Russia and other undemocratic states are difficult to confirm. Indian government statistics are seen as reliable, if somewhat patchy in the more remote or disorganized parts of the country. International monitoring groups, led by the United Nations agency UNAIDS, recently revised downward their estimates of the number of people in India living with HIV/AIDS while warning that the pandemic could still have a significant impact on lifestyles and public health. Whatever the actual number, after years of denial, India is finally coming to terms with the immensity of the problem. In 2001, the prime minister, Atal Bihari Vajpayee, called HIV/AIDS the country's single biggest public health crisis. Unfortunately, as things stand, there are limits on what public officials and politicians can do. India's largely private system of medical provision means that many HIV sufferers have to pay their own way, even if government programs exist to treat them. India is one of the world's largest producers of the antiviral drug cocktails that have been so successful in sustaining life for those with the infection in the West, but so far fewer than 10 percent of Indian patients have access to the right medicines. If a significant number of those now infected with HIV develop full-blown AIDS, the human and monetary costs will intensify. Activists and doctors say a vast awareness and treatment campaign is needed, one far larger than anything tried so far. India's National AIDS Control Programme has been widely praised for its sincerity and commitment, but its efforts remain dwarfed by the scale of the problems it faces.

Yet even HIV/AIDS is a challenge that can be met and overcome. Indian pharmaceutical firms can be persuaded to produce sufficient quantities of the required medicines at an affordable cost, and the mass media are ready, willing and able to take part in campaigns of outreach and advocacy. Migratory laborers, truck drivers and other high-risk groups can be persuaded to start using condoms. Public health systems can be given more resources. Crucially, it isn't just the detail of how India meets challenges that matters, it's the approach itself. There is an almost unbounded sense in today's India that democracy, jurisprudence, activism and goodwill can resolve even the most pressing and chronic problems. It's not precisely what Americans would call a "can-do" attitude—it's more a sense of positive fatalism mixed with an awareness of the scale of all things Indian. In other words, the problem is there and it's vast, but it must be addressed, and not just at the micro level. From partition through the travails of a youthful nation-state, the political upheavals of Indira Gandhi's years, countless natural disasters, the near financial collapse of the 1990s and so many other difficult moments in the past six decades, India has coped, not merely survived. Life for millions of Indians has radically improved, and it seems almost certain to continue to do so. A great many steps will have to be taken though to ensure positive outcomes from India's growth into economic and political influence on a global scale. The suggestions that follow are not meant as a de tailed prescription, merely a series of observations and thoughts gleaned from extensive contacts with India over the past two decades.

It is beyond obvious that the most pressing priority is poverty. It is unacceptable that a country with 250 million relatively affluent members of the middle class should still have a similar or larger tally of malnourished, mistreated, struggling poor people. Poverty has to be tackled on nothing less than a war footing. Two-thirds of the population is dependent on farming. It's tough, unrewarding work for most of them, and pressure and opportunities to leave the land are growing. Those who remain as farmers or farm laborers need various sorts of support and guarantees from government and society at large.

The shoddy system of roads that serves rural areas might be the best place to start. Produce that never makes it to market benefits no one. Of course, experts will have their own imperatives and must be consulted. Food and crop storage facilities need to be improved drastically. These will add immense value to agriculture by allowing the sale of surplus production. Most Indian agriculture is dependent on the monsoon or deep aquifers that are being drawn down by overextraction, so better water policies are a must. This may entail the imposition of fees for water use, perhaps reflecting the ability of users to pay, but that's a matter for Indian democracy to resolve. Most of all, farming has to make economic sense. That means introducing professional cultivation methods, marketing products more effectively and establishing connections with suppliers that actually pay off for farmers. Some crops will be grown for export, but India's vast domestic market has an unending appetite for just about everything that grows in the country, so the real opportunities probably lie within India's borders. Farms will have to become more specialized and depend on commodity trading and a futures system to protect them against bad weather or depressed prices. In short, the future of Indian farming probably lies more with the specialized strawberry farm in the Punjab that sells fruit to a jam factory than with the more traditional cotton or rice crops. Bring on the strawberries.

In the coming years, many Indians now involved in agriculture will migrate to the cities and towns, where they will work as laborers, taxi drivers and maybe even press wallahs, or their twenty-first-century equivalent. They're going to need jobs, jobs and more jobs. Even now, India is facing real problems with unemployment and underemployment. People who hold down a job that doesn't provide enough income to meet nutritional and other requirements are underemployed. The trucks that roll along India's highways, taking goods and commodities to markets, usually have five or six men riding in the cab. This complement includes two drivers, because the vehicle doesn't stop long enough for one to get a good night's sleep, and a mechanic to do roadside repairs. The others are unofficial apprentices, or friends just tagging along, or people who work for a little food just to get by. An Indian shovel is often wielded by two workers, one on the handle and the other tugging on a rope to help the handle wallah fling the dirt. But the job pays only enough for one. Again, statistics pose a problem here. The government doesn't measure underemployment to the satisfaction of most economists, and to simply state that some twenty million Indians don't have jobs is to miss the point. The number of people who are underemployed is far larger, perhaps by a factor of five or more, than the number who actually do not have work, or have given up looking. Meaningful jobs are not being created on anything like the scale that will be necessary. There is an acute demand for graduates in the knowledge economy, but there hasn't been a complementary boom in opportunities for the laborer, artisan or farmhand. Construction and housing bubbles in New Delhi and other cities have pulled in millions of building-site workers and contractors, but this is not steady work. Bubbles burst, booms slow down and laborers are among the first to lose their jobs.

Before 2005, India was growing rapidly, but not fast enough to keep up with the expansion of the labor force. As this book is being written, growth is approaching 10 percent, and there's an opportunity to make sure the job market continues to expand as well. But the requirement for such high overall economic growth will continue for at least a generation, until the demographic bulge of younger Indians reaches middle age and beyond. These people need well-paying, stable work. Public works programs to improve infrastructure are one solution, though the ability of the public sector to pay for them is in doubt. Private investment will be necessary: toll roads, build-own-operate bridges, ports and airports. These innovative approaches to meeting infrastructure needs have a mixed record elsewhere, but they do, in the end, supply the services.

Governments also need to look at ways to encourage and support the growth of low- and medium-skilled jobs in manufacturing, food processing, retailing and other employment-intensive sectors. One good sign could be that Wal-Mart is coming to India. In November 2006, telecommunications entrepreneur Sunil Mittal announced that he was teaming up with global retailing's colossus to open hundreds of shops across the country. India's retail sector—long closed to foreign investment—is only beginning to wake up to its potential. Most of the country's shops remain small family affairs, but mall culture is catching on, as are supermarkets. The middle class has little time or inclination for bazaars and street markets. It may dismay traditionalists, but advanced economies rely on shopping and retail employment as a primary engine for domestic growth.

A lot of India's Wal-Mart workers are bound to be women, and this will be a welcome development. Rigid attitudes toward the role of women in traditional, socially conservative households across the country have gradually relaxed over the country's first sixty years of independence. Now it's time to consider the benefits of equality. As demographer Ashish Bose is fond of pointing out, no society that restricts women to the home can prosper in the absence of vast reserves of petroleum or other commodities. India's people are its most important natural resource, and around half of them are female. When women work, and are treated as men's equals, there is growth for all. Bose calls it "the rocket science equation: patriarchy equals poverty." You don't have to be a rocket scientist to figure it out. This change is already taking place in middle-class quarters of the major cities and—it can be argued—growing prosperity and confidence are the direct results. Women are making advances in rural areas, too, due mainly to political affirmative action rather than economics. The requirement that a third of all municipal and village council seats go to women has to be given the credit here. But there remain vast physical and mental spaces in India where female emancipation is a work in progress. The epidemic of female feticide is a case in point, as is the fact that women continue to lag behind men in literacy and share of family income. Change takes time. The lot of Indian women will have to continue to improve in the twenty-first century.

Outside its borders, India has an array of challenges to confront. Most pressing of these is its poisonous relationship with Pakistan. Since the nuclear tests of 1998, local clashes on at least two occasions have threatened to flare into all-out war, almost certainly involving atomic weapons. This is unacceptable to India, Pakistan, South Asia and the world. For both countries, spending on defense dwarfs that on development and infrastructure and leaves government finances bereft of funds. A comprehensive peace agreement that leads to free trade and travel between India and Pakistan is a pressing need, especially for the people of the disputed region of Kashmir. This should be a pact that demilitarizes Kashmir, sets up political dispute-resolution mechanisms and opens the border between the two countries. South Asia stands to lose in war everything that it has gained in economic terms if these neighborhood issues are not soon resolved.

India's other foreign policy challenges are more nuanced but no less urgent. India lost its war with China in 1962. The shock of that defeat still resonates in Indian security circles, and there are those who would like to prepare for a rematch. This is nonsense. India and China cannot fight another war. There is too much at stake. After decades of animosity, there has been a noticeable thaw. Leaders and ministers from both Asian giants have toured each other's countries.

Trade between them is growing exponentially. Chinese goods are flooding Indian markets and Indian services are being marketed in the Middle Kingdom. War is unimaginable. But still, no peace treaty exists to put to rest the angers of 1962 and one must be drawn up urgently. This will help begin the process of preparing for the future when the two hegemons of Asia must make their regional and international ambitions coincide. China is preparing for superpower status. So is India. If they are to coexist, they must lay the groundwork now.

Beyond Pakistan and China, India needs to continue to focus and fine-tune its foreign policy. It needs to repair relations with its neighbors in South Asia, to play a constructive and generous role in the development of Nepal, Bangladesh and Sri Lanka. A good model might be Canada's relations with the United States. That Canada is among the world's richest economies is due in no small part to its access to U.S. markets and the stability and amity of its relations with Washington. India and its neighbors should work toward this sort of relationship. Being well regarded in its own backyard would help some of India's global aims as well. The country craves a permanent seat on the UN Security Council, but the diplomacy needed to achieve it will be intricate and challenging. The permanent five members hold a veto over any change to the structure of the Security Council, so each will have to be convinced of India's case, or given the incentive to support it. That could mean signing onto an international convention that benefits Washington while agreeing to long-term defense deals with Russia and France. China might want free trade and title to some disputed territory. Britain is an India supporter generally but would need convincing that its own—admittedly inordinate—global power isn't about to be diluted by India's admission to the UN's top table. Alliances with other Security Council aspirants such as Brazil, Germany, Nigeria, South Africa and Indonesia need to be drawn up. As former foreign secretary Shyam Saran has said, India needs to make itself indispensable in global politics by becoming helpfully engaged in all the important transnational issues: public health, fighting terrorism, humanitarian relief, narcotics and people trafficking, international justice, peacekeeping, global trade rules and so on. An India indispensable to the world is an India that is well on its way to realizing its ambitions and potential.

Democracy has served the country well. India met its early challenges not as a directed, authoritarian dictatorship but as a diverse
and cacophonous free society with universal adult franchise and regular elections. It is true, and perhaps unfortunate, that the same political party and family dominated politics for much of that time, but
Indian democracy survived, even thrived, through all of it. Prime
Minister Indira Gandhi's suspension of the constitution between
1975 and 1977 could have been a death blow to democracy, but instead it reaffirmed the commitment of the ordinary Indian voter to
the power of the ballot. Various corruption scandals and political
crises over the years have had much the same effect. Bad or venal
governments have been thrown out of office, sometimes forever, occasionally to learn lessons and return in triumph. Democracy
evolved as India did, in fits and starts, but gradually improving in
execution of policy and outcome. Despite what appear to be rigid
social and economic hierarchies, Indians themselves behave democratically. They debate, discuss and monitor all aspects of policy and
political activity. Nobel laureate Amartya Sen captured the essence of
this in his collection of essays from 2005, *The Argumentative Indian,*
contending that heterogeneous culture, religious tradition and sheer
physical diversity predispose Indian society toward constant public
discourse. This, Sen argues, is a guarantor of the endurance of
democracy.

For Sunil Khilnani of Johns Hopkins University, the democratic
system is nothing less than "the idea of India," the title of a book he
wrote in 1997 that celebrates fifty years of independence and liberal
institutions in his homeland. Khilnani's ideas are still valid. He sees
democracy as akin to a secular religion in India, a central, defining
philosophical concept. Indian voters simply see it as their birthright.
It is clear that India is a functioning democracy and will remain one.
The institutions—parliament, an independent judiciary, the media
and civil society—are firmly established and well protected in law and
by participants themselves. Any attempt to hinder freedom of the Indian press, for example, is met with the most fiery and effective response by journalists and editors.

The challenge is not to guard against overt authoritarianism or
the subversion of fundamental freedoms. It is to ensure that democracy is kept relevant across India's many economic, cultural and so-

cial diversities. The devolution of authority and power must continue. Indian states must acquire more powers, and so must regional, municipal and village councils. At every step, transparency and access must be part of the process. This means a continuing robust role for the media and an ever more vigorous civil society. India's future is federal.

I might be accused, I suppose, of being too optimistic about India's future, of being some kind of Babbitt-like India booster. So be it. Many years of thought, frequent visits and assignments have shaped this book. More importantly, the many, many Indians I have encountered in my travels have inspired my perception that India is going places. Ram the press wallah exists, and his achievement is not a fiction. Raman Roy created over thirty-five thousand jobs, and he's trying hard to double that number. Indian writers and film directors are winning Man Booker Prizes and Oscars and spreading their country's soft-power influence to billions of people. Graduates from the Indian Institutes of Technology are developing miracle cures and nurturing business deals that will change the way we live. The worms raised on Mukesh Gupta's ranch in Rajasthan are propelling a new organic agricultural sector that will revolutionize Indian farming, much to the delight, I'm sure, of Nathi Devi, the low-caste village woman cum international activist for cultivators' rights. The efforts of Infosys, Wipro and, indeed, TutorVista are touching lives all around us. At the same time, J. P. Natraj's efforts in the slums of Bangalore will continue, and they'll bear fruit. The old Communist may not like it, but the people he empowers through his social activism will see their children given a chance to enter a mainstream that has long excluded them. Caste barriers will come down thanks to the efforts of men like Bindeshwar Pathak. Veer Badra Mishra's brand of religious environmentalism is already inspiring change in both religious attitudes and policies that affect the water quality of the sacred River Ganges.

These people whose stories helped propel this narrative represent no more than a sliver of Indian life. There are literally hundreds of millions more like them. They work against a frenetic background of social and economic change. They cope with the challenges thrown their way ingeniously, stoically, indomitably, simply because they must. Whatever the problems, drawbacks and barriers, people not only get by but also frequently manage to improve their lives and the lives of those around them. I have argued extensively in these pages that this is something innate in the nature of Indian society, something that comes from tolerance, diversity, problem-solving skills, argumentativeness, democracy and commitment to family and community growth. This is why the world needs to pay close attention to India, the next liberal superpower.

NOTES

1   Debugging the Millennium

1.   Rudyard Kipling, *Kim* (Macmillan, 1901; New York: Random House, 2004), 59.
2.   The Thursday Interview, with Sam Pitroda, *sify* (January 30, 2003), www.sify.com.

2   From Tech Support to Tutoring

1.   Jay Solomon, "Western Exposure in India's Outsourcing Boom: GE Played a Starring Role," *Wall Street Journal*, May 23, 2005.
2.   Ibid.
3.   Lou Dobbs, Exporting America: Why Corporate Greed Is Shipping American Jobs Overseas (New York: Warner Business Books, 2004), 36–37.
4.   Thomas Friedman, *The World Is Flat* (New York: Farrar, Strauss and Giroux, 2006), 128.
5.   John Boudreau, "Risk Takers Say Now Is the Time to Get In On Ground Floor of India's Tech Boom," San Jose *Mercury News*, January 3, 2006.
6.   Das, Gurcharan, *India Unbound*, New Delhi: Penguin, 1998.

5   Fighting for Freedom

1.   John Keay, *India: A History* (New Delhi: HarperCollins, 2000), 414.
2.   Patrick French, *Liberty or Death: India's Journey to Independence and Division* (London: HarperCollins, 1998), 293.

7   The New Freedom Struggle

1.   Mohandas Gandhi, *Famous Letters of Mahatma Gandhi* (Indian Print Works, 1947), 68–75.

2. Arundhati Roy, "The End of Imagination," *Outlook,* July 27, 1998, p. 26.

8 Educating India Then and Now

1. Sankarshan Thakur, *The Making of Laloo Yadav: The Unmaking of Bihar* (New Delhi: HarperCollins, 2000), xiii.

9 Hinduism and Its Discontents

1. Pankaj Mishra, "How the British Invented Hinduism," *The New Statesman,* August 26, 2002.

11 Becoming Asia's America

1. Strobe Talbott, "Good Day for India, Bad Day for the United States," *Yale Global,* July 21, 2005, p. 17.

Acknowledgments

So MANY CONTRIBUTED to this book. The credit for its strengths go to them; the blame for shortcomings accrues with me. There isn't enough space to thank everyone but a few names cannot be left out. Ashish Bose is one of India's priceless treasures, and my friend. Manjushree Thapa was a pillar of support and strength, and a crucial reader of early drafts. She is also my life partner. Paul Danahar and Bhavna Kumar never stinted on their hospitality and help. Neither did Ben Schonveld, Joel Issacson or Wendy King, all hosts and close friends. Geeta Pandey offered friendship and many insights over the years. Her close namesake, Geetha Panda, both impressed me with her business acumen and welcomed me into her working life in Bangalore. Habib Beary, Mukesh Sinha, Sanjeev Srivastava, Vinod Mehta and a host of other Indian friends and colleagues are people to whom I'm indebted. My agent, John Pearce, and my editors, Diane Turbide and Jonathan Webb, were endlessly patient and insisted on the best at all times. Thanks to David Davidar, we share a passion for his homeland. My family—Katie, Robert, Frank, Dad and Doreen—helped tremendously by allowing me the space to write and by tolerating my travels. I am grateful to the BBC, the world's finest broadcaster, for giving me South Asia. Thanks finally to India. May her people thrive as their society grows into Asia's America and more.

INDEX